Pandemic Surveillance

ELGAR LAW, TECHNOLOGY AND SOCIETY

Series Editor: Peter K. Yu, *Texas A&M University School of Law, USA*

The information revolution and the advent of digital technologies have ushered in new social practices, business models, legal solutions, regulatory policies, governance structures, consumer preferences and global concerns. This unique book series provides an interdisciplinary forum for studying the complex interactions that arise from this environment. It examines the broader and deeper theoretical questions concerning information law and policy, explores its latest developments and social implications, and provides new ways of thinking about changing technology.

Titles in the series include:

Law and Autonomous Machines
The Co-evolution of Legal Responsibility and Technology
Mark Chinen

The Making Available Right
Realizing the Potential of Copyright's Dissemination Function in the Digital Age
Cheryl Foong

The Regulation of Social Media Influencers
Edited by Catalina Goanta and Sofia Ranchordás

Fundamental Rights Protection Online
The Future Regulation of Intermediaries
Edited by Bilyana Petkova and Tuomas Ojanen

Judges, Technology and Artificial Intelligence
The Artificial Judge
Tania Sourdin

Regulating Online Behavioural Advertising Through Data Protection Law
Jiahong Chen

The Future of Copyright in the Age of Artificial Intelligence
Aviv H. Gaon

Pandemic Surveillance
Privacy, Security, and Data Ethics
Edited by Margaret Hu

Pandemic Surveillance
Privacy, Security, and Data Ethics

Edited by

Margaret Hu

Professor of Law, William & Mary Law School, College of William & Mary, USA

ELGAR LAW, TECHNOLOGY AND SOCIETY

Edward Elgar
PUBLISHING

Cheltenham, UK • Northampton, MA, USA

Published by
Edward Elgar Publishing Limited
The Lypiatts
15 Lansdown Road
Cheltenham
Glos GL50 2JA
UK

Edward Elgar Publishing, Inc.
William Pratt House
9 Dewey Court
Northampton
Massachusetts 01060
USA

A catalogue record for this book
is available from the British Library

Library of Congress Control Number: 2022944627

This book is available electronically in the **Elgar**online
Law subject collection
http://dx.doi.org/10.4337/9781800889415

MIX
Paper | Supporting
responsible forestry
FSC® C013604

ISBN 978 1 80088 940 8 (cased)
ISBN 978 1 80088 941 5 (eBook)

Printed and bound by CPI Group (UK) Ltd, Croydon, CR0 4YY

Contents

List of contributors   vii
Introduction   1
Margaret Hu

PART I   DIGITAL PRIVACY, SECURITY, AND
            EMERGING SURVEILLANCE TECHNOLOGIES

1   Mass surveillance in the age of COVID-19   6
       Natalie Ram and David Gray

2   Balancing the pursuit of knowledge against the
       preservation of privacy   27
       Davi Ottenheimer

3   Surveillance and pandemic in Brazil: an essay in three acts   42
       Nathalie Fragoso, Clarice Tavares, and Jade Becari

4   Frictionless pandemic surveillance and social credit systems   64
       Margaret Hu

5   The developing narratives of pandemic surveillance   86
       Joshua Fairfield

PART II   CONTEXTUALIZING CHALLENGES IN
            REGULATING PANDEMIC SURVEILLANCE

6   Pandemic surveillance and US foreign surveillance   105
       Peter Margulies

7   Regulating privacy and data ethics in the context of the
       UK's contact tracing apps   114
       Ian Brown

8   Privacy and pandemic surveillance apps in Latin America   136
       María Soledad Segura

9   Implementing effective digital privacy policy: the road
       ahead in post-pandemic times   148
       Stuart N. Brotman

10   Tracing the invisible: information fiduciaries and the pandemic   158
       Anne L. Washington and Lauren Rhue

PART III   LEGAL AND ETHICAL CONSIDERATIONS
            MOVING FORWARD

11   Pandemic surveillance: ethics at the intersection of
       information, research, and health   187
       Daniel Susser

12   Using personal data and data-driven technologies for
       research and public health in the context of the COVID-19
       pandemic   197
       Bethânia de Araújo Almeida

13   Pandemic ethics: the intersection of technology, trust, and
       privacy, and implications for marginalized communities   204
       Jolynn Dellinger

14   Of pandemics and progress   216
       Andrea M. Matwyshyn

Index   226

Contributors

Bethânia de Araújo Almeida is a sociologist with a PhD in public health. Her interest in the area of health motivated her to work at the Oswaldo Cruz Foundation (FIOCRUZ), an institution affiliated with the Brazilian Ministry of Health, whose institutional actions are designed to generate and disseminate scientific and technological knowledge in order to strengthen the Brazilian Universal Health System (Sistema Único de Saúde, or SUS). She works at the Centre for Data and Knowledge Integration for Health (CIDACS), an initiative that aims to conduct interdisciplinary studies to enrich research efforts in public health to tackle health inequalities.

Jade Becari is a researcher at InternetLab. She has a bachelor's degree in social sciences at State University of Campinas (UNICAMP).

Stuart N. Brotman is the Howard Distinguished Endowed Professor of Media Management and Law and Beaman Professor of Journalism and Electronic Media at the University of Tennessee, Knoxville. He is the author of *Privacy's Perfect Storm: Digital Policy for Post-Pandemic Times* (Miniver Press, 2020).

Ian Brown is the visiting CyberBRICS professor at Fundação Getulio Vargas (FGV) Law School in Rio de Janeiro, Brazil. He is a leading specialist on internet regulation, particularly relating to information security and privacy, digital elements of the election life cycle, and pro-competition mechanisms such as interoperability. His clients since 1999 include the Open Society Foundations, Global Network Initiative, Vodafone, BSkyB, the UK and US governments, the German Bundestag, the European Commission and Parliament, the Council of Europe, the OECD, the Commonwealth, and the United Nations.

Jolynn Dellinger is the Stephen and Janet Bear Visiting Lecturer and Kenan Senior Fellow at the Kenan Institute for Ethics. She also teaches privacy law and policy as a senior lecturing fellow at Duke Law School and as an adjunct professor at UNC School of Law. She is a member of the board of directors for the Triangle Privacy Research Hub and the Future of Privacy Forum Advisory Committee, and she recently served as Special Counsel for Privacy Policy and Litigation for the North Carolina Department of Justice.

Joshua Fairfield is the William D. Bain Family Professor of Law at Washington and Lee University, where he specializes in technology and digital property. He is the author of *Owned: Property, Privacy, and the New Digital Serfdom* (Cambridge University Press, 2017) and *Runaway Technology: Can Law Keep Up?* (Cambridge University Press, 2021).

Nathalie Fragoso is a researcher and Privacy and Data Protection Lawyer. She has a PhD in law from the University of São Paulo Law School (FDUSP) and an LLM from Ludwig-Maximilians-Universität München.

David Gray is Jacob A. France Professor of Law, University of Maryland, Francis King Carey School of Law.

Margaret Hu is Professor of Law and Director of the Digital Democracy Lab at William & Mary Law School. She is also a research affiliate of the Institute for Computational and Data Sciences at Pennsylvania State University.

Professor Peter Margulies is a Professor of Law at Roger Williams University School of Law in Rhode Island, where he teaches national security law. He has analyzed foreign surveillance for the influential *Lawfare* blog and spoken at Harvard, Yale, and Columbia Law Schools on topics including the intersection of surveillance, cybersecurity, and privacy in US and EU law. He has served as co-counsel for amici curiae in prominent cases, including *Humanitarian Law Project v. Holder*, 561 US 1 (2010) (holding that statute prohibiting material support to foreign terrorist organizations did not violate the First Amendment).

Andrea M. Matwyshyn is Associate Dean of Innovation and Professor of Law and Engineering Policy at Penn State Law (University Park); Professor of Engineering Design, SEDTAPP, Penn State Engineering; founding Faculty Director, Penn State Policy Innovation Lab of Tomorrow (PILOT); and founding faculty director, Anuncia Donecia Songsong Manglona Lab for Gender and Economic Equity.

Davi Ottenheimer is Vice President of Trust and Digital Ethics at Inrupt. He brings over 25 years of experience as a head of security and trust managing global security engineering, operations, and assessments, and over a decade of leading incident response and digital forensics. Davi has helped serve customer data protection needs across many industries, including data storage and management, software, investment, banking, and international retail, as well as higher education, healthcare, and aerospace.

Natalie Ram is Professor of Law and the University of Maryland Francis King Carey School of Law, and adjunct faculty at the Johns Hopkins University Berman Institute of Bioethics. She was a 2021 Greenwall Faculty Scholar in Bioethics.

Lauren Rhue, PhD, is an assistant professor of information systems at the University of Maryland's Robert H. Smith School of Business.

María Soledad Segura is licenciada in social communication and has a master's degree in contemporary communication and culture and a PhD in social sciences. She is a professor at the Universidad Nacional de Córdoba and a researcher at the Consejo Nacional de Investigaciones Científicas y Técnicas (CONICET). She has published seven books and more than one hundred scientific articles and journalistic opinion columns about communication and cultural rights and policies.

Daniel Susser is the Haile Family Early Career Professor and an assistant professor in the College of Information Sciences and Technology, a research associate in the Rock Ethics Institute, and an affiliated faculty member in the Philosophy Department at Penn State University.

Clarice Tavares is the head of research at the Inequalities and Identities area in InternetLab. She has a bachelor's degree in social sciences from the University of São Paulo (USP) and is a law student at the Pontifical Catholic University (PUC-SP).

Anne L. Washington, PhD, is Assistant Professor of Data Policy at New York University and is finishing a book on the ethics of predictive data technology. She is a Senior Fellow at the Future of Privacy Forum; is on the Advisory Board of the Electronic Privacy Information Center; and is the founding director of the Digital Interests Lab.

Introduction

Margaret Hu

As the COVID-19 pandemic surged globally in 2020, pandemic surveillance was actively explored and debated as part of the prescription. Questions of data privacy, cybersecurity, and the ethics of the surveillance technologies centered an international conversation on the benefits and disadvantages of the appropriate uses and expansion of cybersurveillance and data tracking. In November 2020, Pennsylvania State University's Institute for Computational and Data Sciences (ICDS), Penn State Law's Policy Innovation Lab of Tomorrow (PILOT), the Kenan Institute for Ethics at Duke University, and InternetLab in Brazil co-hosted an international virtual event to discuss these issues. Experts from the United States, Argentina, Brazil, the Netherlands, and the United Kingdom convened to discuss the ethical challenges we face in adopting emerging technologies to combat the spread of COVID-19.

This book project is an outgrowth of that event. The technological responses proposed to address the pandemic posed and continue to pose critical questions that implicate complex legal, scientific, and ethical issues. This underscores the importance of encouraging international conversations and an informed dialogue on these topics. Panelists touched on the need to balance individual rights with efforts to promote the public good with regard to data collection, usage, and storage during the pandemic and its aftermath. Technologies that are currently being used to track the spread of the virus raise privacy concerns, and the ways in which information is used and stored put people at risk of potential harms. We are grateful that many of the speakers agreed to convert their remarks into the chapters that compose this edited volume.

The book is divided into three sections. Part I frames and defines digital privacy and security in the context of emerging surveillance technologies. Chapter 1, "Mass Surveillance in the Age of COVID-19," by Natalie Ram and David Gray, takes a broad look at mass surveillance during COVID-19, where epidemiological surveillance has been touted as a tool to curb the pandemic despite little evidence of efficacy and at substantial risk to privacy, specifically in light of the United States' Fourth Amendment. Emerging tracking technologies were seen as silver bullets in the early days of the pandemic. However, these technologies have not caught on as much as expected, most notably because of privacy concerns, including concerns over data leaks. The authors note that these technologies could potentially be used for applications such as tracking people to enforce social distancing. There are also concerns about who owns the data collected through these technologies, how long they are stored, and potential uses beyond pandemic surveillance.

Chapter 2, "Balancing the Pursuit of Knowledge Against the Preservation of Privacy," builds on this theme by looking to history to see how the unregulated centralization of technology erodes data privacy and democratic norms—and how past public health crises were addressed in ways that did not violate constitutional rights. Authored by Davi Ottenheimer, Chapter 2 explores the inherent tension between privacy and knowledge, and discusses how we must find ways to align these two values to reach satisfactory solutions.

Similarly, Chapter 3, "Surveillance and Pandemic in Brazil: An Essay in Three Acts," looks to history to draw a path between three "acts" of data collection and processing by the Brazilian state: in the formation of the state, during the yellow fever epidemic, and during the COVID-19 pandemic. The chapter outlines how each period is marked by power asymmetries and paradigm shifts for data collection policies. The authors—Nathalie Fragoso, Clarice Tavares and Jade Becari—describe how the population's distrust is the first operational constraint for a state with limited commitments to democracy and transparency.

In my contribution, Chapter 4, "Frictionless Pandemic Surveillance and Social Credit Systems," I explore how pandemic surveillance accelerated an alignment of incentives between corporate and governmental interests. This lack of friction is antithetical to the separation of powers principles underlying a constitutional democracy and can result in the emergence of invisible social credit systems in democratic nations.

The final chapter in Part I, Chapter 5, "The Developing Narratives of Pandemic Surveillance," by Joshua Fairfield, broadly considers why digital pandemic apps have been so difficult to deploy without contributing to democratic decline: in the United States, for example, narratives about vaccination against COVID-19 have been linked to the country's history of warrantless dragnet surveillance. A legal and regulatory path forward must attend not just to the legal frameworks, but also to the narratives and the communities that drive those narratives.

After this overview of past and present contexts, Part II examines the challenges of regulating pandemic surveillance technologies in various geographical settings. Chapter 6, "Pandemic Surveillance and US Foreign Surveillance," by Peter Margulies, provides a comparative perspective. It points out how the blurring of data collection for epidemiological purposes and national security purposes poses unique challenges for US law and national security under foreign intelligence-gathering authorities, especially for data collection and data-sharing between the United States and European Union.

The scope of US foreign surveillance may hamper data-sharing necessary to combat global health crises. Chapters 7 and 8 examine the on-the-ground implications of contact tracing and other surveillance apps in the United Kingdom and Latin America, respectively. In Chapter 7, "Regulating Privacy and Data Ethics in the Context of the UK's Contact Tracing Apps," Ian Brown argues that inattention to the sociotechnical environment can lead to challenges for technical and regulatory interoperability. The United Kingdom's COVID-19 tracking app, for example, went through several iterations, including centralized and decentralized models, and was hindered by concerns about privacy and logistics as well as by limited governance structures and post-Brexit data-sharing challenges.

Chapter 8, "Privacy and Pandemic Surveillance Apps in Latin America," by María Soledad Segura, surveys COVID-19 apps in multiple Latin American countries, where regulation of both digital access and data and privacy protection varies significantly. Problems that hinder widespread use of these technologies have unintentionally and unexpectedly protected personal data.

Chapter 9, "Implementing Effective Digital Privacy Policy: The Road Ahead in Post-Pandemic Times," by Stuart Brotman, discusses the expansion of digital technology use in the US context during the pandemic, often with little or no regulatory oversight or guidance. The author reviews the political and legal landscape as we approach a "new normal" and considers proposed state and federal privacy law reforms—or the lack thereof.

In Chapter 10, "Tracing the Invisible: Information Fiduciaries and the Pandemic," by Anne Washington and Lauren Rhue, the authors "trace the invisible," discussing the limited efficacy of predictive data technology in the context of COVID-19, which overlooked significant portions of the population and has had many negative consequences for privacy. The authors offer two policy suggestions to discourage behavior that counters public health goals: open data conflict-of-interest notices and a public health fiduciary.

The book's third and final section picks up this theme of forward-looking solutions, exploring legal and ethical challenges in a world with a growing data-surveillance architecture. Chapter 11, "Pandemic Surveillance: Ethics at the Intersection of Information, Research, and Health," by Daniel Susser, outlines the ethical questions and implications that occur at the junction of information ethics, research ethics, and public health. It asks what we must consider in order to balance the social goods of privacy and public health. Chapter 12, "Using Personal Data and Data-Driven Technologies for Research and Public Health in the Context of the COVID-19 Pandemic," authored by Bethânia de Araújo Almeida, provides an overview of the legal and ethical issues presented by data-driven research and technologies, and calls for updated legal concepts and universal policies and regulations.

Chapter 13, "Pandemic Ethics: The Intersection of Technology, Trust, and Privacy, and Implications for Marginalized Communities," by Jolynn Dellinger, focuses on marginalized communities and vulnerable populations, considering how they are affected and often harmed by technology. In the United States, for example, limited data protection and a history of use, misuse, and abuse of data have led to an erosion of trust and compromised public health. The chapter discusses the ethical obligations of pandemic responses and the relevance of trust and privacy. In a pandemic, where a degree of surveillance may be essential to defeating the global health crisis, there may be an ethical obligation to share personal data. However, Dellinger contends that we must pay particularly close attention to the use—and misuse and abuse—of data, especially in relation to vulnerable populations.

Finally, Chapter 14, "Of Pandemics and Progress," by Andrea Matwyshyn, outlines considerations for health technology interventions as we move into the era of an "Internet of Bodies." The chapter underscores a theme that runs throughout the book: there is tremendous potential and significant risk as human bodies come to rely on the internet via devices and processes that affect safety and health.

Taken holistically, *Pandemic Surveillance: Privacy, Security, and Data Ethics* aims to preserve perspectives and reflections during a moment that is likely to be assessed by history as technologically, legally, and socially transformational. This effort was made possible through the generous support of Microsoft Research, the Institute for Computational and Data Sciences and PILOT Lab at Penn State, Duke's Kenan Institute for Ethics, and InternetLab in Brazil. I am grateful for the editorial efforts of Sara Versluis and the careful research support of Blair Johnson, Davi Liang, and Paige Villarreal.

The devastation of the global pandemic led to calls for digital innovation, and the cooperation of technology companies, to address the crisis. The deployment of the most advanced technological tools available to address the pandemic through surveillance and data tracking, however, intersected with a digital revolution that is still underway. I am grateful for the thoughtful attempt of the authors to interrogate the potential legal and ethical consequences of an unprecedented embrace of pandemic surveillance in the earliest months of COVID-19.

PART I

Digital privacy, security, and emerging
surveillance technologies

1. Mass surveillance in the age of COVID-19

Natalie Ram and David Gray

INTRODUCTION

In China, the government has required residents to download a smartphone app that tracks their movements and assigns them a color (red, yellow, or green) corresponding to their asserted public health risk. These color codes regulate access to "subways, malls, and other public spaces" (see Mozur et al., 2020). The methodology by which an individual is color coded is opaque, however, and the app "also appears to share information with the police, setting a template for new forms of automated social control that could persist long after the epidemic subsides" (Mozur et al., 2020). In South Korea, the government reportedly pushes cellphone alerts about infected individuals, sending detailed information including "credit-card history, with a minute-to-minute record of their comings and goings from various local businesses" (Thompson, 2020). That level of detail has led to infected individuals being identified and suffering harassment. Israel has hastily repurposed mass location data secretly collected for counterterrorism purposes to track potentially infected individuals wherever they go (Halbfinger et al., 2020). Meanwhile, in the United States, North and South Dakota have already issued an app for their residents, which gathers location data using cell towers, GPS, and Wi-Fi, and stores that data on a centralized, private server (see Valentino-DeVries et al., 2020; see also NDResponse, n.d.; Care19 App, n.d.). In all, according to one live-tracking site, at least 53 contact tracing apps have already appeared across at least 29 countries (see Woodhams, 2020).

In the United States, the Supreme Court has held that individuals have the right to expect that "the whole of their physical movements" will remain private (*Carpenter v. United States*, 2018). Location data from smartphones and cellphones "provide ... an intimate window into a person's life, revealing not only his particular movements, but through them his familial, political, professional, religious, and sexual associations" (*Carpenter v. United States*,

2018). Yet the explosive growth of COVID-19[1] in this country, and the drastic social distancing measures that have crippled American life and the economy, have triggered increasing interest in harnessing the power of digital location data to track, predict, and control the pandemic.

The U.S. government is already tapping bulk cellphone location data for public health surveillance purposes in the fight against COVID-19. These efforts include tracking the "presence and movement of people in certain areas of geographic interest" (Tau, 2020). Under new legislation, Congress appropriated "not less than $500,000,000" for "public health data surveillance and analytics infrastructure modernization" (Coronavirus Aid, Relief, and Economic Security [CARES] Act, 2020, p. 554).

Private enterprise has been quick to cooperate. Google analyzed location data from its app users' devices to generate "COVID-19 Community Mobility Reports" for every county in the United States. These reports "chart movement trends over time by geography, across different categories of places such as retail and recreation, groceries and pharmacies, parks, transit stations, work-places, and residential" (Google, n.d.). Another much-watched visualization analyzed cellphone location data to show how the spring break population in south Florida dispersed across America. Each dot along a Florida beach during spring break marked a unique cellphone, which was followed for weeks thereafter. Spreading like delicate tendrils, this visualization of individuals' movements illustrated "how massive the potential impact just one single beach gathering can have in spreading this virus across our nation" (Tectonix GEO, 2020). These analyses by Google and others enable the government and others to discern how well the public has complied with social distancing at the individual, county, state, and national level.

The use of cellphone location data for contact tracing in a more targeted, individualized way has also garnered significant interest. Contact tracing is a traditional public health tool. The World Health Organization (WHO, 2017) defines contact tracing as a monitoring process in which an infected individual identifies all other individuals with whom they may have been in contact. Those contacts are then informed, monitored, and sometimes instructed to self-isolate or quarantine. Contact tracing, coupled with effective isolation of relevant contacts, can "prevent further transmission of [a] virus" (WHO, 2017).

---

[1]   COVID-19 is the name for the cluster of symptoms caused by the contagion SARS-CoV-2. In this chapter, we use COVID-19 as a generic term to refer both to the disease and the contagion. We embrace this imprecision because COVID-19 is the more widely recognized term, it is commonly used to refer to both disease and contagion, and in order to avoid any potential confusion with SARS-CoV, which first emerged in 2003, and is the cause of disease symptoms commonly referred to as SARS (see Centers for Disease Control [CDC], 2017).

Traditionally, contact tracing has relied on skilled workers, who interview infected individuals to learn about their activities and the people they encountered after becoming ill, and then monitor those contacts for illness. According to a recent report from the Johns Hopkins Center for Health Security, more than 100,000 contact tracers may be needed nationally to grapple with the COVID-19 pandemic (Watson et al., 2020, p. 8). Massachusetts alone "plans to hire and train roughly 1,000 people to do contact tracing" (Bebinger, 2020).[2]

Other jurisdictions have trained their sights on cellphone data as a new, potentially more powerful, efficient, and accurate tool for contact tracing. With China, South Korea, Singapore, Israel, and others as examples, data brokers and app developers are working to bring digital contact tracing to European and American markets (Thompson, 2020).[3] Their pitch is enticing. In a paper in *Science*, researchers at Oxford argue that COVID-19 spreads too quickly and asymptomatically to be controllable through traditional contact tracing methods (see Ferretti et al., 2020). To alleviate the need for long-term mass social distancing, the authors of that study argue that communities will need to deploy "instant digital contact tracing" (Ferretti et al., 2020, p. 4).

Despite the public health benefits touted by proponents, it is not clear that digital contact tracing can achieve its lavish claims; nor is it evident that it can do so without imposing disproportionate privacy harms. Current technological limitations, as well as limitations in COVID-19 testing and support for quarantining identified contacts, undermine the efficacy of digital contact tracing efforts that its proponents seemingly take for granted (Ram & Gray, 2020, footnote 21). As for privacy, digital contact tracing efforts abroad already raise significant cause for concern. These mass surveillance programs sweep up revealing location data indiscriminately. Although they are defended on grounds of emergency and the urgent need to contend with the present health crisis, experiences in those countries already reveal the potential for abuse. Moreover, our own history amply demonstrates that surveillance powers claimed on emergency grounds frequently remain after the emergency has passed, often morphing into tools of social control targeted against disfavored individuals and groups (see Select Committee to Study Governmental Operations, 1976, pp. 38–39, 90–92).

This chapter assesses whether and under what circumstances the United States ought to embrace the use of epidemiological surveillance programs, including the use of cellphone location data for contact tracing purposes. Section 1 analyzes the constitutionality of programs like digital contact tracing, arguing that the Fourth Amendment's protection against unreason-

---

[2]   Other states have similar plans (see, e.g., NBC New York, 2020).
[3]   Some apps are already in use in parts of the United States and Europe.

able searches and seizures may well regulate the use of location data for epidemiological purposes, but that the legislative and executive branches have significant latitude to develop these programs within the broad constraints of the "special needs" doctrine elaborated by the courts in parallel circumstances. Section 2 cautions that the absence of a firm warrant requirement for digital contact tracing should not serve as a green light for unregulated digital location tracking, whether in the form of individual or aggregate surveillance, and by means of location or proximity tracking.[4] In light of substantial risks to privacy that a digital contact tracing program might entail, this chapter argues for a thoughtful, constitutionally sufficient, legislative scheme that does not indulge the hubris of emergency, assert claims of broad, unchecked power, or follow the siren's song of technovelty. Policymakers must instead ask hard questions about efficacy and the comparative advantages of location tracking versus more traditional means of controlling epidemic contagions, take seriously threats to privacy, tailor programs parsimoniously, establish clear metrics for determining success, and set plans for decommissioning surveillance programs. Should the political branches fail to perform on these duties, then the courts, as guardians of the Fourth Amendment's sacred trust, must act.

1   FOURTH AMENDMENT FRAMEWORKS

In the U.S. context, questions about protecting privacy against threats of government surveillance implicate the Fourth Amendment, which guarantees that "the right of the people to be secure in their persons, houses, papers, and effects against unreasonable searches and seizures shall not be violated ..." (U.S. Const. amend. IV). Would an epidemiological surveillance program that uses cellphone location data to conduct individual contact tracing or to document and predict infection patterns using aggregate data be subject to Fourth Amendment regulation? If so, what form should those regulations take? Answering these questions requires addressing two Fourth Amendment thresholds: whether the program entails state action and whether the conduct at issue constitutes a "search" or a "seizure."

---

[4]   By "location tracking," we mean the use of technologies like cell site location or GPS that monitor the movements of individual persons or devices through space. In the present context, location tracking technologies might be used to trace the movements of individuals who test positive for SARS-CoV-2 and to document potential contacts with others. By "proximity tracking," we mean technologies like geofencing or Wi-Fi that document the presence of individuals or devices in a specific area. Proximity tracking might be used to control the flow of persons in particular spaces, such as malls, grocery stores, or even cities. It might also be used to identify those who have traversed hotspots or other areas of potential contagion.

The Fourth Amendment applies only to governments and their agents. It does not regulate the conduct of private persons or entities. Based on the surveillance programs deployed in other countries and those imagined domestically, data aggregation for contact tracing has been and will be conducted by private entities, principally cellphone service providers and technology companies with access to location data through apps installed on users' devices. This does not necessarily exhaust the Fourth Amendment inquiry, however. Under established doctrine, a private party may be subject to Fourth Amendment regulation to the extent it is acting as an agent of the state.

"Whether a private party should be deemed an agent or instrument of the Government for Fourth Amendment purposes necessarily turns on the degree of the Government's participation in the private party's activities, a question that can only be resolved in light of all the circumstances" (*Skinner v. Railway Labor Executives' Association*, 1989, pp. 614–615). Among the factors relevant to this inquiry are whether a government agent directed, requested, or incentivized the search, whether the private actor believed at the time that she was acting under the direction or authority of a government agent, and whether a government agent had advance notice of the search and believed that the fruits of that search would accrue to the government.

There are good reasons to believe that the cellular service providers and technology companies aggregating data for contact tracing and similar surveillance programs would be acting as state agents for purposes of the Fourth Amendment. Most of these entities are already routinely targets for government demands for user data—sometimes on the order of tens of thousands of requests each year. They may therefore already be acting as state agents when they collect and aggregate location data (see Gray & Citron, 2013, pp. 133–137). That case is even stronger in the narrower circumstance of epidemiological surveillance. These programs require ongoing access to historical data for baseline analysis, recent aggregate data to model population flows and contact patterns, targeted data to trace individual persons, and real-time data to monitor the activities of persons and groups. In short, these programs will entail close, ongoing public–private partnerships, which will have the effect of converting AT&T, Google, and other data collectors and aggregators into government agents for purposes of the Fourth Amendment.[5]

---

[5]   There is, of course, the possibility that a purely private actor with access to individual and aggregate tracking data might attempt to engage in epidemiological surveillance completely independent of any government agent. Although we find this highly unlikely, such a truly private actor would be beyond the reach of Fourth Amendment regulation, although perhaps subject to regulation by state or federal statute. Somewhat more likely is the possibility of a private actor, such as a cellular service provider or technology company, gathering, aggregating, and making available location data,

To the extent doubts about the state agency requirement persist, they are probably mooted by the Supreme Court's recent decision in *Carpenter v. United States* (2018). There, the Court held that the Fourth Amendment governs law enforcement access to historical cell site location data gathered and stored by cellphone service providers (cellphone location data, whether in the form of cell site location or GPS tracking, appears to be a centerpiece of tracing and proximity surveillance proposals because these devices are so often with their users; see *Riley v. California*, 2014, p. 395). As the *Carpenter* Court noted, service providers collect and aggregate this data for their own business purposes (*Carpenter v. United States*, 2018, p. 2212). Nevertheless, the Court held that law enforcement must secure a warrant before accessing that data in the context of a criminal investigation (*Carpenter v. United States*, 2018, p. 2221). The Court was decidedly mealy-mouthed about what constituted the "search" in *Carpenter*, who did it, and when (see *Carpenter v. United States*, 2018, pp. 2217, 2220), but the circumstances contemplated by epidemiological surveillance programs are sufficiently analogous to conclude that the state agency requirement would not be an impediment to applying the Fourth Amendment, even if the precise reasons why might remain a mystery.

But does epidemiological surveillance constitute a "seizure" or a "search"? The Fourth Amendment regulates conduct that threatens the security of the people against "unreasonable searches and seizures." Conventionally, this means that the Fourth Amendment applies only to conduct that constitutes either a "seizure" or a "search."

"Seizures" entail material interference with property or liberty. Depending on the technology used, epidemiological surveillance programs plausibly could constitute seizures of "effects." For example, if the government required citizens to install specific applications on their cellular phones or other electronic devices, then that interference might well amount to a seizure of effects. So, too, if government agents surreptitiously hacked devices to install tracking software (cf. *United States v. Horton*, 2017, pp. 1046–1047). In addition, if a surveillance program was aimed at using personal devices to limit users'

---

which a government agency then accesses. Again, we regard as far more likely a close, ongoing working relationship between government and private actors, but, even in this case of more limited interaction, the private actor would be a state agent for purposes of the Fourth Amendment because it *knows* that its work will be accessed and used by government agents and government agents *know* prospectively that the private actor is gathering location data to which the government will have access (see Gray & Citron, 2013, pp. 133–37). Moreover, the Court's recent Fourth Amendment jurisprudence indicates that the Fourth Amendment regulates government access to location information gathered by private parties (see *Carpenter v. United States*, 2018; *Riley v. California*, 2014, p. 395).

liberty by, say, using geofencing or other proximity tracking to enforce a physical quarantine, then that would constitute seizure of persons.[6]

"Searches" encompass either physical intrusions into constitutionally protected areas (persons, houses, papers, or effects) for the purpose of gathering information (see *Florida v. Jardines*, 2013; *United States v. Jones*, 2012) or intrusions upon subjectively manifested expectations of privacy that society is prepared to recognize as reasonable (see *Katz v. United States*, 1967). Depending on the nature of the program, epidemiological surveillance may qualify as a search under one or both of these definitions. For example, if government agents actively search data on cellular phones or other devices in order to gather location information or to access photographs and other evidence of social contacts, then their conduct might fairly be described as physically intruding upon a constitutionally protected "effect" for the purpose of gathering information.[7] Alternatively, if government agents access location information gathered and aggregated by third parties, such as cellular service providers or technology companies, documenting persons' movements (or lack thereof!) over a period of time, then that would probably qualify as an intrusion upon reasonable expectations of privacy (see *Carpenter v. United States*, 2018, pp. 2217–2220), particularly if it revealed that they were at home (see *United States v. Karo*, 1984, pp. 716–718).

Complications exist, to be sure. For example, what if the Centers for Disease Control (CDC) uses anonymized location data that is aggregated by a cellphone service provider or technology company and made available to researchers or business entities? Is the CDC subject to Fourth Amendment regulation if it has done nothing more than what a private party could do? In one respect the answer is easy: "Yes, of course!" As described above, the state agency requirement highlights the fact that government agents are subject to Fourth Amendment restraints that do not bind private actors. In another respect, however, the answer is less clear. The Supreme Court has long allowed government agents to access through lawful means information voluntarily shared with third parties. For example, law enforcement can access information about a suspect's financial transactions through the suspect's bank or credit card servicer without worrying about the Fourth Amendment because this conduct does not intrude upon reasonable expectations of privacy (see

---

[6]   One question that arises here is whether the attempted use of location surveillance to effect seizures of persons would trigger the Fourth Amendment. For example, what if officials pushed a text to a user's phone notifying her that she had been exposed to the COVID-19 virus then directing her to self-quarantine for 14 days. Would that constitute a "seizure" for purposes of the Fourth Amendment?

[7]   This kind of digital intrusion would be closely analogous to scrolling through the contents of a cellular phone, which is a "search" (see *Riley v. California*, 2014, p. 401).

United States v. Miller, 1976; *California Bankers Association v. Shultz,* 1974). In a similar vein, government agents are free to observe anyone's public movements (see *United States v. Knotts*, 1983) or to access areas open to the public (looking through a trash can placed at the curb for pickup is not a "search"; see *California v. Greenwood*, 1988; entering upon and examining "open fields" is not a search; *Oliver v. United States*, 1984) without subjecting themselves to Fourth Amendment constraints. Would either or both of these lines of cases—colloquially, the third-party and public observation doctrines—exempt epidemiological surveillance programs from Fourth Amendment scrutiny? Probably not.

In *Carpenter*, the Court held that neither the third-party nor the public observation doctrine could relieve law enforcement from the burden of securing a warrant before accessing cell site location data that is routinely gathered and aggregated by cellphone service providers for their own business purposes (*Carpenter v. United States*, 2018, p. 2220). The crux of the Court's reasoning was that location tracking reveals a host of intimate details about private associations and activities (*Carpenter v. United States*, 2018, pp. 2217–2218). The Court also worried that granting law enforcement unfettered access to this kind of data would facilitate programs of broad and indiscriminate search, threatening the right of the people to be secure against threats of arbitrary state power, and conjuring the specters of general warrants and writs of assistance that haunted the minds of the founding generation (*Carpenter v. United States*, 2018, pp. 2213–2214, 2222–2223).

Epidemiological surveillance programs robust enough to conduct individual contact tracing or to document disease progression using aggregate data will trigger these same concerns. This suggests that they, too, would be subject to some form of Fourth Amendment restraint. The fact that some of the data used might be anonymized does not change the calculus. First, as has been amply demonstrated, it is very easy to deanonymize location data (see, e.g., Khazbak & Cao, 2017, p. 1). That is likely to be particularly true in a world where people have been ordered to stay at home because location data will be robustly associated with individual residences. Second, the fact that data is anonymized may salve some of the individual privacy concerns, but it does little to resolve concerns about "arbitrary power" (*Boyd v. United States*, 1886, as cited in *Carpenter v. United States*, 2018, p. 2214) and "permeating ... surveillance" (*United States v. Di Re*, 1948, as cited in *Carpenter v. United States*, 2018, p. 2214), which threaten the Fourth Amendment right "of the people to be secure ... against unreasonable searches and seizures" (Gray, 2017, pp. 146–156).

Accordingly, it is likely that epidemiological surveillance programs proposed amid the current pandemic would be subject to Fourth Amendment regulation. This does not mean that agencies like the CDC would be forbidden from using these tools or that they would be required to seek and secure a warrant based on probable cause. The Fourth Amendment allows for considerable flexibility in terms of the form of regulation it requires (Gray, 2016, pp. 462–483), particularly where searches are conducted to advance public policies ("special needs") separate from criminal law enforcement (*New Jersey v. T. L. O.*, 1985, p. 351).

The epidemiological surveillance programs discussed in recent months, be they individual tracking, location monitoring, or the use of aggregate data, are likely to fall under the special needs doctrine because their purpose is to address public health challenges rather than to effect the goals of traditional law enforcement. The Court has endorsed public health as a legitimate ground for special needs searches on a number of occasions (see, e.g., *Board of Education of Independent School District No. 92 of Pottawatomie County v. Earls*, 2002; *Vernonia School District 47J v. Acton*, 1995) where the programs are sufficiently likely to succeed in serving a legitimate public interest (but see *Chandler v. Miller*, 1997, pp. 320–321) and stayed true to their public health goals (but see *Ferguson v. City of Charleston*, 2001, pp. 79–80). The centerpiece of the special needs doctrine is the balancing of compelling government interests served by searches against the privacy interests of those subject to potential search. In the present context, there is no doubt that there are significant public health interests at stake. Proper interventions could well save thousands, if not hundreds of thousands, of lives while minimizing social, cultural, and economic harm.[8] These weighty public interests cannot sign a constitutional blank check, however. The Fourth Amendment still requires some form of constitutionally sufficient prospective constraint on searches and the discretionary authority of agents to conduct searches.

Special needs searches generally do not require a warrant.[9] In these non-criminal contexts, the Court has endorsed a variety of regulatory approaches that serve legitimate public policy interests while still guaranteeing the right of the people to be secure from threats of unreasonable searches and seizures. Executive agencies and legislatures play a key role in this context.

---

[8]   This seems to be congressional motivation for funding epidemiological surveillance through the CARES Act (2020).

[9]   See *Michigan v. Sitz*, 1990 (roadblock checkpoints to screen for drunk drivers are reasonable in light of the goal of protecting public safety); *National Treasury Employees Union v. Von Raab*, 1989 (the fact that border control agents carry firearms may provide reasonable public safety grounds for drug testing); *Skinner v. Railway Labor Executives' Association*, 1989 (drug testing of railroad workers involved in accidents is reasonable in light of interest in protecting public safety). Cf. *Ferguson v. City of Charleston*, 2001 (municipal program requiring drug testing pregnant women on public health grounds fell outside the special needs doctrine because positive results were reported to law enforcement).

Courts tend to grant the political branches broad latitude to develop and deploy administrative and programmatic structures regulating the use of searches that serve goals such as public health as long as they are narrowly tailored, likely to succeed, strike a reasonable balance between privacy interests and public policy goals, and limit the discretion of government agents conducting search-es.[10] The next section details a framework that policymakers can apply to meet these constitutional demands when deploying and using epidemiological surveillance tools such as contact tracing.

2   LEGISLATING DIGITAL CONTACT TRACING IN THE SHADOW OF THE FOURTH AMENDMENT

The COVID-19 pandemic poses an emergency for public health. Faced with such emergencies, executive agents are wont to assert broad discretionary powers. As the Canadian Freeholder observed in 1779, they are

> fond of doctrines of reason of state, and state necessity, and the impossibility of providing for great emergencies and extraordinary cases, without a discretionary power in the crown to proceed sometimes by uncommon methods not agreeable to the known forms of law. (Maseres, 1779, pp. 243–244)

The Fourth Amendment guards against these threats, "curb[ing] the exercise of discretionary authority" to search and seize (see Davies, 1999, p. 556). To deploy and use epidemiological surveillance tools will therefore require more than executive fiat. What the Fourth Amendment demands is a clear and delib-erative process, weighing the genuine benefits and costs of programs likely to engage in invasive and potentially mass surveillance. This process—which should involve both legislative and agency actors—must identify prospective remedial measures sufficient to safeguard the right of people to be secure against unreasonable searches and seizures while reasonably accommodating legitimate public health goals.

In other work, one of us has elaborated a constitutionally informed frame-work policymakers can apply when designing data surveillance programs (see Gray, 2017, p. 267). This framework challenges the political branches

---

[10]   See, e.g., *Board of Education of Independent School District No. 92 of Pottawatomie County v. Earls*, 2002 (Ginsburg, J., dissenting, expressing concern that subjecting all high school students engaged in extracurricular activities to drug testing casts too broad a net); *Indianapolis v. Edmond*, 2000 (declining to endorse drug inter-diction roadblocks due, in part, to the fact that driving is a relatively common activ-ity and interdicting drugs is not closely tied to automobile safety); *Chandler v. Miller*, 1997, pp. 320–321 (declining to endorse a drug-testing regime aimed at politicians, in part because the program was unlikely to succeed in detecting actual drug use).

to engage critical questions about need, efficacy, parsimony, and discretion before deploying these kinds of surveillance tools. It also provides a guide for courts to evaluate the constitutional sufficiency of the regulatory structures erected around these kinds of surveillance programs (Wiley & Vladeck, 2020).[11] Below, we explain how that framework might guide the development and deployment of public health surveillance programs like digital contact tracing, location monitoring, and data aggregation and analysis.

Pre-deployment review

Before a digital public health surveillance program is deployed, proponents must publicly and transparently identify the goals of the program and establish a reasonable, scientifically grounded fit between those goals, the methods to be used, and the data to be gathered (Wiley & Vladeck, 2020, p. 267). In particular, proponents must clearly articulate why digital methods outperform traditional alternatives in order to justify additional intrusions on privacy.

Contact tracing is a well-established component of ordinary public health measures. Historically, contact tracing has utilized skilled workers to conduct interviews, contact potentially infected individuals, and counsel and diagnose those individuals throughout a monitoring or quarantine period. But there is emerging evidence that digital contact tracing may have substantial benefits over traditional methods of interview and direct contact, given the unique attributes of COVID-19. Recent modelling data comparing traditional and digital contact tracing methods has indicated that COVID-19 spreads too quickly and often asymptomatically to be controllable through traditional contact tracing methods (see Ferretti et al., 2020). According to some researchers, "instant digital contact tracing" will be necessary to transition out of mass social distancing (Ferretti et al., 2020, p. 4).

Digital contact tracing cannot hope to achieve its promised benefits, however, without necessary precursors and responses. For instance, although the United States has expanded COVID-19 testing, its per capita level of testing still lags behind many countries, including several at the forefront of digital contact tracing (see Worldometer, 2020). Effective identification of infected individuals is a prerequisite to effective contact tracing efforts. Absent testing capacity and procedures robust enough to give confidence that infected individuals are likely be identified rapidly, collecting and storing mass loca-

---

[11]   As Wiley & Vladeck (2020) make clear, courts must not abdicate their role in superintending and ensuring compliance with constitutional protections, even in the face of a pandemic.

tion data is likely to impose significant privacy harms without corresponding public health benefits.[12]

Previous infectious disease mitigation efforts reinforce the need to prioritize traditional processes before resorting to technologically enhanced surveillance. In 2014, a West African outbreak of Ebola eventually made its way to the United States (Centers for Disease Control and Prevention, 2019). The first case of U.S. Ebola was Thomas Eric Duncan, who had contact with an Ebola patient in Liberia four days before traveling to the United States. Although Duncan should have been screened before departing Liberia, that screening did not occur. Moreover, when Duncan presented with symptoms at a Texas emergency room, "somehow doctors were unaware that he had recently traveled from one of the West Africa countries where Ebola [was] spreading rapidly. He was sent home, highly infectious" (Roué-Taylor, 2014). Duncan eventually succumbed to Ebola, but not before infecting two of his caregivers. As one commentator concluded, "Ebola is a tragic reminder of the power of the process" (Roué-Taylor, 2014). Efforts to use aggregate digital data in other public health surveillance efforts have reached similar conclusions (see Lazer & Kennedy, 2015).

Reliable processes to identify infected individuals must be followed by efficient procedures to inform and monitor any contacts who may have been exposed. In the case of COVID-19, current proposals for digital contact tracing largely appear to take for granted that identified contacts will immediately and reliably self-isolate for the two-week incubation period of a possible COVID-19 infection. The Oxford research team that advocates "instant digital contact tracing" plainly states that it modeled the impact of "tracing the contacts of symptomatic cases *and quarantining them*" (Ferretti et al., 2020, p. 4, emphasis added). Their model defines its success rate as "the fraction of all contacts traced, assuming perfectly successful quarantine upon tracing, or the degree to which infectiousness of contacts is reduced assuming all of them are traced" (Ferretti et al., 2020, p. 4). That is a generous assumption with no demonstrated grounding in reality.

Our recent experience with social distancing suggests that many people will continue to congregate, whether by choice or necessity, despite prompts to maintain social distance. Pictures abound of crowded subways, public markets, houses of worship, beaches, and parks across the country (see, e.g., Boykin & Konsmo, 2020; Burke, 2020; "Coronavirus news," 2020). Workers

---

[12]   To be sure, contact tracing may hold value even absent a perfectly robust testing regime. But in light of the deep and broad privacy risks that digital contact tracing programs may impose, in particular, the robustness of the testing regime—and other less high-tech matters—substantially affects the balance of benefits and harms at the core of the special needs analysis.

without paid sick leave—let alone paid leave for possible, but unconfirmed, infection—may simply be unable to afford to self-isolate when prompted by public health orders, even if they are otherwise inclined to obey. From a purely practical perspective, then, models grounded in assumptions about compliance with self-isolation instructions offer little in terms of evidence that digital tracing methods will be superior enough to traditional methods to justify the radical costs to privacy attendant to mass surveillance.

Moreover, digital contact tracing may cast so wide and impersonal a net that it will be less effective than traditional means in generating compliance. Depending on the precision of the location data, prompts to self-isolate may become overbroad and routine, which will further reduce compliance. Social distancing recommendations emphasize six feet of distance between people to minimize infection. This suggests that ideal contact tracing would limit its scope to individuals who were within six feet of an infected person. But cell tower and GPS data typically have margins of error of more than six feet. GPS data, which is more precise than cell tower location data, is usually accurate only to within 16 feet, with even poorer performance in crowded urban areas (see *Carpenter v. United States*, 2018, p. 2219; Global Positioning System, 2017).[13] Bluetooth tracking may be more precise, but it is also overinclusive, likely registering contacts between devices despite the presence of walls, car doors, or even whole floors in a building (Romm et al., 2020).

At least for now, these tools are likely to direct into isolation many people who were never actually at risk. Over time, overbroad notifications will fail to prompt appropriate self-isolation even among individuals who are genuinely at risk—the epidemiological equivalent of crying "wolf!" Other difficulties may arise as well, from false or malicious designations of an individual as infected when they are not, to insufficient participation in voluntary programs. Traditional contact tracing, though perhaps a bit slower, may still prove to be more precise, accurate, robust, reliable, and visceral, and therefore may be more effective in generating actual compliance.

In sum, digital contact tracing is unlikely at present to yield its promised benefits due to low testing rates, low compliance rates, and technological limitations. Before requesting or requiring individuals to sacrifice their locational and associational privacy, policymakers must ensure that the screening, testing, and isolating of affected individuals can be done at comparable scale. Similarly, before aggregate location data is gathered or analyzed, policymakers should ensure that there is sound evidence of efficacy and accuracy of such tools, beyond what traditional public health surveillance methods can generate.

---

[13]   Nonetheless, the majority of existing digital contact tracing apps appear to rely on GPS data (see Woodhams, 2020).

Absent such assurances, Americans would be surrendering substantial privacy without concrete gains in public health, safety, or liberty.[14]

Even if an epidemiological surveillance program can establish efficacy, that does not end the Fourth Amendment inquiry. Given the substantial privacy interests at stake, legislators and app developers must take care at all stages of design, deployment, and use to mitigate against privacy harms, beginning with data gathering. Indeed, these later stages—and the need to continue to probe issues of efficacy—will take on increased importance if app developers or policymakers charge ahead before pre-deployment review is completed (see Introduction, above, e.g., Valentino-DeVries et al., 2020; NDResponse, n.d.; Care19 App, n.d.; Woodhams, 2020).

Data gathering and aggregation

Epidemiological surveillance programs such as digital contact tracing should gather the minimum amount and types of data reasonably necessary to facilitate their public health goals. Although GPS data is seemingly ubiquitous, it casts too wide a net and thus exposes a larger population's location data in response to every query. Bluetooth data, by contrast, may be able to register proximity between devices more precisely, alongside or instead of logging location directly (Valentino-DeVries et al., 2020; NDResponse, n.d.; Care19 App, n.d.; Woodhams, 2020). Utilizing proximity data rather than location data could minimize the intrusiveness of the data gathered because this data would reveal *that* two devices were in proximity but not *where*. Limiting the time frame covered by location or proximity data would minimize the scope of information revealed about a person's movements, habits, and intimate associations.[15]

Policymakers should also mandate information siloing to the full extent possible. Information silos "establish or maintain separation between databases,

---

[14]   The American Civil Liberties Union has sounded similar concerns about efficacy in a recent white paper on technology-assisted contact tracing (see Gillmor, 2020, p. 2).

[15]   In addition to satisfying the Fourth Amendment, data gathering, aggregation, and other features of a digital contact tracing effort must also comply with existing statutory privacy protections. For instance, the California Consumer Privacy Act provides California residents with, among other rights, the right to know what information certain businesses have collected about them, the right to request deletion of that data, and the right to opt out of the sale of that data to others (see California Consumer Privacy Act, 1977/2018). Similar statutory constraints exist under Europe's General Data Protection Regulation ("GDPR") (see Regulation [EU] 2016/679, 2016, p. 1; European Data Protection Board, 2020). Guidance under these statutory frameworks may, in significant respects, mirror the approach advocated in this chapter, including preferring proximity data and requiring limited and exclusive purposes for which data may be used (see European Data Protection Board, 2020).

thereby setting limits on the breadth and generality achieved by aggregation" (Gray, 2017, p. 269). Where possible, data should be stored locally on a device or with the entity that initially gathered it. This limits the government's ability to make secondary uses of sensitive data. Congress used this approach in the 2015 USA Freedom Act, which amended the National Security Agency's telephony metadata program so that metadata would remain with telephone companies until queried, rather than being turned over to the National Security Agency in bulk (Gray, 2017, p. 270).

Similarly, keeping digital location trails out of government hands would help mitigate the privacy threats of contact tracing programs. Thus far, digital contact tracing efforts have relied on centralized administration by governments, putting mass location data in government hands. This includes an app for digital contact tracing that the European Union will soon roll out, beginning in Germany (see Doffman, 2020). But there may be alternatives that decentralize data storage, limiting threats of mass surveillance. For instance, a team at University College London designed a framework that "focuses on decentralization and ... stops any personal data leaving a device" (Doffman, 2020). If accurate and effective, a decentralized approach would help mitigate privacy harms while preserving important public health goals.

Data storage
The privacy harms of digital location tracking are exacerbated the longer tracking lasts and the longer data remains available to government agents (cf. *Birchfield v. North Dakota*, 2016, p. 2178). The Supreme Court has recognized that the time-machine nature of digital location tracking is inconsistent with "a central aim of the Framers ... to place obstacles in the way of a too permeating police surveillance" (*United States v. Di Re*, 1948, as cited in *Carpenter v. United States*, 2018, p. 2218). Strict durational limits on data collection, storage, and destruction are vital to minimize threats to privacy posed by epidemiological surveillance programs.

For example, current public health practice recommends a two-week quarantine or active monitoring period for individuals potentially infected with the COVID-19 virus (see Lauer et al., 2020). A similar durational limit would be appropriate for location data utilized for digital contact tracing. Only contacts within that 14-day period are likely to be at risk of infection, with more temporally distant contacts having interacted with the infected person before they were infected or contagious. It therefore seems that location data should be collected and retained only for two weeks at a time, after which it should be destroyed. Insofar as there may be good reasons to extend this window, the point remains that it is important to set limits on how much data is retained and for how long.

Data access, analysis, and use

Access to the data gathered, aggregated, and stored as part of an epidemiological surveillance program—and authority to query that data—should be strictly limited to those whose access is essential for the program to function. This data should not be available to people, groups, or algorithms for purposes unrelated to digital contact tracing and certainly should not be open source. The reason is straightforward: Mission creep imperils the success and constitutional soundness of such a program as does the risk of abuse.

For instance, mass digital location data would surely aid the Department of Justice in investigating and prosecuting crimes or the Department of Homeland Security in tracking and arresting undocumented immigrants in the United States. But these uses would plainly diverge from the purposes undergirding this digital location data program. So, too, would a functionary's use of the data to trace a former spouse's movement and associations. Just as data should be siloed to prevent its misuse, access and authority to query this data should be zealously guarded, privileging public health efforts and excluding law enforcement or other efforts. Absent such segmentation, the Supreme Court's recent epistle on digital location privacy in *Carpenter* would be meaningless.

Similarly, even within the public health arena, the use of this mass surveillance data must be strictly limited to its intended purpose. For instance, while digital location data might be accessible to public health officials engaged in contact tracing efforts, it would be inappropriate for that data to be accessible to government officials charged with enforcing general social distancing orders (but see Volpicelli, 2020). This constitutes a separate purpose requiring independent justification. Moreover, if decentralization of data is possible, then direct access by any government entity might well be unnecessary, and therefore inappropriate.

The program must end

A well-designed and well-justified epidemiological surveillance program designed to combat COVID-19 must be coupled with strict sunset provisions. The War on Terror, launched in the wake of the 9/11 attacks, is instructive in the way that demands for emergency authority can act as one-way ratchets, effecting permanent expansions of surveillance powers, and how crises can metastasize, developing into perpetual claims of emergency. It is telling that, in the midst of the current crisis, Congress once again granted a reprieve to the National Security Agency's troubled Section 215 program, which originated the bulk collection of telephonic metadata (see McKinney, 2020).[16] Once a tool

---

[16] Congress has also repeatedly extended other controversial surveillance programs, despite apparent sunset or reauthorization provisions, including Section 702 of the FISA Amendments Act of 2008 (see Electronic Frontier Foundation, n.d.).

like contact tracing is operational, it will be tempting for public health officials to utilize this tool to combat other infectious diseases. Seasonal influenza, after all, sickens millions and kills thousands each year (see Centers for Disease Control and Prevention, 2020). The ability to more easily track and trace the flu would surely aid public health efforts. Yet this, too, would constitute unjustified mission creep.

Recursive review
Finally, audit procedures should be required to ensure accountability after the fact. Audit trails or other documentation should enable review of who gains access to sensitive location data, on what authority, and for what queries. In addition, program managers should conduct regular reviews to determine whether the promises of a program match its reality.

CONCLUSION

Epidemiological surveillance programs such as digital contact tracing have been touted as a silver bullet that will free the American public from the strictures of social distancing, enabling a return to school, work, and socializing. But these tools also tread on established expectations of privacy while presenting real threats of persistent mass surveillance. In sorting through these promises and challenges, the Fourth Amendment will have a critical role to play. Like all provisions of the Bill of Rights, it imposes limits on what the political branches can do, no matter how popular or seemingly necessary in "providing for great emergencies and extraordinary cases" (Maseres, 1779, pp. 243–244). In particular, the Fourth Amendment will require that epidemiological surveillance programs demonstrate sufficient potential to serve compelling public health goals.

There are good reasons to be skeptical. Unless and until more mundane aspects of contact tracing are operating efficiently—including availability of testing and practical support for appropriate self-isolation by contacts—there is little reason to think that there is enough promise to justify the dramatic expansions in government power and significant costs to personal privacy.

Even if there is good reason to believe in the public health promise of these programs, the Fourth Amendment requires more than blind faith in the judgment of government officials. The Fourth Amendment is genetically skeptical of granting broad, unfettered discretion for state agents to conduct searches and seizures (*United States v. Jones*, 2012, p. 416). To meet Fourth Amendment demands, epidemiological surveillance programs, whether directed at digital contact tracing, location monitoring, or data aggregation and analysis, must be the products of rigorous deliberative processes, weighing the genuine benefits and costs. Robust prospective remedial measures should be put in place to secure privacy and liberty, including limitations on data gathering, aggregation, storage, access, analysis, and use. In addition, programs should be subject to constant review and sunset provisions. Only by adopting these kinds of procedural and substantive safeguards can we hope to achieve legitimate public health goals as we face COVID-19 while also protecting our sacred constitutional trust.

NOTE

Originally published in a slightly different form as N. Ram & D. Gray (2020). "Mass surveillance in the age of COVID-19." *Journal of Law and the Biosciences*, 7(1), 1–17. © 2020 by the Oxford University Press. Reprinted by permission of the publisher.

REFERENCES

Bebinger, M. (2020, April 3). "Why Charlie Baker thinks 'contact tracing' cases may help Mass. slow—or stop—COVID-19." WBUR. www.wbur.org/commonhealth/2020/04/03/contact-tracing-coronavirus-massachusetts-baker

Birchfield v. North Dakota, 136 S. Ct. 2160 (2016).

Board of Education of Independent School District No. 92 of Pottawatomie County v. Earls, 536 U.S. 822 (2002).

Boyd v. United States, 116 U.S. 616 (1886).

Boykin, N., & Konsmo, S. (2020, April 4). "DC mayor closes wharf fish markets after patrons fail to follow social distancing guidelines." WUSA9. www.wusa9.com/article/news/health/coronavirus/wharf-fish-market-packed-on-a-saturday-social-distancing-not-being-practiced/65-334f226a-e56a-45d9-82f3-e6ad129a60fe

Burke, M. (2020, May 2). "Crowds gathered at National Mall to watch Blue Angels, Thunderbirds flyover." NBC News. www.nbcnews.com/news/us-news/crowds-gathered-national-mall-watch-blue-angels-thunderbirds-flyover-n1198706

California v. Greenwood, 486 U.S. 35 (1988).

California Bankers Association v. Shultz, 416 U.S. 21 (1974).

California Consumer Privacy Act, California Civil Code § 1798.100–1798.199 (1977 & rev. 2018).

Care19 app. (n.d.). "COVID-19 in South Dakota." Retrieved April 30, 2020, from https://covid.sd.gov/care19app.aspx

Carpenter v. United States, 138 S. Ct. 2206 (2018).

Centers for Disease Control and Prevention. (2017, December 6). "Severe acute respiratory syndrome (SARS)." Department of Health and Human Services. www.cdc.gov/sars/index.html

Centers for Disease Control and Prevention. (2019, March 8). "2014–2016 Ebola outbreak in West Africa." Department of Health and Human Services. www.cdc.gov/vhf/ebola/history/2014-2016-outbreak/index.html

Centers for Disease Control and Prevention. (2020). "Disease burden of influenza." Department of Health and Human Services. www.cdc.gov/flu/about/burden/index.html

Chandler v. Miller, 520 U.S. 305 (1997).

Coronavirus Aid, Relief, and Economic Security (CARES) Act, Pub. L. No. 116-136, 134 Stat. 281 (2020). www.congress.gov/116/plaws/publ136/PLAW-116publ136 .pdf

"Coronavirus news: Social distancing is not happening on the NYC subway." (2020, April 1). ABC7NY. https://abc7ny.com/overcrowded-subway-train-nyc-social -distancing-coronavirus/6068366

Davies, T. Y. (1999). "Recovering the original Fourth Amendment." *Michigan Law Review*, 98, 547–750.

Doffman, Z. (2020, April 7). "COVID-19's new reality—these smartphone apps track infected people nearby." *Forbes*. www.forbes.com/sites/zakdoffman/2020/ 04/07/COVID-19s-new-normal-yes-your-phone-will-track-infected-people-nearby/ #790dd4b17f0d

Electronic Frontier Foundation. (n.d.). "Decoding 702: What is Section 702?" Retrieved April 30, 2020, from www.eff.org/702-spying

European Data Protection Board. (2020, April 21). "Guidelines 04/2020 on the use of location data and contact tracing tools in the context of the COVID-19 outbreak." https://edpb.europa.eu/sites/edpb/files/files/file1/edpb_guidelines_20200420 _contact_tracing_covid_with_annex_en.pdf

Ferguson v. City of Charleston, 532 U.S. 67 (2001).

Ferretti, L., Wymant, C., Kendall, M., Zhao, L., Nurtay, A., Abeler-Dörner, L., Parker, M., Bonsall, D., & Fraser, C. (2020). "Quantifying SARS-CoV-2 transmission suggests epidemic control with digital contact tracing." *Science*, 368(6491). https://doi .org/10.1126/science.abb6936

Florida v. Jardines, 569 U.S. 1 (2013).

Gillmor, D. K. (2020, April 16). "Principles for technology-assisted contact-tracing." American Civil Liberties Union. www.aclu.org/report/aclu-white-paper-principles -technology-assisted-contact-tracing

Global Positioning System. (2017, December 5). "GPS Accuracy. U.S. Space Force. www.gps.gov/systems/gps/performance/accuracy/

Google. (n.d.). "COVID-19 Community Mobility Reports." www.google.com/ COVID19/mobility/

Gray, D. (2016). "Fourth Amendment remedies as rights: The warrant requirement." *Boston University Law Review*, 96, 425–483.

Gray, D. (2017). *The Fourth Amendment in an age of surveillance*. Cambridge University Press.

Gray, D., & Citron, D. (2013). "The right to quantitative privacy." *Minnesota Law Review*, 98, 62–144.

Halbfinger, D. M., Kershner, I., & Bergman, R. (2020, March 18). "To track coronavirus, Israel moves to tap secret trove of cellphone data." *New York Times*. www .nytimes.com/2020/03/16/world/middleeast/israel-coronavirus-cellphone-tracking .html

Indianapolis v. Edmond, 531 U.S. 32 (2000).

Katz v. United States, 389 U.S. 347 (1967).

Khazbak, Y., & Cao, G. (2017). "Deanonymizing mobility traces with co-location information." *2017 IEEE Conference on Communications and Network Security*, 1–9. https://doi.org/10.1109/CNS.2017.8228621

Lauer, S. A., Grantz, K. H., Bi, Q., Jones, F. K., Zheng, Q., Meredith, H. R., Azman, A. S., Reich, N. G., & Lessler, J. (2020). "The incubation period of coronavirus disease 2019 (COVID-19) from publicly reported confirmed cases: Estimation and application." *Annals of Internal Medicine*. Advance online publication. https://doi.org/10.7326/M20-0504

Lazer, D., & Kennedy, R. (2015, October 1). "What we can learn from the epic failure of Google flu trends." *Wired*. www.wired.com/2015/10/can-learn-epic-failure-google-flu-trends/

Maseres, F. (1779). *The Canadian Freeholder: In Three Dialogues between an Englishman and a Frenchman, Settled in Canada: Vol. 2*. B. White.

McKinney, I. (2020, March 18). "Enough is enough—let it expire." Electronic Frontier Foundation. www.eff.org/Enough-is-enough-let-215-expire

Michigan v. Sitz, 496 U.S. 444 (1990).

Mozur, P., Zhong, R., & Krolik, A. (2020, March 1). "In coronavirus fight, China gives citizens a color code, with red flags." *New York Times*. www.nytimes.com/2020/03/01/business/china-coronavirus-surveillance.html

National Treasury Employees Union v. Von Raab, 489 U.S. 656 (1989).

NBC New York. (2020, April 22). "What you need to know about New York's 'monumental' contact tracing program." www.nbcnewyork.com/news/coronavirus/what-you-need-to-know-about-new-yorks-monumental-contact-tracing-program/2385611/

NDResponse. (n.d.) "Care19". State of North Dakota. Retrieved April 30, 2020, from https://ndresponse.gov/covid-19-resources/care19

New Jersey v. T. L. O., 469 U.S. 325 (1985).

Oliver v. United States, 466 U.S. 170 (1984).

Ram, N., & Gray, D. (2020). "Mass surveillance in the age of COVID-19." *Journal of Law and the Biosciences*, 7(1), 1–17. https://doi.org/10.1093/jlb/lsaa023

Regulation (EU) 2016/679 of the European Parliament and of the Council of 27 April 2016 on the protection of natural persons with regard to the processing of personal data and on the free movement of such data and repealing Directive 95/36/EC (General Data Protection Regulation). 2016 O.J. L. 119. https://gdpr-info.eu/

Riley v. California, 573 U.S. 373 (2014).

Romm, T., Harwell, D., Dwoskin, E., & Timberg, C. (2020, April 10). "Apple, Google debut major effort to help people track if they've come into contact with coronavirus." *Washington Post*. www.washingtonpost.com/technology/2020/04/10/apple-google-tracking-coronavirus

Roué-Taylor, J. (2014, October). "Ebola shows it is process—not technology—that will protect us." *Wired*. www.wired.com/insights/2014/10/ebola-process-not-technology/

Select Committee to Study Governmental Operations with Respect to Intelligence Activities. (1976, April 26). "Final report together with additional, supplemental, and separate views."

Skinner v. Railway Labor Executives' Association, 489 U.S. 602 (1989).

Tau, B. (2020, March 28). "Government tracking how people move around in coronavirus pandemic." *Wall Street Journal*. www.wsj.com/articles/government-tracking-how-people-move-around-in-coronavirus-pandemic-11585393202

Tectonix GEO [@TectonixGEO]. (2020, March 24). "Want to see the true potential impact of ignoring social distancing? Through a partnership with @xmodesocial, we analyzed secondary locations" [Tweet]. Twitter. https://twitter.com/TectonixGEO/status/1242628347034767361

Thompson, D. (2020, April 7). "The technology that could free America from quarantine." *The Atlantic*. www.theatlantic.com/ideas/archive/2020/04/contact-tracing-could-free-america-from-its-quarantine-nightmare/609577

United States v. Di Re, 332 U.S. 581 (1948).

United States v. Horton, 863 F.3d 1041 (8th Cir. 2017).

United States v. Jones, 565 U.S. 400 (2012).

United States v. Karo, 468 U.S. 705 (1984).

United States v. Knotts, 460 U.S. 276 (1983).

United States v. Miller, 425 U.S. 435 (1976).

U.S. Const. amend. IV.

Valentino-DeVries, J., Singer, N., & Krolik, A. (2020, April 29). "A scramble for virus apps that do no harm." *New York Times*. www.nytimes.com/2020/04/29/business/coronavirus-cellphone-apps-contact-tracing.html

Vernonia School District 47J v. Acton, 515 U.S. 646 (1995).

Volpicelli, G. (2020, April 7). "The NHS coronavirus app could track how long you spend outside." *Wired*. www.wired.co.uk/article/nhs-coronavirus-tracking-app

Watson, C., Cicero, A., Blumenstock, J., & Fraser, M. (2020). "A national plan to enable comprehensive COVID-19 case finding and contact tracing in the US." Johns Hopkins Bloomberg School of Public Health: Center for Health Security. www.centerforhealthsecurity.org/our-work/publications/2020/a-national-plan-to-enable-comprehensive-covid-19-case-finding-and-contact-tracing-in-the-us

Wiley, L. F., & Vladeck, S. (2020). "Coronavirus, civil liberties, and the courts: The case against 'suspending' judicial review." *Harvard Law Review*, 133(9). http://dx.doi.org/10.2139/ssrn.3585629

Woodhams, S. (2020, April 28). "COVID-19 digital rights tracker." Top10VPN. www.top10vpn.com/research/investigations/covid-19-digital-rights-tracker/

World Health Organization. (2017, May 9). "Infection prevention and Control: Contact tracing." United Nations. www.who.int/features/qa/contact-tracing/en/

Worldometer. (2020, April 30). "COVID-19 coronavirus pandemic." www.worldometers.info/coronavirus/#countries

2. Balancing the pursuit of knowledge against the preservation of privacy

Davi Ottenheimer

Examining the global pandemic through a historical lens is the best way to support a meaningful path forward. Computer science and engineering can indisputably help achieve the immediate social and public health needs presented by COVID-19; however, relying on historic lessons can allow us to do so without repeating tragedy. The moment we now face offers us a brilliant opportunity to shift our relationships with technology, if we seize and act upon it intelligently. Conversely, if we fail to accurately assess and mitigate the risks posed by pandemic surveillance, we may tip power balances in ways that may permanently nullify the privacy rights of citizen users.

Because the historical moment of the global pandemic coincides with the historical moment of the best platforms in the world, it affords an inflection point. The coronavirus pandemic starkly exposes many of the flaws and limitations of current approaches to data-centric sources of knowledge and tech-driven solutions. The crisis of COVID-19 has driven some companies to promote "new" powerful and big data platforms as essential to addressing the pandemic. A look at history reveals the opposite. Fundamentals of managing disease information have changed little, whereas allowing growth in unregulated centralization of technology erodes both data privacy and the democratic norms that depend on informational privacy protections.

PRIVACY VERSUS PUBLIC HEALTH

There is a trade-off between privacy and public health when it comes to pandemic surveillance. In public health debates, data privacy is presented as essentially in opposition to pandemic knowledge. On one hand, individuals may reject pandemic surveillance technologies: they may not feel comfortable compromising their information privacy and security for public health purposes. On the other hand, public health mandates may require mass collection of citizen data to track the pandemic and stem the spread of the COVID-19 virus. What we want is a balance that keeps both knowledge and privacy at the forefront. The contradiction between them makes it difficult, especially for technologists. If someone builds digital contact tracing technology and says, "We have given you all this public health knowledge necessary to slow the spread of the virus," someone else might come and say, "Where are the privacy controls?" That is exactly what happened with pandemic surveillance technologies as they were deployed at the start of the pandemic.

Part of the complexity in the "privacy versus public health" debate is a failure to grasp the extent to which information technology is essentially an exercise in economics. The rapid deployment of pandemic surveillance technologies at the start of the COVID-19 crisis was a convergence of the economics of privacy and the economics of public health technologies. And that convergence obscured the true nature of the debate. Tech companies presented the digital contact tracing technologies as privacy enhancing. Public health officials demanded digital contact tracing technologies as a critical part of the solution. Consequently, the economics of technology prevailed. Business considerations drove the decisions about what knowledge to procure from data collection and how to produce public knowledge. However, because of the compelling need for a pandemic prescription, the business model driving the expansion of the data surveillance made possible by the state of emergency did not appear to present itself as an economic driver.

Yet, as is common in our digital economy, how power is negotiated is often a business decision and a product of the tech economy. Providing more storage, more processing memory, more connectivity, and so on enhances business and can result in higher margins or a better product. To put COVID-19 surveillance and public health concerns in a historical context, the pandemic apps present an opportunity like that of the 19th-century California Gold Rush: they have the capacity to mine the health data of our digital bodies like mountains of gold.

Without closely examining the business model and in a moment of premature faith in technology thanks to exigencies, the risk is that we fail to demand a sufficient scientific reason or proof of efficacy to justify pandemic surveillance. We risk blindly accepting that the solution lies with Big Tech tools. However, even solutions that claim to be anonymized and decentralized may not be ethically designed to handle mountains of human information. Who really owns the value of personal data being sifted and sorted from our digital selves? In enforcing the social contract in a democracy, economics and the market must be based in some sense of ethics. And that is where security comes in. Essentially, the security person or data privacy professional might say, "Well, let's not give more power to the platform owners. They don't deserve it. They're not authorized to have that power." This is the difficult tension for some technology companies. The power-loss game dynamic in privacy versus knowledge is essentially one of ethics. The ability to navigate an ethical course of action, especially in an emergency and with ubiquitous data technologies presented as a magic bullet, demands a deliberative process of consideration and analysis. This is where lessons from history become essential.

CENTRALIZED PLATFORMS

In the recent past, two major economic shifts gravitated the world toward centralized digital platforms. The first was the dot-com crash in 2000 and 2001 (Wray, 2010). Before the crash, smaller yet heavily funded start-ups were demonstrating that the web was extremely successful at exactly what it was meant to accomplish—the technical processes of decentralization. However, the success brought an overheated rise in investment that led to the dot-com bubble. After the crash, many of the small companies were absorbed by big companies. Their ideas were sound, but their financials were not, and centralization became an act of financial survival. Today, companies like Amazon that draw on established funding, alternate revenue streams, and centralized platforms have built highly successful versions of what web-based shopping companies like Webvan tried to do 20 years earlier in a decentralized form (see, e.g., Hansell, 2001; Barr, 2013).

The second economic shift was the mortgage crisis of 2008. The rapid shift of money into mobile apps locked people into web-based platforms, or "digital moats" (Grant, 2017). Venture capitalists love this term because the structure ensures a high rate of return on high-risk investments they make. Digital moats defend against competition in the form of interoperability and portability. It is the opposite of what moats are supposed to mean, because it locks people in digital castles. The moat is essentially a prison as opposed to the thing that protects you from adversaries.

These two economic shifts have taken our internet, our web, our world of mobile devices, our independence, and centralized them in ways that are profitable and useful to a specific group of people.

Notably, the Google-Apple API that facilitated pandemic surveillance was championed by the companies and some privacy experts as privacy protecting because it adopted a decentralized data model (Apple, 2020). However, there was little connection to the epidemiological necessities within a pandemic. In many discussions between the companies and the German government, for example, Apple and Google said that because of privacy concerns, they would not go forward with the German plan for a centralized, low-energy Bluetooth contact tracing app (Scott et al., 2020). But the primary criticism of decentralization was that it would not give epidemiologists control of the design and use of the platforms (White & van Basshuysen, 2021). The subtext of these discussions was that Apple wanted to maintain greater control over its devices. Apple did not want to lose control over the user experience and interaction with devices. Loss of product control was more of a concern than privacy. Privacy was a kind of shield put up to protect the control of Apple's engineering practices.

The issue is not so much whether the data collected from pandemic surveillance, made possible through the Google-Apple API, is centralized or decentralized. The more critical issue is whether the concept of privacy is being exploited to serve corporate interests that champion technological control and profit maximization by the tech company over epidemiological interests. Many technologies have been abysmal failures because they were not designed with the right objectives—saving human lives. Instead of centering their collaboration around human life, for example, Apple and Google focused on battery life (Greenberg, 2020). They seemingly cared more about the battery life of a device than they did about human life. Furthermore, their movement toward a decentralized platform fostered innovations around consent, but not a form of consent that is fully autonomous by the user. While users could choose whether to download the COVID-19 tracking app, the Google-Apple API rolled out as an automated update, forcing consumers to adapt their devices to accommodate COVID-19 tracking apps and other similar apps through the adoption of new updates (Amadeo, 2021; Etherington, 2020).

In essence, the security update, the technology itself that had enabled the pandemic surveillance tracing technologies, was coerced under the rhetoric that the decentralization of data would be privacy enhancing through the Google-Apple API. And now that the API has been developed to minimize battery drain caused by the surveillance technologies embedded within the COVID-19 tracing apps, the question is whether future surveillance apps can maximize this new "battery sipping" API. The API facilitates surveillance technology innovations. In other words, a technological barrier had prohibited the adoption of Bluetooth-based tracing and tracking technologies. The pre-API technology created a barrier to certain surveillance technologies because the adoption of those technologies would have resulted in excessive battery drain.

Centralization is unjust or non-beneficial to a large number of people. It is not necessarily the fault of centralization inherently, but the practice of centralization. The efficiency, the margin, and the scale serve a certain group of people, and they may not have any concept or sense of who is harmed. There is an efficiency in centralization, as it allows a centralized authority to make a unilateral decision on behalf of multitudes of users. Centralizing data to accommodate many people requires the central authority to decide that it is going to invest in those models. But if you have a standards-based technology, the efficiency is oriented to being closer to the needs of a local application developer. For example, a pandemic management app made in any regional hospital could fund its own development around models that best suit the needs of the providers or patients in that area.

Instead of novel solutions to this ancient problem of aligning our identity with common technologies, the technologies introduced during the pandemic shed light on how pandemic surveillance risks permanently shaping identity. Efforts to build applications are forced into either aggressive centralization or extreme localization, making it difficult to navigate identity choices because both limit users in shaping their identity (see, e.g., Criddle & Kelion, 2020). One kind of application doesn't share data well, the other doesn't allow the user data integrity control. The gap between approaches is palpable, as people also discuss a flip-switch or a "data dump" as the only compromise, which presents a wholly unsafe and unsatisfactory situation. How does anyone really cross a one-way bridge in reverse, or undo a hard switch from private to shared? This is a question everyone should be asking. How do we maintain consent and control after we dump our "digital bodies" into hands we don't and won't perpetually trust?

Many are right to suggest that more regulation and greater pressure for transparency of the biggest big data platforms (Facebook, Apple, Amazon, Google, Microsoft, Twitter) can move us closer to safe consent; in other words, we collect data about them to stop unsafe collection of data about us. Greater transparency pressure on big data platforms is good, yet the problem with a detective approach is always that too little is discovered too late. We need prevention strategies.

A better answer is that data consent controls in software should technically always stay in the hands of the data owners, not only theoretically or by policy. Better standards and protocols (e.g., W3C Solid, which aims to allow users full control of their data within a decentralized standards-based system) have the necessary concepts built in today that facilitate a shift to wider access when necessary, while at the same time being safer and revocable (Lohr, 2021; Berners-Lee, 2018). We could already be writing apps that move our world toward a data fabric that is run by owners where a no really means no.

LESSONS FROM THE PAST

Again, the core challenge is building technology that can represent the natural balance between sharing knowledge and privacy in our everyday lives, even during times of crisis. We want to share knowledge, but we also want to protect our privacy. The value of knowledge that comes from sharing information widely has to come from flexible and responsive control by data owners and their local service providers, such as doctors or clinics. Comfort and guidance for these current difficult times can sometimes be found by examining past moments of extraordinary changes. To that end, it is useful to consider some simple examples from health and human rights crises in mid-1800s Europe.

In a widely retold story from 1846, a Hungarian doctor named Ignaz Semmelweis noticed that more women died in childbirth when a doctor was present than ones who gave birth unaccompanied by a doctor. Semmelweis surmised from some basic analysis that use of a disinfectant by doctors would decrease fatality risk to women (Kadar et al., 2018, p. 521). He developed and applied an innovative yet simple disinfection routine. A steep and immediate reduction in deaths proved him right. Unfortunately, germ theory had not yet been developed, and Semmelweis was not well received by the conservative medical establishment he directly challenged. He suffered greatly while pursuing a virtuous campaign that he correctly believed would dramatically reduce unnecessary deaths (Kadar et al., 2018, p. 522).

The lesson we must consider today is whether we are in a similar position to derive answers that significantly and immediately reduce death rates. This manifests in many of the debates around washing hands, use of masks, and drug and vaccine trials. All of it needs better data, and our technology can serve us the way that Semmelweis used the technology of his day.

Adolf Fischhof was also a young doctor in Austria at the same time as Semmelweis. In 1848, Fischhof advocated for a constitution that would protect citizens from human rights abuses (Lagi, 2017, pp. 350–351). Historians refer to the "Neoabsolutist" government of the time as "centralization with a vengeance." It was in effect a surveillance society that was a precursor to the data collection of today's Big Tech firms. Fischhof's call for liberty was revolutionary in his time, as he decried his country's becoming a "standing army of soldiers, kneeling army of worshippers, and crawling army of informants" (Britannica, n.d.).

Fischhof, like Semmelweis, started spreading concepts to protect people from harm. He promulgated a constitution as a step toward enshrining human rights. In that context the question for him was whether he could lead a movement against technology that was facilitating vengeful centralization under an unjust authority that used pervasive surveillance.

And in a third example, Dr. John Snow analyzed disease with technology. In 1854 in London, he led a practice of interviewing survivors and compiling resulting data; his mathematical approach today is considered a trailblazing example of data visualization and contact tracing through health data collection and analysis (Rogers, 2013). His work not only pioneered social regulation of tech—in this case, removing a community water pump handle to disable the well responsible for a cholera outbreak (Vinten-Johansen et al., 2003, p. 294)—but also delivered insights essential to ending decades of political delays in securing approval to build the greater public sewer system for London (Cook, 2001).

Semmelweis, Fischhof, and Snow contextualized and utilized the technology of their time. How would modern technology be used in the hands of each? What would they be promulgating in the modern context? Put these stories together and they bear amazing resemblance to our modern dilemmas as well as policy decisions during the COVID-19 pandemic. The doctors applied themselves using state-of-the-art technology to foment positive change and public good. And it should not go unmentioned that they ultimately were rejected and, in the case of both Semmelweis and Fischhof, incarcerated by the very systems they aimed to improve.

These stories make us consider whether an application of more rational, compassionate, and moral human guidance to technology of any day brings faster and broader positive outcomes, both for the advocates of science and for the vulnerable populations they serve.

A BALANCED APPROACH TO FORWARD PROGRESS

Given such celebrated efforts of Semmelweis, Fischhof, and Snow in data collection and analysis for social good and medical advancements in public health and epidemiology, why is there such a lack of trust in Big Technology companies who could deploy modern versions of their work? The dilemma is an ethical one. It is not a question of whether technology itself can be trusted in data collection. The question is whether self-interested companies that have been centralizing power over data for years will continue taking away privacy and ignore inherited rights by building ever-invasive tools and operating them unethically.

Useful technology solutions should mean engineers start from a foundation of ethics to guide innovations through necessary and proportionate steps. COVID-19 tools ought to emerge from epidemiological expertise, not force epidemiologists to squeeze into business boxes unfit for public health purposes. After all, Dr. Snow's aim clearly was to understand and prevent disease. He was not pushed by private companies to suit their aims. Data owners, as with epidemiologists, should not be forced to compromise to suit the technologists' whims and profits. Epidemiological prescriptions and public health prognostications based on personal health data are societal questions and must be tied directly to technical controls that honor basic consent of the data owners.

The global COVID-19 crisis has Big Tech companies weighing in with their view of solutions that probably seem a long way from the 1850s, yet the fundamentals haven't changed. We need to discuss ways to reinvent and reimagine how everyone generates, stores, and consumes data. Had Android or iOS been available in the time of Semmelweis, Fischhof, and Snow, I am certain that today we would be discussing the same topics and reflecting on the same choices made by these men—although, to be fair, we are seeing more volume, more variety, and more velocity of data than they could have imagined.

Intelligence should not mean to pursue all this data for its own sake, but rather should mean to strive to answer questions or give some knowledge specific to a warning. The latter is how we will make our best decisions. The latter also is far less risky than the mad accumulation of information by aggressive centralists. The unregulated corporate collection of information, without representation or accountability, has led people to rightfully wonder how "Don't be evil" is even attainable as Google's (former) motto. Now is a great time to wonder this aloud more than ever.

Uncertain times force us to think more purposefully about our future desired world because our normal pace of current activities experiences an abnormal end. We suddenly acknowledge our habits as we process their loss, which moves us toward an unavoidable reflection on what we had taken for granted.

History clearly shows that an unbridled novelty approach to technology during times of rushed solutions translates to powerful elites expanding mistreatment of vulnerable populations, and to mass atrocities (e.g., the 1882 Chinese Exclusion Act led to the 1887 mass murder of Chinese Americans, and later to the targeted "papers, please" movement restrictions during World War II; Nokes, 2006, p. 332; Hu, 2011). In the United States, for example, this is why COVID-19 data collection must operate in the context of both science and the nation's struggle with systemic racism in its corporations and government. We must embrace the good while avoiding predictable repetitions in the unjust and inhumane use of technology.

Corporations today operate with wildly unbalanced collection tools and have minimal or missing ethical consent, representation, or accountability models. Big Tech has long operated within selfish "legal" interpretations of unlimited data access and purpose, feigning a false separation of engineering from ethics. It has been far too easy for tech companies to take unfair advantage of vulnerable groups and users by sidestepping consent in complex social relationships and ignoring the human right to privacy (Newman, 2013; Richards & King, 2014).

The pressure to act quickly during the pandemic thus brings to mind many glaring flaws and limitations of the current approaches by the largest data platforms. Why would any Big Tech company be trusted to collect private health data, under what circumstances, and when? Who is allowed to responsibly access the data, and for how long? What is the proper response to insights found? How can data remain private to the individual while serving a shared public good?

The sensible access model during a pandemic is based on community service provider roles and attributes (e.g., doctor, nurse, lawyer), and this further illuminates how current Big Tech COVID-19 models are misguided (Cohen et al.,

2020). A health officer should lead public health technology product features. Just as doctors ascribe to standards of care and elected officials to public oaths, so an oath or standard of care should be required of engineers and operators, such as restricting use of location or movement tracking, and in service of public objectives.

The Apple-Google system claims to handle risks by completely disengaging from authorities. They force absolute decentralization as privacy preserving without any real evidence of effectiveness for either protecting privacy or advancing public health. In fact, studies indicate that most of the new COVID-19 apps are not privacy preserving (Hatamian et al., 2021). And it has been reported that contact tracing is already being repurposed to favor the objectives of those with political power, consistent with the United States' historical abuse of identity technology (e.g., Singer & Sang-Hun, 2020; Zhong, 2020).

COVID-19 is a forcing function for us to radically reimagine the way that user data is stored, accessed, and utilized. Theorizing is not enough. Responsible data ownership requires us to think in terms of real-world complex attributes and role access models to allow knowledge while limiting collection and use of data to reasonable norms set by owners. We need engineers ready to build something guided by nuance and the data ethics of scientists like Semmelweis, Fischhof, and Snow.

A COVID app that honored privacy would have better results than one designed by Google and Apple engineers with an exclusivity bubble as a goal. They just engineer something whole cloth to serve the people, which has failed repeatedly. Google has yet to come up with an innovative product since their initial use of search to index the web, which in and of itself was simply an application of the Beowulf cluster technology and the concept of peer review. Google took two existing ideas, put them together, and then used advertising to fund it. Since that time, Google has produced very little innovation. Google takes other people's ideas and makes them better, but that does not put the company in a position to solve COVID. Instead, what we need to do is ask, "Who are the modern Drs. Snow and Semmelweis, and what would they use technology for? How would they use technology to find disease, find the source, and better address people's needs?" In that sense, informed consent becomes based on who you're talking to, what they are doing, and how they are doing it: "Would I allow this doctor, would I allow this group, or would I allow this nation to help me protect myself and my family?"

This is a very different consent decision from saying, "Let's let Apple or Google decide what to do with my data through mechanisms we can't even see." The mechanisms and algorithms are highly opaque. Open standards, as the web has proven, are a foundation of building better technology. The fact that Google and Apple had to work together to find a way to interoperate is shameful. They should have been able to recognize right away that they already interoperate on internet communication protocols like TCP/IP, HTTPS, and TLS.

Open standards are essential to the success of any technology that is going to serve both knowledge purposes to improve the human condition and privacy purposes to protect the right to privacy. The first is the open standard for technology, but the second is essentially an open standard for privacy rights. We must embrace a universal concept of privacy as a human right. Open standards for both technology and privacy are taken for granted because we benefit so much from them. Yet the fact that we take them for granted leaves room for pushback. People want to create proprietary standards because doing so is beneficial for them even if it hurts others. They see some benefit to themselves and so they push proprietary standards for technology and for privacy rights.

Some researchers ask, "What harm is there for privacy loss?" (Caprio et al., 2018). In some sense, exposing harm from privacy loss is itself a loss of privacy. It requires revealing that you have been harmed. Some may claim there is no evidence of privacy loss actually harming anyone, but that is a shift away from the framing of privacy as a priceless right. Many of us have a clear sense of the importance of privacy and the dangers of exposing our personal information. The protection of information in the form of intellectual property or physical assets is one type of quantifiable privacy protection, but arguably, privacy as a human right is not quantifiable. Open standards for technology allow us to interoperate open standards for rights, and allow us to interoperate. We should use these standards to implement these universal concepts on a relativist basis.

Fortunately, efforts are already underway, and there is real opportunity for social good using technology that both pre-dates Big Technology and yet is new again. Instead of any single giant repository, data can be "recentralized" around owners and accessed via consent. Not only does this human relationship-based model of tech generate healthcare knowledge, but it assuages concerns of users wary of data abuse. It also alleviates burdens placed on organizations who currently lack viable alternatives to the Google and Apple models that force reductions in privacy to use services.

If Dr. Snow were here today, he would design a data acquisition and storage model to study and end COVID-19 very different from the Google and Apple framework. His long-standing goal was the demonstrable and fast reduction in harm, not imposing and operating his tools on citizens for personal gains. We should continue that legacy of service to others.

SOLUTIONS FRAMEWORK

There are three essential considerations for developing technology solutions for public health. First, we need to level the field for software and hardware developers by building open standards for data access. We must move data ownership away from proprietary platforms and apps. The web has been successful because it relies on being open, and we must reignite that legacy to reach our better future.

We need to invigorate the market for technology by leveling the field for software and hardware developers. Standardization is the tried and tested solution for interoperability and expansion of ideas, because it encourages wider and deeper research in technology options. If the market continues to have only a handful of self-centered giants set the terms and conditions of software development (with their SDK lock-in and inflexibility), we will prolong human suffering by squelching technology innovation opportunities.

Second, we need to universally start projects with protection rights, such as data privacy and data consent, in formal terms that can be monitored and enforced. The COVID-19 apps should fit within the norm of human-centric data storage with consent controls, not be a special panic-driven rushed design that promises safety with no guarantees.

After all, we can benefit from Snow's research without delving into the personal information of the cholera outbreak victims or the neighborhoods Snow mapped in 1854 (Vinten-Johansen et al., 2003, p. 310). Mapping the outbreak didn't necessitate the exposure of personal information. We have medically appropriate research generated by Snow without excessive need or want for underlying data to be revealed. Why wasn't that an initiative of Google and Apple five or even ten years ago? Pandemics are not new, and epidemiology has a clear purpose for access to big data.

We need to protect rights, such as privacy and safety, more universally, in formal terms that can be monitored and enforced. As we have explored here, preservation of privacy seems to be an inherent contradiction to accumulation of knowledge, yet the two can coexist when striving for a balanced (role-based authorization) approach. Again, think of Semmelweis and Snow explaining the outbreaks to us without exposing personal information. To this day we have knowledge generated by them with no real data about their patients or the people they studied.

Third, the questions of who should be authorized to see your data, when they can access it, and for how long are all fundamental considerations for future innovation—and questions that implicate fundamental human rights. The kind of data detective work pioneered by Dr. Snow requires skilled judgment by trained health professionals accountable to an ethical code. Big Tech unfortunately and repeatedly has proven itself unqualified to lead in this context. The moment we face offers a brilliant opportunity to reorient and reassess responsible data ownership standards, if only we have the determination and insight to do so.

HISTORY VERSUS TECHNOLOGY

Developing technology in a far more humane way is in fact possible if we make the right decisions now. Decisions that reflect the human condition of change, rehabilitation, reflection, and the creation of who we are and who we are perceived to be are increasingly tied up in technology. Data collection and analysis risks with the new contact tracing apps are adding fuel to long-running debates about privacy as well as ownership and control. At the same time, we should be asking an even more fundamental question about the role of technology in our lives. Can we control access to data so it doesn't become an unfair means of control over us?

Trying to squeeze humanity into uncomfortable shortcomings of technology boxes made by Apple or Google is exactly backwards. Big Tech expects the virus to behave in a way convenient to mobile phones such that everyone could own one, always keep it on them, charged, with Bluetooth enabled—a set of assumptions as unreasonable as they are unrealistic.

Contemporary attempts to fight the global pandemic aspire to capitalize on the "three *vs*"—high volume, variety, and velocity—of big data (Gewirtz, 2018). The tricky part is to safely yet dynamically shift a balance of power from an individual's generated data to the many incoming layers of desire for knowledge (from doctor to hospital, from regional health services to national or even global one). Who should be authorized to see your data, when, and for how long are fundamental questions we must not lose sight of when enabling technology that examines our "digital bodies." Data collection and examination of our digital bodies can be done right if we do not lose sight of lessons from history—and if we do the hard work to build platforms and technologies ready to support market growth through socially responsible innovation in engineering.

With that in mind, here is some simple logic to illuminate why the Big Tech coronavirus mobile app models are misguided. They would be justified if they were effective. Yet definitions of "effectiveness" are either vaguely pitched by Big Tech companies themselves or left open to debate.

Even if a definition of "effective" could be derived from fieldworkers (e.g., human contact tracers), they would depend on massive adoption of a very few mobile apps using Bluetooth that are always on and never run out of battery. That uptake, aside from technical barriers, would happen only if people had some degree of trust in the project. And trust requires the kind of transparency in data collection that Big Tech companies cannot achieve.

Now imagine instead if Semmelweis, Snow, and Fischhof were to time travel and design an application meant to study and end human suffering from disease. Their definition of effectiveness seems fairly clear, given hindsight. They were searching for a demonstrable reduction in harm in a short time that would not violate the rights of citizens under a constitutional framework of law. Their wise vision is within our immediate grasp, should we humbly choose to accept the challenge.

REFERENCES

Amadeo, R. (2021, June 21). "Even creepier COVID tracking: Google silently pushed app to users' phones [Updated]." ArsTechnica. https://arstechnica.com/gadgets/ 2021/06/even-creepier-covid-tracking-google-silently-pushed-app-to-users-phones/

Apple. (2020, April 10). "Apple and Google partner on COVID-19 contact tracing technology." www.apple.com/newsroom/2020/04/apple-and-google-partner-on-covid -19-contact-tracing-technology/

Barr, A. (2013, June 18). "From the ashes of Webvan, Amazon builds a grocery business." Reuters. www.reuters.com/article/net-us-amazon-webvan/from-the-ashes-of -webvan-amazon-builds-a-grocery-business-idUSBRE95H1CC20130618

Berners-Lee, T. (2018, October 22). "One small step for the web …" Inrupt. www .inrupt.com/one-small-step-for-the-web

Britannica. (n.d.). "Austria, History, Neoabsolutist era, 1849–60." www.britannica .com/place/Austria/Neoabsolutist-era-1849-60

Caprio, D., Freund, L., Jerome, J., Sepulveda, D., & Stemaier, G. M. (2018, June 1). "The US impact of the GDPR" [Panel discussion]. Sixth Annual Symposium on the Law and Economics of Privacy and Data Security, George Mason University, Arlington, VA, United States.

Cohen, J. E., Hartzog, W., & Moy, L. (2020). "The dangers of tech-driven solutions to COVID-19." Brookings. www.brookings.edu/techstream/the-dangers-of-tech -driven-solutions-to-covid-19/

Cook, G. C. (2001). "Construction of London's Victorian sewers: The vital role of Joseph Bazalgette." *Postgraduate Medical Journal*, 77(914), 802–802. http://dx.doi .org/10.1136/pgmj.77.914.802

Criddle, C., & Kelion, L. (2020, May 7). "Coronavirus contact-tracing: World split between two types of app." BBC. www.bbc.com/news/technology-52355028

Etherington, D. (2020, May 20). "COVID-19 exposure notification settings begin to go live for iOS users with new update." TechCrunch. https://techcrunch.com/2020/05/ 20/covid-19-exposure-notification-settings-begin-to-go-live-for-ios-users-with-new -update/

Gewirtz, D. (2018). "Volume, velocity, and variety: Understanding the three V's of big data." ZDnet. www.zdnet.com/article/volume-velocity-and-variety-understanding -the-three-vs-of-big-data

Grant, N. (2017, May 17). "'Moat' is the latest jargon encircling Silicon Valley." Bloomberg. www.bloomberg.com/news/articles/2017-05-17/-moat-is-the-latest -jargon-encircling-silicon-valley

Greenberg, A. (2020, April 10). "How Apple and Google are enabling Covid-19 contact-tracing." *Wired.* www.wired.com/story/apple-google-bluetooth-contact -tracing-covid-19/

Hansell, S. (2001, February 19). "Some hard lessons for online grocers." *New York Times.* www.nytimes.com/2001/02/19/business/some-hard-lessons-for-online -grocer.html

Hatamian, M., Wairimu, S., Momen, N., & Fritsch, L. (2021). "A privacy and security analysis of early-deployed COVID-19 contact tracing Android apps." *Empirical Software Engineering*, 26(3), 1–51.

Hu, M. (2011, November 15). "'Show me your papers' laws and American cultural values." Jurist. www.jurist.org/commentary/2011/11/margaret-hu-immigration -papers/

Kadar, N., Romero, R., & Papp, Z. (2018). "Ignaz Semmelweis: The 'savior of mothers': On the 200th anniversary of his birth." *American Journal of Obstetrics and Gynecology*, 219(6), 519–522. https://dx.doi.org/10.1016%2Fj.ajog.2018.10 .036

Lagi, S. (2017). "Adolf Fischhof and the national question in the Habsburg Empire: A problem of 'trust' and 'collaboration' amongst the nationalities of Austria (1869–1885)." In L. Kontler & M. Somos (eds.), *Trust and Happiness in the History of European Political Thought* (pp. 345–368). Brill.

Lohr, S. (2021). "He created the web. Now he's out to remake the digital world." *New York Times.* www.nytimes.com/2021/01/10/technology/tim-berners-lee-privacy -internet.html

Newman, N. (2013). "The costs of lost privacy: Consumer harm and rising economic inequality in the age of Google." *William Mitchell Law Review*, 40, 849. http://dx.doi .org/10.2139/ssrn.2310146

Nokes, R. G. (2006). "'A most daring outrage': Murders at Chinese Massacre Cove, 1887." *Oregon Historical Quarterly*, 107(3), 326–353. www.jstor.org/stable/ 20615657

Richards, N. M., & King, J. H. (2014). "Big data ethics." *Wake Forest Law Review*, 49(2), 393–432. https://ssrn.com/abstract=2384174

Rogers, S. (2013, March 15). "John Snow's data journalism: The cholera map that changed the world." *The Guardian.* www.theguardian.com/news/datablog/2013/ mar/15/john-snow-cholera-map

Scott, M., Braun, E., Delcker, J., & Manacourt, V. (2020). "How Google and Apple outflanked governments in the race to build coronavirus apps." Politico.

Singer, N., & Sang-Hun, C. (2020). "As coronavirus surveillance escalates, personal privacy plummets." *New York Times.* www.nytimes.com/2020/03/23/technology/ coronavirus-surveillance-tracking-privacy.html

Vinten-Johansen, P., Brody, H., Paneth, N., Rachman, S., Rip, M., & Zuck, H. D. (2003). *Cholera, Chloroform, and the Science of Medicine: A Life of John Snow.* Oxford University Press.

White, L., & van Basshuysen, P. (2021). "Privacy versus public health? A reassessment of centralised and decentralised digital contact tracing." *Science and Engineering Ethics*, 27(2), 1–13.

Wray, R. (2010, March 13). "Ten years after the crash, the dotcom boom can finally come of age." *The Guardian.* www.theguardian.com/business/2010/mar/14/ technology-dotcom-crash-2000

Zhong, R. (2020). "China's virus apps may outlast the outbreak, stirring privacy fears." *New York Times*. www.nytimes.com/2020/05/26/technology/china-coronavirus -surveillance.html

3. Surveillance and pandemic in Brazil: an essay in three acts

Nathalie Fragoso, Clarice Tavares, and Jade Becari

This chapter concatenates facts at different times in which state surveillance practices motivated by health emergencies are evident in the public debate or historical record. We do not assume that the management of a COVID-19 pandemic is simply a product of historical legacies. We observe and argue, however, that in order to understand it, it may be useful to observe other critical moments that synthesize power relations and are built and reconstructed from common elements and indicate important interpretative keys for the Brazilian case.

The first case of COVID-19 in Brazil was registered in late February 2020. Brazilian authorities' responses to the emerging crisis were uncoordinated. While the federal government took a negationist position, local governments, with significant variation in effectiveness, sought to implement measures to contain the spread of the virus in the country. Between the attempts by state and municipal governments to implement lockdowns, social distancing, and use of technological tools with the most varied purposes and the federal government's commitment to collective immunization through rampant contamination and the investment of material and symbolic resources in treatments known to be ineffective (Centro de Estudos e Pesquisas de Direito Sanitário [CEPEDISA], 2021), in August 2021, the country surpassed 570,000 deaths by COVID-19, according to official data ("Brasil ultrapassa 570 mil mortes," 2021).

Even in this uncoordinated way, as in many countries worldwide, Brazilian authorities have invested heavily in the use of technological tools to fight the pandemic. Contact tracing apps such as Coronavírus SUS, telemedicine apps such as Atende em Casa (Home Service), and apps for granting the minimum income benefit, such as Emergency Aid, were part of the repertoire of public policies implemented during the health emergency that implied new uses of Brazilians' personal data (Gomes et al., 2020).

However, Brazil had low adherence to some of these tools and other COVID-19 containment measures. The divergent orientations of the different public bodies added to the country's structural inequalities—which made both the realization of a lockdown and remote access to services difficult—can be attributed, at least in part, to distrust of the actions of public authorities in confronting the pandemic. Regarding the use of technological tools, a survey carried out by the Painel TIC COVID-19 showed that over half of Brazilians believed that the risks in making their personal data available outweighed the benefits (Painel TIC COVID-19, 2020). Among the reservations regarding the data availability presented by the interviewees were the risks of digital crimes and surveillance, both from public authorities and from the private sector.

The use of data to fight the pandemic by controlling social distancing and use of contact tracing tools, or even the sharing of data for research purposes and serious episodes of leaks, led to concerns regarding surveillance and privacy. Even when presented as necessary, in a context that demanded, in fact, urgent measures, several episodes showed excessive and unlawful data treatment and a scenario of some legal uncertainty. Because of the pandemic, an attempt was made to postpone the entry into force of the General Personal Data Protection Law (Lei Geral de Proteção de Dados Pessoais, or LGPD; Serpro, 2020), and there was a substantial delay in establishing the National Data Protection Authority (Kuo, 2020). The entire debate showed how the meaning and normative horizon of a data protection legal framework in the country are still under construction. There is also a historical-institutional liability to be addressed by the authorities responsible for data protection enforcement and effectiveness.

As for this liability crystallized in public policies, it is worth noting how certain practices related to the processing of personal data in the context of the health emergency of the COVID-19 pandemic mirror government actions in the formation of the Brazilian state, which forged defining features of the country and its society, government, and culture. The objective of this chapter is to briefly analyze these three *acts*—data collection and processing actions (a) in the formation of a national state, (b) in the management of the yellow fever epidemic, and (c) in the management of the COVID-19 pandemic—and the coincident power asymmetries on which they sit. An opaque and democratic deficient state, we argue, finds its population's distrust as its first operational constraint.

DATA PROCESSING IN THE FORMATION OF THE BRAZILIAN NATIONAL STATE: RACISM AND POPULATION MANAGEMENT IN DECREES NOS. 797 AND 798/1851

Carvalho (2012) reports how in the first session of the first parliamentary legislature after the declaration of independence in Brazil (1822), the congressman Custódio Dias complained about the lack of statistics on the public service and the society to be governed: "We don't have the precise data to know the evils that must be remedied, and without the necessary knowledge we can do nothing" (p. 37).[1] The collection and processing of data on the country's population, public health, and economic activities, perceived as a condition for the planning, formulation, and implementation of state action, were demanded, but not provided quickly or effectively (p. 38).

Despite the urgency conveyed by the congressman, only the yellow fever epidemic in the years 1849–1850 produced the first effects on the issue, breaking the informational inertia and offering a cause for the organization of a census. The statistics of those killed by the epidemic needed to be compiled with information from public hospitals. These statistics were marked by underreporting, as many deaths took place outside hospitals and wards, and without recording the cause of death.

In 1850, Law No. 586 was enacted, authorizing the country's first census (art. 17, §3). The urgency of the epidemic resulted in the edition of decrees making compulsory the civil registration of births and deaths and prescribing a "general census of the Empire." Decree No. 797/1851 instituted the General Census of the Empire; Decree No. 798/1851 created a system for the civil registration of births and deaths. These regulations centralized in the state, for the first time, the functions of recording and collecting data on all people who inhabited Brazil, whether free or enslaved. Until then, the functions of registration of births, marriages, and deaths were the responsibility of the Catholic Church, which kept these data in ecclesiastical books, separated according to the condition of enslaved person or free person (Oliveira, 2005, p. 121).

Under the new regulations, civil registries would no longer have separate registration books for enslaved people and free people. Under the new system, the justice of the peace in each district would be responsible for registering births and deaths. The religious sacraments, both for the newborn and for the deceased, could be performed only after registration was made by the imperial authorities (Saavedra, 2015, p. 92). In addition, for free newborns, data was collected on day and place of birth, gender, name, parents' names, profession and domicile; in the case of enslaved people, the name of the "master," date and place of birth, sex, race, and parents' names if they were married, or only the mother's name if they were not. Race, therefore, was not included for the freeborn, and in the records of the enslaved, if freedom was granted, it was to be registered with a specific note. In the book of deaths, race was required to be recorded only for enslaved people.

---

[1] Our translation. In the original:
Não temos os dados precisos para sabermos dos males que se devem remediar, e sem os conhecimentos necessários nada poderemos fazer.

The law did not catch on. Popular uprisings broke out in Pernambuco, Paraíba, Alagoas, Sergipe, Ceará, and Minas Gerais (Saavedra, 2015; Carvalho, 2012). The most famous resistance movements in Paraíba and Pernambuco, known respectively as Ronco das Abelhas (figuratively, the Roar of the Bees[2]) and Revolta dos Marimbondos (Revolt of the Hornets),[3] were led by black and brown, poor and free men. The motivation for the revolt was the fear that such records, which no longer differentiated between enslaved and free people in separate books, could subject poor men to the condition of slavery, especially in a context where being registered as black could be risky, even if the register did not record the person as enslaved (Oliveira, 2005, p. 121).

The background to this fear was the unstable enslavement regime and the constant infractions of the laws that were beginning to criminalize slavery in the country. Brazil was the last country in the American continent to abolish slavery, and it did so gradually and without offering reparations or guarantees to the newly freed people. With the promulgation in 1831 of the Feijó Law, the first law to abolish slavery in the country, the trafficking of enslaved people became forbidden. Years later, with Law No. 581/1850, known as the Eusébio de Queirós Law, measures were established for the repression and criminalization of people engaged in the trafficking of enslaved people. However, even though slavery began to be illegal in this period, these laws did not offer any guarantees to enslaved individuals, since the enslavers acted outside the law. Thus, the condition of an enslaved or a free person could easily be changed. In this sense, Saavedra (2015, p. 105) states that an individual could be submitted to the condition of slavery, manage to become free, and then, whether by an illegal process or not, become enslaved again:

In Brazilian 19th-century society, especially between 1830 and 1860, "no African or African descendant—black or brown, free or freed—could remain safe from threats to his freedom by the customary landlord right to reduce people to slavery regardless of the law" (Chalhoub, 2010, p. 100). For black and brown people in Brazil in those years, freedom was a "very risky undertaking" (Idem. p. 107).[4]

---

[2] Translation according to Loveman (2007).

[3] Revolt movements similar to those that occurred in Paraíba and Pernambuco were registered in other states in the northeast, such as Alagoas, Ceará, and Sergipe (Oliveira, 2005, p. 120).

[4] Our translation. In the original:
    Na sociedade oiticentista brasileira, principalmente entre 1830 e 1860, "nenhum africano ou descendente de africano—preto ou pardo, livre ou liberto—poderia permanecer a salvo de ameaças à sua liberdade pelo direito costumeiro senhorial a reduzir pessoas à escravidão independentemente da lei" (Chalhoub, 2010, p. 100). Para pretos e pardos no Brasil desses anos, a liberdade constituía um "empreendimento muito arriscado" (Idem. p. 107).

Thus, the free black and brown men who rebelled during the Ronco das Abelhas and Revolta dos Marimbondos understood that the imperial decrees could imply their slavery. With protests that could gather up to 4,000 people, the rebels invaded churches, tore up edicts, and intimidated the authorities responsible for collecting data (Oliveira, 2005, p. 121). Historians record that the law came to be nicknamed the "Law of Captivity" and that it supported the belief that "the purpose of registration was only to enslave the colored people" (Carvalho, 2012, p. 40). In a document of the Pernambucan rebels, who identified themselves as "we, poor black and brown people," the "news of the paper of slavery" was recorded and the veracity of the information was questioned directly to the municipal authority (Carvalho, 2012, p. 40).

In that same year, the civil registry and the General Census of the Empire were suspended by Decree No. 907/1852. The authorities' perception was that, for the newly established Brazilian state, it was more convenient to postpone the data collection than to risk losing its legitimacy. However, the lords who illegally kept enslaved people were also cautious about collecting data about the population, since it could evidence the illegality of their actions (Oliveira, 2005, p. 123). Thus, as Loveman (2007) points out, with the Revolta dos Marimbondos and the Ronco das Abelhas, "the Brazilian State's effort to lay the foundations for a modern, centralized, statistics-gathering infrastructure was abandoned—if, in retrospect, only temporarily—in response to this revolt" (p. 7). Brazil's first census would not take place until 1872, 20 years after its first attempt, and its results became known only in the years 1876/77. The urgency for knowledge of the population would then be related to the Paraguayan War and the discussion of gradual abolition policies.

The resistance movements of the Ronco das Abelhas and Revolta dos Marimbondos indicate resistance to a decaying slave state and the precariousness of the state of freedom of black people in a racist society (Saavedra, 2015, p. 105). To a large extent, these revolts marked a resistance to the centralizing effort of a slave state, which excluded most of its population from the condition of citizen and subject of the law. More than a broad refusal to collect and process data—since this resistance was not registered when similar recordkeeping was carried out by the ecclesiastical authorities—the refusal of the rebels is presented in relation to the surveillance of a violent state that did not prevent and in fact endorsed "constant threats to freedom" (Saavedra, 2015, p. 105). This state, marked by authoritarianism, inequality, and violence, faced distrust from the population as its first operational limitation.

The case of Decrees Nos. 797 and 798, according to Loveman (2007), as an attempt to react to the lack of information about the population, evidences a "blindness" of the Brazilian state to local realities, which created an obstacle for the administrative development of the imperial government. According to the author, these modernization projects clashed with on-the-ground realities, and as a consequence, "socially marginalized populations disproportionately bore the costs of the State's blindness to the local context." Thus, Loveman states:

> The blindness of twentieth-century high modern state technocrats to local knowledge—foreshadowed by their nineteenth-century predecessors' disregard for local modes of life—continues to echo in many state-led development projects today. This suggests that if the technical vision of modernizing states improved with the adoption of various "tools of legibility," the blindness brought on by modernist convictions—the inability to see in "traditional" relationships or ways of life potential allies or resources in the pursuit of progress—was not cured by taking a census or standardizing weights and measures. If anything, as Scott's (1998) analysis confirms, with respect to the modernizing state's blindness to contextualized needs and concerns, legibility projects were apt to make things worse. (p. 34)

These characteristics—although largely addressed in the development of the Brazilian state, especially since 1988, with the emergence of policies based on data and more attentive to the grammar of rights—can still be observed in some public initiatives, which produce legibility of citizens—that is, identification and visiblity of citizens by the state—without promoting as a counterweight and safeguard the transparency and limitation of state power. This "blindness," combined with an always renewing history of violence of the Brazilian national state, ends up imposing an operational limitation, as the authorities encounter strong resistance from the population. As Saavedra (2015) writes,

> More than understanding the Guerra dos Marimbondos as a social movement of negotiation with the State in the mid-nineteenth century, the study of this revolt *allows us to think about the current Brazilian State, a State that is other, but that retains its inabilities of legibility and "classification" of the social, its inability to reconcile security and rights.* (p. 109, emphasis added)[5]

THE YELLOW FEVER EPIDEMIC: STATISTICAL REASONING AND DATA COLLECTION FOR EPIDEMIOLOGICAL PURPOSES

As noted earlier, data collection in Brazil reached new dimensions with the yellow fever epidemic. In 1849, a second wave of the disease emerged in the

---

[5] Our translation. In the original:
Mais do que compreender a Guerra dos Marimbondos como movimento social de negociação com o Estado em meados do século XIX, o estudo dessa revolta permite pensar sobre o Estado brasileiro contemporâneo, um Estado que é outro, mas que conserva suas inabilidades de legibilidade e "classificação" do social, sua incapacidade de conciliar segurança e direitos.

country, along with new hygienic practices.[6] With the spread of the disease throughout the country, the imperial government created the Junta de Higiene Pública (Public Hygiene Council; Decree No. 598, 1850), the first governmental organization against yellow fever. In this period, the Serviço de Estatística Demográfica (Demographic Statistics Service) was created, which was linked to the Council and had the objective of controlling the death records of the epidemic. It was the first of its kind in Brazil and throughout South America. In addition, the Demographic Statistics Service recorded the environmental conditions, as well as the "sanitary status of individuals" (Costa et al., 2011, pp. 12–13).

The main yellow fever control measures at that time were linked to the control of individuals through the isolation of infected people and quarantine. However, these practices were added to "a disciplinary component for urban spaces in terms of public salubrity" (Costa et al., 2011, pp. 12–13), especially regarding the actions of the Council and the Demographic Statistics Service. According to the health authorities, poor people's housing, characterized by tenements and inns, was the epicenter of epidemics and therefore needed to be controlled (Camargo, 2016, p. 299). Thus, with the disciplinary measures in urban spaces and the control of deaths, the authorities raised funds to develop public policies aimed at fighting the disease and, at the same time, mapped the distribution of the disease in the territory.

In the transition between the Second Empire (1840–1889) and the First Republic (1890–1930), with the permanence of the epidemic of yellow fever in the country and the spread of other diseases throughout the national territory, a medical elite—mostly doctors with doctorates in public health or epidemiology—organized statistical agencies that aimed to produce and analyze data for disease prevention and public policymaking. The doctors involved in this emergence of *statistical rationale* in Brazil became known as *demographer-sanitarians* (Camargo, 2012, p. 1). These demographer-sanitarians shared ideals of modernizing the state's organization, which had been consolidating in Brazil since the 1850s, and its milestone Decrees Nos. 797 and 798.

The work of these professionals was essential for the consolidation of data collection and processing practices in Brazil. According to Camargo (2012), "the statistical program in force in this period [was] greatly informed by sanitary, urbanistic and epidemiological issues that guided Public Health"

---

[6] The first cases of yellow fever in Brazilian territory were recorded in 1685, when Brazil was still a Portuguese colony. Around 1691, the epidemic was controlled in the region through isolation and quarantine measures. New cases of yellow fever infection were recorded again only in 1849 (Costa et al., 2011).

(p. 2).[7] Data collection, however, still faced many of the same challenges since registering Decrees Nos. 797 and 798. As mentioned earlier, civil registration and census were viewed with great distrust by the population, which led to a significant under-registration. In addition to this resistance, government authorities made it difficult to access administrative records, such as data from customs, hospitals, police stations, courts, and so on. Consequently, demographer-sanitarians "recalculated the census results and pressed for reform of the civil register, and soon ascended to the command of national statistics, to promote its desired restructuring."[8]

In 1899, with the creation of the Oswaldo Cruz Institute, the country reached a new level in its consolidation of statistical rationale based on data collection and data processing. The Oswaldo Cruz Institute was the first microbiology research center in Latin America and raised Brazil's scientific reputation. The institute had the collaboration of demographer-sanitarians, who provided logistical support to combat epidemics (Camargo, 2012, p. 20). According to Costa et al. (2011), the Oswaldo Cruz era was marked by the "strength of the sanitary police," with the adoption of repressive measures against those who hid sick people and with the surveillance of houses (p. 13). There was, in this period, a strengthening of sanitary surveillance through the preparation of statistical bulletins, supervision of cases, and organization of health services. These data legitimized the authorities' actions:

> In São Paulo, during the period from 1903 to 1915, the Demographic and Health Statistics Section was consolidated, which allowed transformation of the interpretation of the data published in the Demographic Yearbooks into true manifestos in defense of the action of the São Paulo Health Service. These data supported and justified the measures and interventions taken for disease interventions, presenting the results and their effects, that is, their efficacy (Alves, 2012). (Oliveira et al., 2017, p. 225)[9]

---

[7]   Our translation. In the original:
O programa estatístico vigente nesse período é grandemente informado pelas questões sanitárias, urbanísticas e epidemiológicas que pautavam a Saúde Pública.

[8]   Our translation. In the original:
Recalculavam os resultados dos censos e pressionavam pela reforma do registro civil, e logo ascenderiam ao comando das estatísticas nacionais, para promover sua desejada reestruturação.

[9]   Our translation. In the original:
Em São Paulo, durante o período de 1903 a 1915, foi consolidada a Seção de Estatística Demógrafo-Sanitária, a qual permitia transformar a interpretação dos dados publicados nos Anuários Demográficos em verdadeiros manifestos em defesa da ação do Serviço Sanitário paulista. Estes dados sustentavam e justi-

The measures adopted by the demographer-sanitarians were successful. Yellow fever became the first disease whose notification was mandatory, and in the years that followed, the disease lost its epidemic character (Costa et al., 2011, p. 13).

The first attempts at data collection and processing by the Brazilian state took place, back and forth, during the Second Empire; but it was with the yellow fever epidemic that the state extensively incorporated such procedures, based on medical and statistical knowledge. The data collected were efficient for controlling the epidemic in the Brazilian territory and legitimized the restructuring of data collection by the state. Although this process faced difficulties from the perspective of nationalization and dissemination within Brazil, it marked a turning point in the mentality of the Brazilian government (Camargo, 2016).

The difficulties of nationalization occurred for two reasons: (a) in the first decade of the 20th century, this statistical rationale was institutionalized mainly in Rio de Janeiro and São Paulo (Camargo, 2012, p. 20), and this rationality would penetrate the interior of Brazil only around 1915 (Santos, 1985); and (b) the Constitution of 1891 established that the centralization of hygiene was the responsibility of the states, and the Union was responsible only for the sanitary control of ports (Camargo, 2016, p. 361).

However, even with these obstacles, Camargo (2016) argues that in the Brazilian case, the centralized political authority—that is, the state—is constituted "through the formation of a medical-sanitary network around the fight against diseases and epidemics" (p. 400),[10] which takes place through medical consensus and demographic-sanitary statistics, establishing the ground for the interpretation of data and its use in government actions. With the successful control of the yellow fever epidemic, there was a generalization of the "medical-sanitary perspective to the society as a whole" (p. 400). Thus, the sanitarian-demographic movement became associated with national progress and was intrinsically linked to the centralization of political authority. The sociologist states:

> The centralization of political authority was built by professional categories—first the sanitarists, then the educators—who, initially located outside the state, integrated specialized bureaucracies to impose their definition of the situation and expand their position and frontier of action. In this movement, the population will

---

      ficavam as medidas e intervenções tomadas para as intervenções das doenças, apresentando os resultados e seus efeitos, ou seja, a sua eficácia.

[10] Our translation. In the original:
     Por meio da formação de uma rede médico-sanitarista em torno do combate às doenças e epidemias.

be reconfigured as the visual field of government. In turn, the quantitative discourse will strengthen political authority, for which it depends on being amplified as a public referent, becoming a support for the translation of the interests of professional groups, whose recognition depends on their knowledge about the population. (Camargo, 2016, p. 400)[11]

In this sense, medical-demographic knowledge represented an important paradigm for data collection by the Brazilian state. While state initiatives to collect data were viewed with suspicion during the Second Empire and the early First Republic, which is evident with the emergence of movements such as the Revolta dos Marimbondos and Ronco das Abelhas, the use of data (especially statistical data, in this historical context) took on a new centrality after the yellow fever epidemics. Mobilized to solve public health problems, and based on a medical-sanitary rationality, data collection started to integrate the state power and justify government actions. This new rationality of the Brazilian government has been maintained and accentuated throughout its history, with an increase in data processing, which serves to give legitimacy to the power of political authorities and to justify the implementation of new techniques and technologies.

Santos (1985) points out that the sanitation movement at that time was the most important project in the construction of Brazilian nationality. In this same sense, Hochman (1993)[12] argues that in the First Republic, public health

---

[11]   Our translation. In the original:
A centralização da autoridade política foi construída por categorias profissionais— primeiro os sanitaristas, depois os educadores—que, inicialmente situadas fora do Estado, integraram burocracias especializadas para impor sua definição de situação e expandir sua posição e fronteira de ação. Neste movimento, a população será reconfigurada como campo visual do governo. Por sua vez, o discurso quantitativo irá fortalecer a autoridade política, da qual ele depende para se amplificar como referente público, tornando-se suporte para a tradução de interesses de grupos profissionais, cujo reconhecimento depende de seu saber sobre a população.

[12]   Hochman, disagreeing with some of his peers (such as Nilson Rosário Costa and Eliana Labra), understands that the relationship between sanitarian rationality and the construction of the Brazilian state is not guided by the success of public policies promoted to contain the diseases that ravaged the country, since many of these measures failed. According to the historian,
health policies are constituent parts of a broader and more complex process, in which the State and state elites have specificities that give them autonomy in relation to societal interests, and also have specific objectives, diverse and even divergent from those of societal elites. Thus, the long-term results of a policy that benefits dominant groups may be the future inability of those same groups to autonomously continue to influence and obtain benefits from that state policy. (Hochman, 1993, p. 41)

policies were central to the creation and increase of the intervention capacity of the Brazilian state, because at that moment, health became a public good that required public, compulsory, and national responses, and for that, it was necessary to create and develop administrative structures. Thus, the process of nationalization and collectivization of healthcare in the early 20th century was reflected in the creation of social security mechanisms (p. 55). In this way, the Vargas era (1930–1945) inherited this state and bureaucratic structure. Hochman states:

> The regulatory capacity of the Union on the health field expanded considerably especially in the 1920s, leaving to the Vargas period an administrative structure with an expanded power of intervention on public health that did not undergo significant changes just at a time when centralization and expansion of the State occurred in an unprecedented way in Brazilian history. (p. 41)

This sanitary-informational apparatus was combined with state control devices and produced unequal results. The process of tackling yellow fever carried, in addition to the impetus for data collection, violent urban interventions, such as the destruction of tenements, popular collective dwellings considered to be foci of disease dissemination, and the displacement of poor people from city centers. Experiences and strategies of resistance also marked this process, to the extent that its burden fell mainly on the most vulnerable populations, black people in particular.

Chalhoub (1996) argues that the hygienists' discourse against collective housing was appropriated by business groups interested in the construction of housing and infrastructure. The hygienists' science would have legitimized radical urban interventions, and the reduction of the presence of "dangerous classes" in the city center (Chalhoub, 1996, p. 26). In one of the most famous episodes, in the early republic (1893), the Cabeça de Porco, a tenement in Rio de Janeiro that housed 4,000 people, was destroyed with the participation of infantry troops and police cavalry, who surrounded the dwelling while its inhabitants fled and the building was demolished (Chalhoub, 1996, p. 15). The tenements housed people who were poor and often black (Chalhoub, 1996, p. 26).

In this sense, the sanitary-informational drive, crucial to the formation and maturation of the Brazilian bureaucracy, as an action of a strongly asymmetric state, was not compliant with basic rights but rather was armed and inequitable. There are records of resistance to such methods, including, at the beginning of the First Republic, the Revolt of the Vaccine (1904), when vaccines were compulsorily and violently applied as a measure to combat smallpox.

THE COVID-19 PANDEMIC IN BRAZIL

The COVID-19 pandemic hit Brazil in a different historical moment, with a different institutional and political structure. There is, on the one hand, significant political instability and persistent inequality. On the other hand, the redemocratization has accumulated significant institutional legacies, among which are guarantees and fundamental rights and universal public policies, such as the Brazilian public health system, Sistema Único de Saúde (SUS), and the maturing of some discussions related to information management and personal data treatment.

The Federal Constitution protects the right to inviolability of communications, inviolability of the home, secrecy of communications, and *habeas data* (respectively, arts. 5, X, XI, XII and LXXII). There is, therefore, constitutional protection to the "right not to be subjected to arbitrary or illegal interference in one's private life." These guarantees aim to protect the subjective right of the citizen against the supervisory and surveillance capacity of the state.

SUS, the Brazilian health system, is characterized by universal coverage, free access, integrality of assistance, decentralization of management and administrative functions, and the supply of services throughout the national territory. These characteristics explain why its existence had—and has—the potential to reduce damage in the pandemic by offering free testing, hospitalization, care in basic health units, and monitoring and dissemination of information on care measures in the most remote regions through community health workers, in addition to vaccine distribution. The technological measures that were already part of SUS's repertoire of tools were mobilized in the context of the pandemic. New tools were also developed and made available.

Such tools, however, often seem to have been implemented by default and disconnected from the public health strategy, under the still eloquent and pertinent rationale of confronting a health emergency, in this case the pandemic of COVID-19.

It is still not possible to be certain about the long-term consequences of these data-processing initiatives for health purposes in the context of the coronavirus pandemic. However, in view of previous experiences in dealing with sanitary crises and the way they were important milestones for the organization of the Brazilian state, we focus here on the measures adopted by the government to fight the COVID-19 pandemic and how these actions relate to constitutive features of Brazil.

As we discuss below, the COVID-19 pandemic evidences an attempt to expand technological solutions by the government, even though these measures do not seem to be compatible with the inequalities that mark the country. Furthermore, COVID-19 technologies have intensified concerns about the normative framework for data protection and privacy in the country, which is still under construction.

1   The Use of Technologies to Fight the Pandemic

With the need to maintain social isolation to curb the spread of the coronavirus, Brazilian authorities, especially at the state and municipal levels, have invested in technologies to offer telemedicine services, online public services, and information about the disease. Technological tools, which use aggregated data of citizens' mobility, have been mobilized to monitor population displacement and rates of social isolation.

Of the technologies implemented by SUS, the Coronavírus SUS app stands out. The digital app was initially launched to increase public awareness about COVID-19 and to provide information on symptoms, forms of prevention, guidelines for cases of suspicion and infection, maps indicating nearby health units, and the Ministry of Health's official news page about the pandemic (Gomes et al., 2020). Its initial goal, therefore, was to perform the SUS tasks of information and awareness about diseases, betting at an early moment of the epidemic on information as a means to control contagion. In addition, the app presented figures on the epidemiological situation of the states and country.

Updates transformed the app's scope and function. The functionality of numbers on the epidemiological picture and information on the user's health status were excluded, and later the map of the SUS care network and the dissemination of news about COVID-19 were added. The app then began to track contact with infected people through a partnership between the Ministry of Health and Google and Apple. Since then, the app has focused essentially on exposure notification.

Contact tracing apps were launched by authorities worldwide for the rapid and early identification by public health authorities of as many contacts with COVID-19-infected persons as possible for quarantine, testing, and isolation. Another elementary goal of this strategy is to obtain anonymized, aggregated data on epidemiological patterns in order to enact effective containment measures.

The Brazilian app, however, seems to have been implemented at odds with the federal public health strategy. The use of contagion data to seek focused and specific solutions has never been a priority of the federal executive. With the dizzying increase in cases and deaths in June 2020, the Health Ministry started to omit data related to COVID-19. The lack of transparency is not anecdotal: The president issued Medida Provisória (MP) No. 926 on March 23, 2020, amending Law 13.979/2020—the Quarantine Act—to provide that government authorities are not obliged to answer any request for access to information during the state of public calamity if the agency is adopting a telework and quarantine regime, in contradiction with the Access to Information Law.

As a technological solution, the app's implementation did not have a concrete plan of action or execution. The low number of downloads in relation to the total Brazilian population and the lack of dissemination and a coordinated campaign to expand the app's use contributed to its being forgotten. In this vein, the lack of technical studies by Ministry of Health authorities, the lack of integration of the app with other measures, and the use of data for answers in public policies reveal that little effort was made to instrumentalize this tool.

Only a small fraction of the population accessed the app. The Coronavírus SUS was downloaded by a little over 5 million users, representing 2.3% of the Brazilian population. From an effectiveness perspective, as mentioned, a policy based on contact tracing requires considerable penetration in the lives of the population, and expressive adherence to the apps. This adherence cannot be observed in Brazil because of broad inequalities in the country, including inequitable internet access.

Although health experts believe that contact tracing via the app can be effective if mobilized properly and in combination with other tools, the limited number of downloads and negligible usage undermine its effectiveness. Nor is there any official data to contradict these impressions. The extent of the digital contact tracking measure remains limited by the digital divide in Brazil (Fragoso et al., 2021).

This picture also points out a contradiction and the fragility of the federal public health policies: on one hand, technological solutions are implemented to optimize control of the contagion and reduce deaths and infections; on the other hand, there is a low disposition not only for the use of health data in the execution of confrontation actions but also for the dissemination of these data as a means of information and awareness (Fragoso et al., 2021).

In addition to the Coronavírus SUS, more than seven other apps were also made available by the public administration at the municipal, state, and federal levels with functions of remote medical care, provision of public services, or contact tracing (Fragoso et al., 2021). Through various public–private partnerships, monitoring services for social isolation were also used. One of the most prominent partnerships was between the Government of the State of São Paulo and four telephone companies. They signed an agreement to create the São Paulo Intelligent Monitoring Information System (SIMI-SP),[13] which

---

[13]   Even with the formal execution of the agreement on April 14, 2020, the promulgation of an appropriate legal instrument for the implementation of SIMI took place on May 5, by Decree No. 64.963/2020 (Intelligent Information and Monitoring System, 2020).

would develop social isolation indexes using data from telephone service users captured by antennas, enabling managers to identify isolation percentages and population concentration zones to issue guidance via SMS and conduct analysis for decision-making on targeted policies.

Governments also established partnerships with the start-up Inloco (see its privacy policy at Incognia, 2021), which provides states and municipalities with daily updates on the population indexes that remained in their neighborhood, allowing focused contingency administrative decision-making. In both partnerships, the data provided are statistical and volumetric, made available in an anonymized form and aggregated through heat maps. State governments announced that there would therefore be no risks to privacy, since it would not be possible to identify natural persons, preventing the processing of their personal data.

However, location data, even in an anonymized and aggregated form, can expose characteristics, behaviors, and conditions of individuals that, when crossed with other public administration databases, can provide information such as race and ethnicity and facilitate the identification of individuals. These issues raise concerns about security, privacy, and ethics, as much of this data is sensitive, and its processing can compromise civil liberties such as autonomy, equality, and data protection. They also affect future service delivery models that increasingly move toward the use of technologies and personal data, making it essential that these technologies undergo, before implementation, an assessment of proportionality, necessity, and other principles of constitutional protection and regulation of data protection.

Furthermore, when it comes to data collection by state authorities, there is an even greater problem because of the vulnerability of users and power asymmetry, as their bargaining power is limited to the terms of use of services in a public emergency situation. That is, as the user's choice is to accept or not accept the terms of use, if a user does not accept the terms, the person is impeded from using the service. The user's power of choice is reduced, which is aggravated in emergencies.

The Brazilian population itself identified risks associated with the use of personal data by COVID-19 information apps, according to the Painel TIC COVID-19 survey on online public services, telehealth, and privacy, carried out in October 2020 (Painel TIC COVID-19, 2020). According to the research, more than half of Brazilians believe that the risks of making their data available outweigh the benefits. Among the risks identified by the use of personal data, most pointed to bank fraud (32%) and identity theft (23%), showing a greater concern regarding cybercrime compared to risks associated with the use of health data in a pandemic context and surveillance power enacted by public or private initiatives. By making a class division, the research shows that AB classes, with higher incomes, understand financial loss from bank fraud as the main risk; and the DE classes, with lower incomes, are especially concerned about identity theft and the invasion of privacy. When asked what measures they might take, 84% said they would denounce companies or governments that made use of their data without their permission.

Added to the above are the data incidents and invasions suffered by the federal government (Temóteo & Militão, 2020), including the leak of the Ministry of Health's password that unduly exposed data from more than 16 million patients infected by COVID-19, including information such as their taxpayer registry number, address, and preexisting diseases (Cambricoli, 2020). This leak resulted from the archiving of information without proper protection. Other failures regarding proportionality and necessity in data collection and processing have intensified the debates over the regulation of data use in the country, which is still in its early stages, with the recent entry into force of the General Personal Data Protection Law (LGPD) and later establishment of the National Data Protection Agency (ANPD).

2   Data Protection in the Pandemic: Occasion and Agenda

In parallel and concatenated with the health crisis, there was some legal uncertainty regarding the regulatory framework for data protection in Brazil. Proposals to postpone the entry into force of the LGPD, initially scheduled for August 2020, were presented, debated, and considered. One of the proposals was presented by Senate Bill No. 1179 (2020), which intended to regulate legal and private relations during the pandemic, establishing exceptions clauses to avoid damage to citizens and companies. One of the bill's provisions, which was withdrawn during its passage, provided for the postponement of LGPD's effectiveness by six months in order "not to burden companies in view of the enormous technical and economic difficulties arising from the pandemic." Soon after the presentation of the project, the LGPD was postponed until May 2021 by the executive act issued by the president of the Republic (Medida Provisória No. 959/2020), which Congress denied.

Crucial to the outcome of this debate was the Federal Supreme Court response to exceptional data treatment initiatives. In April, the federal government issued Medida Provisória No. 954/2020, which provided for the sharing of landline and mobile phone data between telecom operators regulated by Anatel and the Brazilian Institute of Geography and Statistics Foundation (Instituto Brasileiro de Geografia e Estatística [IBGE]). The executive act[14]

---

[14]   The executive act, which can be issued by the president of the Republic in cases of relevance and urgency (art. 62 of the Federal Constitution), was motivated by the "need for the timely production of data for monitoring the COVID-19 pandemic,"

determined that telecom companies should share data such as the name, phone number and address of all consumers, in order to support statistical research conducted to combat the pandemic. This data sharing, however, would not comply with a series of obligations related to security, privacy, and transparency, taking the discussion to the Supreme Court through actions of unconstitutionality proposed by political parties and the Brazilian Bar Association (Ordem dos Advogados do Brasil [OAB]; Direct Unconstitutionality Actions [ADIs] 6387, 6388, 6389, 6390, & 6393, 2020).

On April 24, 2020, STF Minister Rosa Weber granted an injunction "to prevent irreparable harm to the intimacy and secrecy of the private life of more than a hundred million users of fixed and mobile telephony services"[15] in the face of Precautionary Measure No. 6.387 (Agência Senado, 2020). The other ministers then endorsed the decision and highlighted the existence of a fundamental right to data protection, pointing out the importance of informational self-determination and the need for attention to data protection principles also and especially during crisis—even before the General Personal Data Protection Law (LGPD), Law 13.709/2018, which came into effect in September 2020.

The court's decision has resonated in the public and legislative debate. The LGPD's full deferral was suspended and, as noted, came into force in September 2020. The National Data Protection Agency was effectively created in August, and its board of directors appointed in October. Notably, despite the uncertainty of specific regulation at the beginning of the pandemic, the International Health Regulations (IHR), incorporated into national legislation in Decree 10.212/2020, already brought some answers to the concern about data protection applicable to measures instituted in this context by determining that data processing must be adequate, relevant, and compatible with the defined purpose.

In force, the LGPD provides ten legal bases for processing nonsensitive personal data and seven more-restrictive legal bases for sensitive data. For the use of data-based technologies in the pandemic context, the most appropriate ones seem to be (a) data processing for public policies provided for in laws and regulations; and (b) data processing for the protection of life of the data subject or third parties. The LGPD imposes obligations on controllers and other processing agents and safeguards aimed at promoting informational self-determination. Its opposite, informational alienation, has been the norm in

---

to ensure the implementation of PNAD Continuous (an annual household survey in Brazil) and preserve the basic historical series, and in the choice of form, to make it possible to obtain the requested data quickly.

15   Our translation. In the original:
      Danos irreparáveis à intimidade e ao sigilo da vida privada de mais de uma
      centena de milhão de usuários dos serviços de telefonia fixa e móvel.

the data-processing initiatives reported here: this results from lack of transparency; lack of knowledge about the specific treatments to which the collected data will be subjected; unequal exposure of the most vulnerable and most policy-dependent people to informational risks, such as leaks, and massive and proactive disclosure of beneficiary data; and difficulty exercising data rights (see Ceará & Bilenky, 2021). Therefore, informational alienation is based on and reproduces inequality.

This shows that even with the General Data Protection Law in force, the trajectory of construction and maturing in the normative sense of a legal framework for data protection in the country is just beginning, and effort is still needed to engage the authorities in charge of its application and to guarantee its effectiveness.

CONCLUSION

In analyzing these three "acts" of different historical moments in Brazil, we find not exact similarities but persistent features of the Brazilian state and its informational action on citizens.

The specificity of slavery, the history of Brazilian institutions, and the state's modernization process are fundamental to understanding contemporary Brazil. In all three acts, a threat to life and health constitutes and is harnessed as a drive to collect data and reinforce state intelligence; in all three acts there are notable inequalities in the unequal exposure to the collection, either in the legibility scheme (i.e., citizen identification systems) or in the dependence on public policies; in all three acts, unequal results (i.e., interventions or policies) produce or reproduce discrimination. Rather than heritage, the persistent inequality of the majority is the result of a historical process, which has an informational dimension.

The first attempts to build a database about its population, still in the first half of the 19th century and soon after Brazil's independence, were frustrated because of the population's strong resistance to and distrust of the then slave-holding Brazilian empire. The regime's authoritarianism, the racial record in the legibility scheme, the lack of transparency about the newly adopted measures, the absence of rights guarantees, and the legal insecurity that was part of the daily life of the Brazilian population, both free and enslaved people, impeded the state's actions in collecting data.

It was with the yellow fever epidemic in the second half of thc 19th century that the Brazilian state consolidated its capacity for data collection and processing, focused on population management and public health. There was, at that moment, a change of paradigm, in which politics based on data started to integrate the structure of state power and justify government actions. This paradigm shift was not necessarily because of success in disease containment, but because of the emergence of new rationality based on medical and statistical knowledge. This rationality created a bureaucratic structure for data collection to confront the yellow fever epidemic, which became part of all later regimes in Brazil. However, the informational drive and policy implementation coexisted and were made possible by a discriminatory and violent repressive apparatus.

The health emergency of COVID-19 has occurred in a context quite different from the one registered during the yellow fever epidemic. Guarantees linked to the collection and processing of personal data are beginning to be structured more robustly, and the country's bureaucratic structure, both for data collection and for public health, is already quite solid. Nonetheless, the country simultaneously faces strong political instability and a constant threat of democratic rupture by the president of the Republic. Inequality, a persistent mark of the country, has deepened during the pandemic, including informational asymmetries and unequal access to data rights.

It is in this scenario that the public authorities, at the federal, state, and municipal levels, invested in data-driven technologies as a strategy to face the health emergency. Technological solutions and data collection have even been adopted by the spheres of power that have taken negative positions concerning the pandemic, as is the case with the federal government.

These technological solutions also raise concerns regarding data protection, since it allows intensive data treatment. Furthermore, the attempts to postpone the entry in force of the General Personal Data Protection Law (LGPD), and the later establishment of the National Data Protection Agency (ANPD), created juridical insecurity at the beginning of the COVID-19 pandemic. In this sense, many early decision processes about data collection and treatment to fight the pandemic were made without those legal protections.

The government's attempt to implement technological and data-driven solutions cannot be considered successful, from the point of view of controlling the pandemic—which has run out of control, killing more than half a million people—and in terms of adherence by the population. Surveys also show a distrust of the population toward apps developed by governments. We add as a hypothesis: This is related to a lack of transparency and an asymmetry of power, especially in the face of an unresolved democratic deficit and persistent inequality.

The failure of these strategies, from an epidemiological point of view, does not mean, however, that these techniques are being abandoned by the public authorities. Brazil, like other places in the world, has been on a growing trend of digitalization and centralization of data by the public power. The pandemic of COVID-19 represents an intensification of the construction of public policies based on data, and it is likely that many of these technologies will become part of the state bureaucratic structure.

If the yellow fever epidemic represented a paradigm shift for health statistics data collection and for the policies that result from it, the question that remains is what marks will be left by COVID technological solutions whose capacity for data collection, data treatment, and surveillance is significantly higher.

REFERENCES

Agência Senado. (2020, May 8). "STF suspende eficácia de MP sobre compartilhamento de cadastros telefônicos com o IBGE" [STF suspends effectiveness of MP on sharing phone records with IBGE]. Senado Federal. www12.senado.leg.br/noticias/materias/2020/05/08/stf-suspende-eficacia-de-mp-sobre-compartilhamento-de-cadastros-telefonicos-com-o-ibge

"Brasil ultrapassa 570 mil mortes por Covid e 20,4 milhões de casos" [Brazil surpasses 570 thousand deaths by Covid and 20.4 million cases]. (2021, August 17). *Folha de S.Paulo*. www1.folha.uol.com.br/equilibrioesaude/2021/08/brasil-ultrapassa-570-mil-mortes-por-covid-e-204-milhoes-de-casos.shtml

Camargo, A. P. R. (2012). "Demografia sanitária e a emergência de um estilo de raciocínio estatístico na Primeira República" [Health demography and the emergence of a style of statistical reasoning in the First Republic]. In *Anais XVIII Encontro Nacional de Estudos Populacionais*. Associação Brasileiras de Estudos Populacionais (ABEP).

Camargo, A. P. R. (2016). "A construção da medida comum: Estatística e política de população no Império e na Primeira República" [The construction of the common measure: Statistics and population policy in the Empire and the First Republic]. Doctoral dissertation, Instituto de Estudos Sociais e Políticos, Universidade do Estado do Rio de Janeiro.

Cambricoli, F. (2020, November 26). "Vazamento de senha do Ministério da Saúde expõe dados de 16 milhões de pacientes de covid" [Ministry of Health password leak exposes data from 16 million COVID patients]. ESTADÃO. https://saude.estadao.com.br/noticias/geral,vazamento-de-senha-do-ministerio-da-saude-expoe-dados-de-16-milhoes-de-pacientes-de-covid,70003528583

Carvalho, J. M. de. (2012). "Introdução: As marcas do período [Introduction: The marks of the period]. In J. M. de Carvalho (ed.), *A construção nacional 1830–1889: Vol. 2*. Objetiva.

Ceará, L., & Bilenky, T. (2021, June 4). "Invasão de privacidade com chancela oficial" [Invasion of privacy with official seal]. *Revista Piauí*. https://piaui.folha.uol.com.br/invasao-de-privacidade-com-chancela-oficial/

Centro de Estudos e Pesquisas de Direito Sanitário. (2021, May 28). "A linha do tempo da estratégia federal de disseminação da COVID-19" [The timeline of the federal COVID-19 dissemination strategy]. https://static.poder360.com.br/2021/06/CEPEDISA-USP-Linha-do-Tempo-Maio-2021_v2.pdf

Chalhoub, S. (1996). *Cidade febril: Cortiços e epidemias na Corte Imperial* [A feverish city: Tenements and epidemics at the Imperial Court]. Companhia das Letras.

Costa, Z. G. A., Romano, A. P. M., Elkhoury, A. N. M., & Flannery, B. (2011). "Evolução histórica da vigilância epidemiológica e do controle da febre amarela no Brasil" [Historical evolution of epidemiological surveillance and control of yellow fever in Brazil]. *Revista Pan-Amazônica de Saúde*, 2(1), 11–26. http://dx.doi.org/10.5123/S2176-62232011000100002

Direct Unconstitutionality Action No. 6387. (2020, April 20). http://portal.stf.jus.br/
processos/detalhe.asp?incidente=5895165
Direct Unconstitutionality Action No. 6388. (2020, April 20). http://portal.stf.jus.br/
processos/detalhe.asp?incidente=5895166
Direct Unconstitutionality Action No. 6389. (2020, April 20). http://portal.stf.jus.br/
processos/detalhe.asp?incidente=5895168
Direct Unconstitutionality Action No. 6390. (2020, April 20). http://portal.stf.jus.br/
processos/detalhe.asp?incidente=5895176
Direct Unconstitutionality Action No. 6393. (2020, April 22). http://portal.stf.jus.br/
processos/detalhe.asp?incidente=5896399
Fragoso, N., Tavares, C., Roberto, E., & da Silveira J. F. (2021). "Privacy and data
protection in the pandemic: Report on the use of apps and alternative measures in
Brazil." InternetLab. www.internetlab.org.br/wp-content/uploads/2021/04/Privacy
-and-Data-Protection-in-the-Pandemic_05.pdf
Gomes, A., Luciano, M., Fragoso, N., & Pavarin, V. (2020, April 30). "COVID-19:
Apps do governo e seus riscos à privacidade" [COVID-19: Government apps
and their privacy risks]. InternetLab. www.internetlab.org.br/pt/privacidade-e
-vigilancia/covid-19-apps-do-governo-e-seus-riscos/
Hochman, G. (1993). "Regulando os efeitos da interdependência: Sobre as relações
entre saúde pública e construção do Estado (Brasil 1910–1930)" [Regulating the
effects of interdependence: On the relationship between public health and state building (Brasil 1910–1930)]. *Revista Estudos Históricos*, 6(11). http://bibliotecadigital
.fgv.br/ojs/index.php/reh/article/view/1956/1095
Incognia. (2021). "Política de privacidade COVID-19: Inloco × COVID-19"
[COVID-19 Privacy Policy: Inloco × COVID-19]. www.incognia.com/pt/politicas/
covid
Intelligent Information and Monitoring System—SIMI, aimed at fighting the
COVID-19 pandemic, Decree No. 64.963/2020. (2020). www.al.sp.gov.br/
repositorio/legislacao/decreto/2020/decreto-64963-05.05.2020.html
Kuo, J. (2020, May 4). "Brazil postpones enforcement of new privacy law in response
to COVID-19." Taft's Privacy & Data Security Insights. www.lexology.com/library/
detail.aspx?g=6d3b2eff-948c-4879-be6a-267413e5d68b
Loveman, M. (2007). "Blinded like a state: The revolt against civil registration in
nineteenth-century Brazil." *Comparative Studies in Society and History*, 49(1),
5–39. https://doi.org/10.1017/S0010417507000394
Medida Provisória No. 954/2020 (2020, April 17). www.planalto.gov.br/CCIVIL_03/
_Ato2019-2022/2020/Mpv/mpv954.htm
Medida Provisória No. 959/2020 (2020, April 29). www.planalto.gov.br/CCIVIL_03/
_Ato2019-2022/2020/Mpv/mpv959.htm
Oliveira, M. L. F. D. (2005). "O Ronco da Abelha: Resistência popular e conflito na
consolidação do Estado nacional, 1851–1852" [Ronco da Abelha: Popular resist-
ance and conflict in the consolidation of the national state, 1851–1852]. *Almanack
Braziliense*, 0(1), 120–127. https://doi.org/10.11606/issn.1808-8139.v0i1p120-127
Oliveira, S. G., Safranski, C., Santos-Junior, J. R. G. D., Velleda, K. L., Oliveira, A.
D. L. D., Felipe, M. D. A. A., & Sella, M. A. (2017). "Discursos referentes à febre
amarela no contexto da Primeira República" [Discourses referring to yellow fever
in the context of the First Republic]. *Revista Contexto and Saúde*, 17(33), 215–230.
https://doi.org/10.21527/2176-7114.2017.33.215-230
Painel TIC COVID-19. (2020, October). *Pesquisa sobre o uso da internet no brasil
durante a pandemia do novo coronavírus* (2nd edn.) [Survey on internet use

in Brazil during the new coronavirus pandemic]. Regional Center for Studies for the Development of the Information Society, Information and Coordination Nucleus, & Internet Steering Committee. https://cetic.br/media/docs/publicacoes/2/20200930180249/painel_tic_covid19_2edicao_livro eletrônico.pdf

Saavedra, R. (2015). "Recenseamento e conflito no Brasil Imperial: O caso da Guerra dos Marimbondos" [Census and conflict in imperial Brazil: The case of the Revolt of the Hornets]. *Revista de Pesquisa Histórica*, 33(1), 90–113. www.academia.edu/36051878/Recenseamento_e_conflito_no_Brasil_Imperial_o_caso_da_Guerra_dos_Marimbondos

Santos, L. A. C. (1985). "O pensamento sanitarista na Primeira República: Uma ideologia de construção de nacionalidade" [Sanitary thought in the First Republic: An ideology for the construction of nationality]. *Dados—Revista de Ciências Sociais*, 28(2), 193–210. www.bvshistoria.coc.fiocruz.br/lildbi/docsonline/antologias/eh-594.pdf

Serpro. (2020, April 4). "Medida provisória adia a LGPD para 2021" [Provisional measure postpones the LGPD to 2021]. www.serpro.gov.br/lgpd/noticias/2020/medida-provisoria-adia-a-lgpd-para-2021

S. Lei [Bill] No. 1179 (2020). https://legis.senado.leg.br/sdleg-getter/documento?dm=8081779&ts=1609782720111&disposition=inline

Temóteo, A., & Militão, E. (2020, November 5). "Após STJ, hackers atingem sistemas do Ministério da Saúde e governo do DF" [After the STJ, hackers reach the Ministry of Health and the DF government's systems]. UOL Notícias. https://noticias.uol.com.br/politica/ultimas-noticias/2020/11/05/apos-stj-hackers-paralisam-sistemas-do-ministerio-da-saude-e-governo-do-df.htm

4. Frictionless pandemic surveillance and social credit systems

Margaret Hu

INTRODUCTION

This chapter examines how pandemic surveillance policies unfolding in the United States and other democracies could lead to similar surveillance risks as those posed by the China Social Credit System. Between the two nations, China's pandemic surveillance apparatus is considered the more privacy-intrusive system (Cadell, 2020). State surveillance under the China Social Credit System already involves constant monitoring of citizens' behavior and the well-known implementation of behavioral modifiers (Mozur et al., 2020). The China Social Credit System can be described as a hybrid surveillance system, combining elements of both hard and soft surveillance techniques. Hard surveillance has been described as traditional surveillance methods and technologies, including video monitoring, wiretapping, and intercepting communications (Levi & Wall, 2004). Soft surveillance, in contrast, not only captures data-driven and AI methods of surveillance, but also encapsulates behavioral modification objectives of the surveillance (Kerr et al., 2006). Examples of soft surveillance include behavioral modification and use of psychological influence to shape consumer habits through targeted advertising that might result from online tracking.

China's pandemic surveillance response has one attribute that differentiates it from that of the United States: as a state surveillance method, it is prominent and obvious (Mozur, 2018; Yang & Zhu, 2020). The citizens of China are preemptively aware of privacy intrusions under both the China Social Credit System (Ahlam, 2021, pp. 814–815, 818) and the pandemic surveillance techniques that have been integrated into the preexisting system (Mozur et al., 2020; Yang & Zhu, 2020). The invitation of tech companies into pandemic surveillance policy in the United States risks creating a similar system of behavioral modification without the same level of citizen awareness (Zuboff, 2019, pp. 295–299).

Some experts observe that there is a preexisting and rapidly emerging soft social credit system in the United States (Tate, 2021; Poulos, 2021), one that in the future could support the integration of pandemic surveillance. Because the pandemic surveillance response in the United States has introduced not only additional layers of hard surveillance architecture but also behavioral modification goals and incentives, the way the pandemic policy reinforced a burgeoning soft surveillance system is largely opaque. Specifically, digital contact tracing systems in both the United States and China created techno-logical innovation that facilitated longer-term data tracking consequences that are hidden and veiled from the public, and that may still lead to an ongoing surveillance impact.

This chapter encompasses four sections. Section 1 examines the technolog-ical components of the application program interface (API) and exposure noti-fication system jointly developed by Apple and Google, presented to the public to support privacy enhancing pandemic tracking apps, as well as other imple-mentations of digital contact tracing technology. Section 2 provides an over-view of the China Social Credit System and Chinese pandemic surveillance. Section 3 discusses how pandemic surveillance created a state of emergency in the United States and other democracies and compares the U.S. approach to that of China to illuminate similarities and consequences of surveillance. I contend that the conditions of the global pandemic emergency allowed for frictionless alignment between the motivations that guide citizens, technology companies, and government institutions. This alignment removes the checks and balances necessary for effective oversight of the deployment of new sur-veillance systems. As the final section concludes, these systems, purportedly implemented for a limited purpose to address a public health emergency, are likely to result in longer-term surveillance consequences and a warping of democratic norms through an invisible shift in governance philosophy.

1   COVID-19 AND BLUETOOTH-BASED DIGITAL TRACING

Under traditional human-based contact tracing, conducted by skilled health professionals, patients with infectious diseases are interviewed to determine with whom they may have been in contact and who may be at risk of infection through exposure (see, e.g., Zastrow, 2020). The speed of transmission of COVID-19 combined with the asymptomatic spread of the virus led some experts to claim that digital contact tracing tools (Halbfinger et al., 2020) would be more effective than human contact tracing (see, e.g., Ferretti et al., 2020; Thompson, 2020). This conclusion has been challenged (Ram & Gray, 2020). Experts note that, to date, no definitive evidence establishes the efficacy of digital tracking methods (see, e.g., Ram & Gray, 2020). Nonetheless, multiple governments have embraced the use of digital contact tracing (Zastrow, 2020) and other surveillance technologies such as pandemic drones, facial recognition systems, and thermal imaging (Selinger & Leong, 2020). Privacy experts, however, have warned that the technological solutions offered to combat the pandemic may violate the spirit and letter of data privacy laws (Ram & Gray, 2020, pp. 4–7).

Privacy laws and privacy concerns unique to each state, in the United States and globally, have led to the adoption of different methods of contact tracing and exposure notification. The most common methods for digital contact tracing have been split between centralized and decentralized approaches. Tracing programs adopted by nations around the world range from limited systems to highly intrusive methods that track all avenues of information possible.

The tech companies Google and Apple both had a major hand in conceptualizing and releasing smartphone software that enabled a widely adopted notification system for digital contact tracing. In April 2020, Apple and Google announced their collaboration on a common platform for apps to enable Bluetooth-driven "proximity tracing" (Zastrow, 2020). The technology companies explained that they intended to alter the operating systems of iPhones and Android phones to allow battery-efficient continuous access to Bluetooth to COVID-19 app developers. Apple and Google attempted to "decentralize" contact tracing through their system to alleviate privacy concerns (Gurman et al., 2020).

In May 2020, Apple and Google announced their new system, originally called the "Exposure Notification Application Programming Interface," and now referred to as GAEN (Ratnam, 2020; Google, n.d.). GAEN supports several widespread COVID-19 digital tracing tools, which were presented as limited contact tracing apps. This system was introduced to iPhone and Android users in the form of a software update. Under the system, an iOS and Android smartphone or device "regularly broadcasts a random string of characters that serves as a pseudonym to other phones using Bluetooth's low-energy specification for sending short bursts of data" (Zastrow, 2020). Every 15 minutes, the phone changes the string of characters to further anonymize the user. As the phone passes near other phones, it logs character strings "as well as information about the signal strength to estimate how close they are" (Zastrow, 2020); this is also referred to as a "Bluetooth handshake" (Bradford et al., 2020, p. 9). If a user who has voluntarily downloaded a Bluetooth-based tracing app is diagnosed with COVID-19, the user can consent to post on the app's database the recent history of pseudonyms through the Bluetooth handshake (Ratnam, 2020). The system requires express user consent to report a positive diagnosis for COVID-19 through the app, which then reports this information to other users who were within close proximity of the reporting user's phone at particular points in time.

Apple and Google claim that the system facilitates important privacy protections—for example, the geolocation data of the user is not retained (Nellis & Dave, 2020). To better protect users' privacy and data, the two companies announced that they would explicitly require data collected from tracing apps built on their system to be kept on the users' individual phone instead of in a central database (Criddle & Kelion, 2020). GAEN allowed the "optional collection of additional data ... including ZIP codes and user phone numbers" (Gurman, 2020). This feature allowed public health authorities to gather additional information from exposed users and conduct outreach, but this optional collected data may not be shared unless users give express permission.

The Bluetooth-based digital contact tracing approach was considered to be privacy protective in that it was voluntary for users. It depended on the user to voluntarily download the appropriate tracing app for their physical location (Ratnam, 2020). The information from the Apple-Google API platform was accessible only to public health officials seeking data from the contact tracing apps (Ratnam, 2020; Gurman et al., 2020). The platform, as noted, also requires express user consent "to report a positive diagnosis for COVID-19 through the app" (Ratnam, 2020). The platform's design also grants significant control to local public health authorities because "the system is designed to work with one app per region, such as a country or state, to avoid fragmentation" (Gurman et al., 2020). Each individual region or nation has autonomy to build their own app, and each can "set parameters for what constitutes a [COVID-19] exposure," measuring factors such as the length of time spent near another user or the distance between users (Gurman et al., 2020).

At the same time, the security updates that facilitated the new API were practically mandatory. The underlying API was installed on Android and Apple smartphones by default as part of regular updates. The GAEN system was added to Android phones via an update to Google Play Services (Google, n.d.), and added to iOS devices as part of the iOS 13.5 update (Etherington, 2020). While exposure notifications, public health apps, and exposure logs can be removed from a phone's local storage, removing the API itself requires rolling the operating system back to a prior version at the risk of reintroducing security flaws that may have been patched by the update (Winder, 2020). Therefore, although the choice to download and use digital contact tracing apps in the United States may be voluntary, the technological infrastructure that supports the apps was not.

Apple and Google stated that the exposure notification data would be limited and that apps would be removed at the conclusion of the global pandemic (Ng, 2020). However, ambiguity remains over when such apps will be removed. And the underlying technology and API will potentially remain on smartphones indefinitely. There is the possibility that a similar Bluetooth handshake system will be retained, or reimplemented into future devices, for precision tracking, enabling the collection of greater and additional movement data.

In contrast to the decentralized GAEN framework, some proposed protocols and apps store all user data on government servers, which perform the data analytics and contact tracing (Zastrow, 2020). Tracing and notification systems designed from the centralized approach offer a clear advantage of allowing health workers and government authorities "to use the database to piece together a view of the network of contacts, enabling further epidemiological insights such as revealing clusters and superspreaders" (Zastrow, 2020). Providing this additional data to try to enable further data analysis comes with clear risks of providing too much information beyond users' preferences, enabling state surveillance, and heightening the harms that data breaches and leaks could cause through deanonymization by hostile hackers.

Germany was initially one of the loudest proponents of the centralized approach, creating a European consortium called Pan-European Privacy-Preserving Proximity Tracing (PEPP-PT), which championed the centralized model (Zastrow, 2020). However, in response to widespread criticism of the privacy risks associated with these centralized protocols, Germany adopted the decentralized model proposed by Apple and Google. Other European nations, including Norway and the United Kingdom, designed and tested centralized apps (Albergotti & Harwell, 2020). Similarly, France favored the centralized approach while petitioning Apple and Google for access to GAEN without agreeing to the full gamut of data restrictions, which Apple and Google refused.

Outside of Europe, several other countries utilized centralized protocols and apps. For example, India (Woodhams, 2020) and Singapore (Access Now, 2020, p. 18) used a centralized app. China also used a centralized approach to pandemic surveillance that utilized government surveillance data, including drones and CCTV systems integrated with thermal-imaging cameras (Woodhams, 2020; Meaker, 2020).

2   THE CHINA SOCIAL CREDIT SYSTEM AND PANDEMIC SURVEILLANCE

China's surveillance of the COVID-19 pandemic has led to "a bold mass experiment in using data to regulate citizens' lives" (Mozur et al., 2020). For example, in Hangzhou, citizens were required to reveal their Alipay payment platform code as a method to track movements. Travel restrictions were imposed through color-coded instructions on the Alipay app: a green code indicated travel was permitted, whereas a yellow or a red code indicated travel restrictions or requirements to report to authorities immediately. Further, the pandemic "provided ideal conditions for exploiting and adapting" the China Social Credit System (Khalil, 2020).

Like the GAEN system, the China Social Credit System, or SCS, illustrates a collaboration between the government and tech firms to collect and exploit big data (Liang et al., 2018, p. 418; Xin, 2018). The social credit ratings systems span multiple regions and comprise overlapping systems under the SCS umbrella. They are implemented by both corporate and governmental entities for different sectors, typically to impose consequences in either public or commerce contexts (Liang et al., 2018, Table 1). The SCS focuses on social behavior for the purposes of behavioral modification (Liang et al., 2018, p. 425; Backer, 2019, p. 2). Determann (2020) summarizes, "The Chinese government seeks to ease access to personal data for the Chinese government, to safeguard social stability, to facilitate censorship and surveillance, and to protect domestic industries from global competition."

The SCS was first conceptualized in the 1990s and reached the stage of formalized proposals in 2011 (Liang et al., 2018, pp. 424–425). The SCS was initially proposed to cover "government affairs, commercial behaviors, social activities, and judicial affairs" (Liang et al., 2018). It was later expanded to full development and implementation in 2014, transitioning into a mass surveillance and social control system. Development of SCS would also include Chinese tech companies, including giants like Alibaba, Baidu, and Tencent, that would contribute user data and monitoring technologies.

As an example, Alibaba, the e-commerce giant, deployed its massive database of consumer information to develop and assign Sesame Credit scores to everyone in their database (Wong & Dobson, 2019, p. 223). Financial information akin to Western credit systems is used to rate individuals, as well as interpersonal relationships, item purchases, and other behavior. Such ratings can alter people's behavior in "nudges" with tangible government-provided incentives and punishments for having good or bad social credit scores, enabling a level of social control (Backer, 2018, pp. 18–19; Backer, 2019, p. 5). Unlike Western democracies that assume autonomous nudges in a "choice architecture" (Thaler & Sunstein, 2009), SCS assumes that nudges facilitate governance objectives through centralized mandates (Cong, 2021).

In the United States, for example, a life insurance company can base premium determinations on information gleaned from social media posts (Elgan, 2019). Any data gleaned about risky behaviors can provide justification for higher insurance rates (Elgan, 2019). This type of behavior modification is considered noncoercive in that the "choice architecture" theoretically provides consumers with the autonomy to pay higher insurance premiums if they choose to post images or information about their risky behaviors. Similarly, the China

Social Credit System imposes consequences on citizens when surveillance determines they are engaging in risky behaviors. For instance, an SCS pilot project in Rongcheng applies restrictions on individuals who fall below certain scores, such as having their names added to a public blacklist, being subject to increased surveillance, and being prohibited from managerial occupations, while other regions restrict train and airline travel (Wong & Dobson, 2019, pp. 223–224).

While the Chinese government intended to launch the SCS nationwide by 2020, it is still provisional, and several social credit systems within China operate independently (Wong & Dobson 2019, pp. 222–223). As of the end of 2020, data sharing issues as well as disparate regional programs and data collection methods have created challenges to fully integrating the SCS on a national scale (Reilly et al., 2021).

Pandemic surveillance systems in China were developed with the aid of Chinese tech companies and act as an extension of social credit systems, offering rewards and punishments for quarantine-connected behavior (Cong, 2021). Pandemic surveillance included less technologically sophisticated methods, including the use of existing public camera surveillance and facial recognition that relied on human monitoring and reporting (Cadell, 2020). Phone apps were also designed for contact tracing, using more invasive methods of monitoring and tracking, and with limited transparency in how tracing and data collection was performed. One of the primary contact tracing apps was developed in collaboration between the Chinese government and Ant Financial, a developer of Alipay and its sister company Alibaba (Mozur et al., 2020).

China's implementation of contact tracing apps permitted significant government access to detailed location data, purporting to aid public health objectives through granular location tracking and other pandemic surveillance tools. Data from Chinese contact tracing apps may have been shared with law enforcement, raising concerns that the apps were utilized for expanding social control beyond the premise of public health (Mozur et al., 2020). Some reports have indicated that, rather than solely revealing contagion risks, the system "also appears to share information with the police, setting a template for new forms of automated social control that could persist long after the epidemic subsides" (Mozur et al., 2020).

Legal scholar Larry Backer (2018) suggests two primary ways to conceptualize the Chinese social credit regime. The first is as a legal and regulatory mechanism that was created and operated by the Chinese government with affiliated companies (Backer, 2018, p. 5). The second is as an emerging form of social governance that bridges the public and private realms in a recombinant form that is likely to upend basic principles of social regulatory systems. Historically, regulatory systems have been grounded in law and oversight by government entities. Under social credit systems, a social regulatory regime is technologically mediated, displacing the traditional role of law and government. A social credit system turns data into a measurement that guides regulatory systems, attempting to motivate individual action through rewards or punishments, to conform to legal and regulatory frameworks (Backer, 2018, pp. 4–5). The social credit system turns the mass of information gathered about a population into ways to control the population's behavior at the individual level (Backer, 2018, pp. 18–19). Essentially, write Liang et al. (2018), the Chinese government "aims to score the 'creditworthiness' and 'trustworthiness' of each individual and organizational actor by a computational score based on their historical and ongoing social and economic activities, and these credit scores will determine whether the actor can obtain benefits or punishments" (p. 416).

Backer (2018) argues that at its furthest extent, the development of social credit will lead to a negation of the law as a privileged system without socioeconomic and political structures. Instead, the resulting governing structure will be one where the constitution turns into mechanics, principles become data, and norms become statistics (p. 5). This process is now possible with modern computing.

> The SCS relies on the use of big data collection, sharing and analysis methods to secure enhanced control over market and social processes on the behalf of the government. If successful in containing the pandemic or at least portraying itself as such, the CCP [Chinese Communist Party] may strengthen domestic and foreign appeal for this new model of surveillance. (Trauth-Goik, 2020)

The dramatic public health concerns raised by the global pandemic increased the acceptance of the widespread adoption of ubiquitous surveillance methods (Ignacio, 2021, p. 225; Zhang et al., 2020, p. 1). Social credit systems, and government surveillance and monitoring, were commonplace in China before the pandemic. Hard surveillance systems were commandeered to provide the ingrained contact tracing and pandemic surveillance needed for effective quarantine measures. As Meaker (2020) writes, "Initially, China's use of surveillance technology to track people's movements was branded 'excessive' by critics—an example of typical authoritarian overreach." But as death tolls from the virus grew worldwide, governments "scrambl[ed] to save lives [and] started to see the appeal of using location data to put the coronavirus—and its potential carriers—under surveillance" (Meaker, 2020).

3   FRICTIONLESS PANDEMIC SURVEILLANCE:
      A COMPARATIVE PERSPECTIVE

As in China, the corporate surveillance infrastructure in the United States integrates digital contact tracing into a preexisting surveillance architecture. In China, the citizenry already understands the consequences of failing to follow pandemic surveillance rules because it is the state that metes out penalties both for noncompliance for pandemic surveillance and for those tethered to the China Social Credit System (Wong & Dobson, 2019, pp. 223–224; Liang et al., 2018, pp. 415–416). In the United States, the corporate surveillance structure, with limited regulation and limited public knowledge of the technology itself, obscures the incestuous relationship between law and technology (Citron & Pasquale, 2014, pp. 18–19). Big tech, in the earliest stages of the digital revolution, remains underregulated. The absence of both comprehensive data privacy legislation and a data protection regime assures a lack of legal controls to curb the misuse and abuse of the data collected pursuant to the purported public health goals (Li, 2019; Hartzog & Richards, 2020, pp. 1702–1704). Big tech companies are not treated as surveillance systems per se, and therefore are not subject to U.S. privacy and surveillance laws that are focused on restraining government surveillance capacities. This creates a parallel "secret law" system (Balkin, 2008) for corporate entities that fall outside of the formal surveillance law restraints that exist in the United States, permitting technology firms to continue operating in obscurity and extralegally.

The lack of transparency in companies and poorly considered "consent" from clickwrap contracts enable technology firms to implement new data-gathering systems with limited oversight. Data surveillance, as part of soft surveillance and soft social credit systems, is executed in exchange for free services offered by tech companies (Wong & Dobson, 2019, pp. 222, 225; Andrejevic, 2007). The primary difference between this privately held data and China's plans for data governance is that the data is not yet publicly planned to be centralized in the hands of the U.S. or other democratic governments, but all the other systems for collecting and processing the data exist.

The current and long-term consequences of big tech surveillance systems in the United States are unknown. To the extent that the soft social credit systems' architecture, philosophy, and consequences remain unknown, the potential for future harms will also remain unknown. Similarly, to the extent that the architecture, philosophy, and consequences of the soft surveillance of big tech in the United States remain unregulated, many legal and constitutional consequences will be unresolved and unseen. Because the Chinese government controls the consequences under the China Social Credit System, there is a direct link between the surveillance technology and the government.

Under soft social credit systems proliferating in the United States, big tech in conjunction with the government can collude to implement potential consequences. Consequently, there is often no direct link between the soft surveillance technology and the government, making an unpredictable and uncertain environment of compliance and penalty. As this section explores, one way to render the consequences of U.S. pandemic surveillance and soft social credit systems more visible is by assessing comparisons between the United States and China.

Soft social credit systems in the United States are sometimes formed entirely by private entities (Elgan, 2019), and sometimes by collaboration between big tech and the U.S. government (Hu, 2016, p. 1740). Big tech has been described as generating forms of behavioral modification, not unlike the China Social Credit System (Buckley, 2019). The pandemic surveillance combined the behavioral modification goals of big tech and the U.S. government. Both big tech and the government sought to incentivize the implementation of the data tracking technology. Both big tech and the government discouraged failure to adopt the data tracking technology. And both big tech and the government argued that adoption of pandemic surveillance was in the public's best interest (Ahlam, 2021).

Additionally, rather than rely on behavioral modification by the government, soft social credit systems in the United States and other democracies can delegate behavioral modification to private entities. Pandemic surveillance, for example, allowed employers and universities to impose consequences or experiment with behavioral modifying tools on employees and students. There were reports that employees who failed to download the COVID-19 app were terminated (Johnson, 2021). Some universities required during the pandemic that all students download an app that tracked the students' location or risk being suspended or removed from campus (Whittaker, 2020).

The U.S. pandemic surveillance response arguably compounds the opacity challenges because it is hidden by a soft surveillance system that feeds data and potential consequences into a soft social credit system. Like the opacity of the surveillance consequences in the United States, the apparent merger between pandemic surveillance and the China Social Credit System means that it may be increasingly difficult for those in China to fully understand the nature of the surveillance or the nature of the behavioral modification. Even though Chinese citizens know the China Social Credit System is intended to modify their behavior, they may not understand how the pandemic surveillance structure is working toward specific modifications (Mac Síthigh & Siems, 2019, 17; Mozur et al., 2020). Chinese citizens, like U.S. citizens, may not know how data is shared, whom it is shared with, or how privately constructed or government-managed algorithms process that data (Keane & Su, 2019).

For example, the GAEN, purportedly implemented only for pandemic surveillance, may result in a partnership between big tech and the government that
creates new systems of data governance with new forms of behavioral modification and penalties. First, the promises made by Apple, Google, and regional
app makers to preserve data privacy and to remove COVID-19 apps at the end
of the public health emergency do not guarantee that the exposure notification
technology will not persist as a tracking tool beyond the pandemic (Morrison,
2020). Under current law, tech companies are not bound to maintain data protections or remove pandemic surveillance apps. Regardless of promises made
during the height of the pandemic, data privacy assurances presented by these
private entities will not be enforced without a statutory mandate or other legal
authority. Historical precedent indicates that digital trust may be difficult after
the conclusion of the pandemic. This potential for abuse of the technology is
especially ripe when, as here, two critical conditions are present. The first is
the fact that the smartphone technology itself was modified through a security
update that accommodated more pervasive data tracking capacities in the form
of COVID-19 apps. As described earlier, this technological transformation of
the smartphone will be permanent even if the COVID-19 apps are removed.
The second condition is the philosophical alignment between big tech, government, and the citizen. This philosophical transformation in surveillance
interests, which I explore further below, may also lead to enduring shifts in
governance, less reliant on checks and balances as the democratic norm.

The cooperation between Apple and Google to develop a joint contact
tracing API should have raised red flags for the privacy minded, as the companies are market competitors and would normally have a market incentive to
work against each other's interests. Cahn and Selinger (2020) explain: "We
should be wary of technological corporations claiming to be altruistic." The
program was reportedly developed to provide an alternative to overreaching
pandemic surveillance systems, such as those developed in China and other
Asian countries at the start of the pandemic (Cong, 2021). It was also reported
that the system was developed from the ground up to follow best data privacy
practices, including the General Data Protection Regulation (GDPR). Apple
and Google announced that the system would avoid the possibility of assisting
state surveillance. Yet the lack of oversight and regulation in the United States
to guarantee privacy allowed Apple, Google, and third-party cell phone manufacturers and service providers possible access (or ability to grant access) to
data generated by the API (*Diaz v. Google LLC*, 2021; Reardon, 2021).

The GAEN system was only superficially privacy enhancing. Enhanced
battery life protocols now allow for more invasive location tracking, including logging visits by local shops, a practice that is already performed using
Bluetooth beacons (Kwet, 2019). In *Diaz v. Google, LLC*, a case filed in
2021, the plaintiffs alleged in federal court that GAEN had included a security

flaw that "exposed … participants' private personal and medical information associated with contact tracing," which "is personally identifiable," "to third parties." As noted earlier, millions of smartphones changed overnight because the API was embedded as a security update that could not be avoided and changed the infrastructure to be more invasive. As it applies to all iOS and Android devices, comprising virtually all smartphones, the Apple-Google system now changes what any app can do for generations afterward. The infrastructure has fundamentally allowed the API to enable far more invasive apps than was possible before this modification was released. Few people understand that when this API was released as a security update, it was not only in support of a public health emergency, but also supported a change in the technological infrastructure of smartphones that can be utilized for far more than public health purposes. For example, "Google's implementation of GAEN logs [allowed for] crucial pieces of information to [be entered into] the system log, which can be read by hundreds of third-party apps" (Reardon, 2021). Apple and Google had, according to some reports, solved multiple challenges from the past, including addressing "problems that led previous apps to quickly drain a phone's battery" (Paul, 2020). The global pandemic, therefore, created a public health emergency that made the technological update seem well justified.

Big tech firms have long aspired to expand geolocational and pinpoint tracking for adtech purposes. Adtech companies and apps were proponents of this technological change to iOS and Android devices, as this modification is worth billions. Beyond COVID-19 apps, other apps can possibly utilize the Bluetooth handshake technology that was built for digital contact tracing purposes, superseding the limitations of prior beacon-based Bluetooth location tracking systems (Nicholas & Shapiro, 2021, pp. 479–480). Imagine running a phone app, then closing it, but having it continue releasing Bluetooth signals in the background, allowing Bluetooth beacons to receive and store contact pings that enable precise triangulation. Even the anonymization protocols promised to preserve privacy are not guarantees of anonymity, as other forms of anonymized location data have been proven to be vulnerable to deanonymization attacks (Kondor et al., 2018; de Montjoye et al., 2013). The GAEN framework itself may also be vulnerable as well, and the IP address of the app user can also lead to revelation of personally identifiable data (*Diaz v. Google LLC*, 2021; Reardon, 2021).

Through multiple pandemic surveillance technologies adopted globally, both corporate and government entities became vested with the types of tools needed to replicate social credit system goals—for instance, allowing a more ubiquitous view into the behaviors and movements of those being tracked for public health purposes. Some claimed that data privacy concerns during the pandemic "focus … too much on individual privacy and not enough on what is needed to prevent potential dangers to the health of the patient or others" (Determann, 2020, p. 267). This potentially facilitated the implementation of the structure of a social credit system in the private sector that could parallel the goals and structure of the China Social Credit System. A U.S.-based social credit system, for instance, could affect consumer credit scores and travel restrictions, and have other possible consequences that mirror those in China. More accurate phone tracking in the United States could also enable greater government surveillance if the uses of new technology aren't appropriately limited (Thompson & Warzel, 2019, Ram & Gray, 2020, pp. 15–16), which the GAEN framework prevents only via weak promises of limited data sharing and obfuscation and encryption guarantees (Albergotti & Harwell, 2020). The intelligence community and law enforcement, for example, are also likely to be interested in new streams of data to build up new data governance systems, predictive policing, or new methods of surveillance. In the criminal procedure context, Bluetooth tracking may become an alternative to cell site location information for law enforcement, accessing it through the Stored Communications Act (*Carpenter v. United States*). Just like cell site location information, Bluetooth data can be transferred to third parties, potentially under a reduced expectation of privacy under the third-party doctrine.

It is a mistake to assume that China's pandemic surveillance tools have seamlessly integrated into a preexisting surveillance architecture whereas the United States and other democracies have developed the independent implementation of pandemic surveillance by private companies like Google and Apple. If we assume that democracy provides the requisite oversight and protections to stop the harms of surveillance capitalism, then we assume that abuses seen in an authoritarian state will not be possible. But this overlooks surveillance harms that may be invisibly woven into the fabric of the digital economy and are thus minimized or excused. For example, because the "choice architecture" of digital nudging is assumed to be voluntary, the behavioral modification is either unseen or is dismissed as consumer preference. The lack of regulation over both the surveillance and the behavioral modification allows harms to proliferate in the United States.

Applying the lens of digital authoritarianism gives insight into how pandemic surveillance technology applies stress points to democracy (Bloomfield, 2021). The state of emergency created by the public health crisis masked the market realities of pandemic surveillance: the clear market incentives driving the creation of pandemic surveillance technologies (Calo, 2014; Ottenheimer, Chapter 2 of this book). The market incentives create uncomfortable parallels between pandemic surveillance tech adopted in the United States and the China Social Credit System where big tech, the government, and social and market incentives line up in concert. During the pandemic, the same alignment was found in both the United States and China—yet the originating governance structure of the former relies on friction among powers to establish checks and balances and ensure the prominence of the democratic rule of law. When government and big tech enjoy perfect alignment and cooperation, there is diminished oversight of both. Healthy tension between governmental and big tech interests is critical to maintain the checks and balances that protect the social contract between the citizen and state.

The global pandemic, and the propulsion of big government and big tech solutions to address the state of emergency, facilitated frictionless alignment between the goals and objectives shared by both. The dangers of this alignment were not immediately understood, as the necessary cooperation presented itself as life-preserving and an example of effective public–private cooperation. In the rush to embrace technology advances and data collection and analysis for the purposes of mitigating pandemic harms, what was difficult to witness was the erosion of checks and balances at a theoretical level as well as a practical one.

Privacy specialist Bruce Schneier presents the challenge to democracies in the following way: "As we move toward greater [pandemic] surveillance, we need to figure out how to get the best of both: how to design systems that make use of our data collectively to benefit society as a whole, while at the same time protecting people individually" (Crabtree et al., 2020). Apple and Google claimed they would not directly share data with government entities, and that their project was a privacy-protecting API to decentralize the data and mitigate the risks of centralizing it in ways that can be abused and misused by government entities or hackers. As discussed above, the true privacy protections are limited. Furthermore, that level of individual user protection doesn't protect against a shift of theory in data governance. The philosophical shift in data governance that allows for a full alignment of market, technology, social ordering, and government is what may pose a hegemonic challenge to a democratic republic. Consequently, the acceleration of pandemic surveillance and frictionless implementation should be understood as a silent data governance revolution that entrenches and extends the surveillance powers of private companies and the state.

In short, pandemic surveillance systems, purportedly implemented for a limited purpose to address a public health emergency, are likely to result in longer-term surveillance consequences. For this reason, it is critical to analyze how, on a philosophical level, pandemic surveillance can potentially shift democracies one step closer to that of the China Social Credit System.

4   THE SILENT DATA GOVERNANCE REVOLUTION

Both China and the United States are driven by similar market forces, including the volitional impact of technological innovation and surveillance capitalism (Zuboff, 2019, pp. 388–394). Both countries also embraced pandemic surveillance as one method to combat the spread of COVID-19. The governmental structures of China and the United States differ, yet surveillance systems can operate similarly. For this reason, scholars such as Shoshana Zuboff encourage citizens to keep their eye on the market incentives that may guide innovation and social control. As the business model of algorithmic and AI-centered power drifts closer to data resources, historical moments that accelerate motivations for mass data collection must be interrogated closely. The terrorist attacks of September 11, 2001 incentivized the acceleration of the adoption of ubiquitous surveillance technologies to address the state of emergency. The pandemic has presented another state of emergency. Both historical moments hastened the embrace of surveillance technologies—but some experts predict that the response to the pandemic may be even more drastic than the impact of the 9/11 terrorist attacks (Schneier, 2020; Swire, 2020). "Like other life-transforming crises," explains Robert Kaplan, "the coronavirus pandemic will likely ignite an urge for the protective embrace of big government" (Crabtree et al., 2020).

What was lost in the focus on public health was how surveillance justifications facilitated a theoretical shift in governance. Citizens, policymakers, and big tech representatives largely agreed that technological advancements in human contact tracing were necessary to curtail the devastating harms presented by COVID-19. The global health policymaking role of GAEN transformed big tech into quasi-governmental entities (Safdar & Poulsen, 2020; Sharon, 2020). Google and Apple effectively became gatekeepers, "de facto regulators of virus apps, deciding which of the many developers can offer services in their stores" (Safdar & Poulsen, 2020). The Google app store's policies, which required COVID-19 apps to include privacy policies, were not enforced. Additionally, some apps included codes that facilitated targeted advertising or allowed for the processing of online purchases through interaction with social media.

As discussed above, the architecture and philosophy of the China Social Credit System is less obscure to Chinese citizens than the architecture and philosophy of big tech surveillance in the United States (Mac Síthigh & Siems, 2020, p. 10; Tufekci, 2014). It purportedly matches the architecture and structure of other Chinese governance models (Keane & Su, 2019). The architecture and philosophy of big tech surveillance in the United States was not designed to be consistent with constitutional democracy. Ironically, the types of behavioral modification goals embraced by the China Social Credit System were enabled by the increasing integration between the governance objectives of both big tech and Western governments. It is conceivable that the kinds of deprivation, stigmatization, and limitation on rights and freedoms seen in China can occur in the United States and other democracies that adopted the proposed big tech pandemic surveillance technologies. As a result of normalizing these soft social credit systems—before, during, and after the pandemic—U.S. citizens may also be subjected to the types of behavioral modification deployed in China under state-run surveillance. Pandemic surveillance can result in soft surveillance consequences, misleading the citizenry that may be unaware and uninformed of these consequences.

Unlike the China Social Credit System, which is intended to support local and national governance objectives, big tech surveillance in the United States supports big tech governance objectives. The mission of surveillance capitalism in the United States serves the big tech market (Zuboff, 2019, pp. 293–294; Foer, 2020). Because the architecture and philosophy of big tech surveillance in the United States is largely taken for granted, it operates invisibly within the digital economy and capitalism. It can also be characterized as a soft surveillance system, as the behavioral modification model for the monetization of data fuels the profit. The presentation of the technology as a mere extension of the market further means that the soft surveillance system in the United States is mostly unrecognized as a governance system.

Whether an underlying cybersurveillance structure for social credit systems has already taken root in Western democracies is a topic of active dialogue. Some experts have expressed concern that with pandemic surveillance providing the foundations for more advanced data-driven governance systems, social credit systems will follow and transform democracy. The current state of corporate self-regulation exacerbates concerns regarding whether big tech pandemic surveillance can be regulated to control and properly guide data-driven governance in a way that sufficiently protects privacy and democracy.

The ways in which we experience deprivations of our rights, increased stigmatization, and limitations on social credit platforms are opaque in democracies like the United States where the consequences of surveillance capitalism and big tech surveillance systems are unclear. Social pressures from private individuals can amount to stigmatization that is never publicly voiced but is subtly applied. A constitutional ethos of strong individual rights and the separation of powers is at risk of breaking down when there are greater social pressures to sacrifice private rights and power alliances appear justified to combat an emergency. The pandemic and other states of emergency facilitate conditions that bring the United States and other democracies closer to a Chinese-type pandemic surveillance and social credit system (Backer, 2019), but one run by big tech rather than the state (Mac Síthigh & Siems, 2019).

The implementation of full data collection is enabled by both the government that seeks the data and the tech companies that use the increased accessibility to data for private market purposes. Data privacy protections that limit the power of big tech and government to collect and use data acquired from pandemic surveillance are currently limited in scope. Using China as an example, there is a far end of data utilization that the Chinese government has encouraged under the China Social Credit System. The pandemic accelerated the frictionless alignment between technology and the state in the exploitation of China's preexisting Social Credit System. China's rapid rollout of more intrusive data collection and a capitalization of the existing surveillance architecture represented a phenomenon which could be, and has been, repeated in other nations.

CONCLUSION

The pandemic presented a significant global health challenge that overshadowed and made opaque the market-driven motivations behind the mass data collection of locational or proximity location data for public health purposes. Unlike the China Social Credit System, which operates as a hard surveillance system in architecture and philosophy, the pandemic surveillance system in the United States can be conceptualized as a big tech soft surveillance system in both architecture and philosophy. The consequences of a soft social credit system in the United States are rendered more visible through a comparative perspective, viewing the discomforting similarities between the philosophical impact of pandemic surveillance in the United States and the China Social Credit System. Frictionless pandemic surveillance risks digital authoritarianism. And because data surveillance unfolds almost invisibly, not only do the data tracking technologies render themselves nearly invisible, but the philosophies that guide data governance, such as frictionless alignment, are also rendered nearly invisible (Kampmark, 2020; Tufekci, 2014).

The market demands for pandemic surveillance and technological responses to that demand removed tensions between big tech and government, leading to a type of frictionless alignment in the United States, and moving it one step closer to the philosophy of the China Social Credit System. To disable the soft social credit system embraced by pandemic surveillance, democracy demands oversight and friction. Dangers to democracy tend to unfold stealthily where perceptions of what serves the public good rely on surveillance and behavioral modification, and where governance fuses with technology firms to advance a new kind of social contract that excludes the citizen.

REFERENCES

Access Now. (2020, March). "Recommendations on privacy and data protection in the fight against COVID-19." www.accessnow.org/cms/assets/uploads/2020/03/Access -Now-recommendations-on-Covid-and-data-protection-and-privacy.pdf

Ahlam, R. (2021). "Apple, the government, and you: Security and privacy implications of the global encryption debate." *Fordham International Law Journal*, 44, 771.

Albergotti, R., & Harwell, D. (2020, May 15). "Apple and Google are building a virus-tracking system. Health officials say it will be practically useless." *Washington Post.* www.washingtonpost.com/technology/2020/05/15/app-apple -google-virus/

Andrejevic, A. (2007). "Ubiquitous computing and the digital enclosure movement." *Media International Australia*, 125, 106–117. www.dhi.ac.uk/san/waysofbeing/ data/citizenship-robson-andrejevic-2007.pdf

Backer, L. C. (2018, October 30). "Next generation law: Data driven governance and accountability based regulatory systems in the West, and social credit regimes in China." http://dx.doi.org/10.2139/ssrn.3209997

Backer, L. C. (2019, October 11). "Blacklists and social credit regimes in China" [Symposium session]. Super-Scoring? Data-Driven Societal Technologies in China and Western-Style Democracies as a New Challenge for Education, Cologne, Germany. www.backerinlaw.com/Site/wp-content/uploads/2019/08/Blacklists-and -Social-Credit-Regimes-in-China.pdf

Balkin, J. M. (2008). "The constitution in the national surveillance state." *Minnesota Law Review*, 93, 1.

Bloomfield Jr., L. (2021). "Let them eat smartphones: Reflections on the wealth-information paradox." *Fletcher Forum of World Affairs*, 45, 17.

Bradford, L., Aboy, M., & Liddell, K. (2020). "COVID-19 contact tracing apps: A stress test for privacy, the GDPR, and data protection regimes." *Journal of Law and the Biosciences*, 7(1).

Buckley, F. H. (2019, August 28). "'Social credit' may come to America." *Wall Street Journal*. www.wsj.com/articles/social-credit-may-come-to-america-11567033176

Cadell, C. (2020, May 26) "China's Coronavirus campaign offers glimpse into surveillance system." Reuters. www.reuters.com/article/us-health-coronavirus -china-surveillance/chinas-coronavirus-campaign-offers-glimpse-into-surveillance -system-idUSKBN2320LZ

Cahn, A. F., & Selinger, E. (2020, April 17). "Tracking coronavirus with smartphones isn't just a tech problem." *Boston Globe.* www.bostonglobe.com/2020/04/17/ opinion/tracking- coronavirus-with-smartphones-isnt-just-tech-problem/

Calo, R. (2014). "Digital market manipulation." *George Washington Law Review*, 82, 995.

Carpenter v. United States, 138 S. Ct. 2206 (2018).

Citron, D. K., & Pasquale, F. (2014). "The scored society: Due process for automated predictions." *Washington Law Review*, 89, 1.

Cong, W. (2021, April 14). "From pandemic control to data-driven governance: The case of China's health code." *Frontiers in Political Science*, 3, 627959. www .frontiersin.org/articles/10.3389/fpos.2021.627959/full

Crabtree, J., Kaplan, R. D., Muggah, R., Naidoo, K., O'Neil, S. K., Posen, A., Roth, K., Schneier, B., Walt, S. M., & Wrage, A. (2020, May 16). "The future of the state: Ten

leading global thinkers on government after the pandemic." Foreign Policy. https://
foreignpolicy.com/2020/05/16/future-government-powers-coronavirus-pandemic/

Criddle, C., & Kelion, L. (2020, May 7). "Coronavirus contact-tracing: World split
between two types of app.*"* BBC. www.bbc.com/news/technology-52355028

de Montjoye, Y. A., Hidalgo, C. A., Verleysen, M., & Blondel, V. D. (2013). "Unique
in the crowd: The privacy bounds of human mobility." *Scientific Reports*, 3(1), 1–5.
www.nature.com/articles/srep01376

Determann, L. (2020). "Healthy data protection." *Michigan Technology Law Review*,
26, 229.

Diaz v. Google, LLC, 5:21-cv-3080 (N.D. Cali. 2021).

Elgan, M. (2019, August 26). "Uh-oh: Silicon Valley is building a Chinese-style social
credit system." Fast Company. www.fastcompany.com/90394048/uh-oh-silicon
-valley-is-building-a-chinese-style-social-credit-system

Etherington, D. (2020, May 20). "COVID-19 exposure notification settings begin to
go live for iOS users with new update." TechCrunch. https://social.techcrunch.com/
2020/05/20/covid-19-exposure-notification-settings-begin-to-go-live-for-ios-users
-with-new-update/

Ferretti, L., Wymant, C., Kendall, M., Zhao, L., Nurtay, A., Abeler-Dörner, L., Parker,
M., Bonsall, D., & Fraser, C. (2020, May 8). "Quantifying SARS-CoV-2 transmission suggests epidemic control with digital contact tracing." *Science*. https://science
.sciencemag.org/content/early/2020/04/09/science.abb6936/tab-pdf

Foer, F. (2020, July/August). "What Big Tech wants out of the pandemic." *The Atlantic*.
www.theatlantic.com/magazine/archive/2020/07/big-tech-pandemic-power-grab/
612238/

Google. (n.d.). "Android Help: Use the COVID-19 Exposure Notifications System on
your Android phone." Google. https://support.google.com/android/answer/9888358
?hl=en

Gurman, M., De Vynck, G., & Bloomberg. (2020, May 20). "Apple, Google's
COVID-19 tracing tool is one big step closer to being put to use." Fortune. https://
fortune.com/2020/05/20/apple-google-covid-19-tracing-tool/

Halbfinger, D. M., Kershner, I., & Bergman, R. (2020, March 18). "To track coronavirus, Israel moves to tap secret trove of cellphone data." *New York Times*. www
.nytimes.com/2020/03/16/world/middleeast/israel-coronavirus-cellphone-tracking
.html

Hartzog, W., & Richards, N. (2020). "Privacy's constitutional moment and the limits of
data protection." *Boston College Law Review*, 61, 1687.

Hu, M. (2016). "Big data blacklisting." *Florida Law Review*, 67(5), 1735–1809.

Ignacio C. (2021). "Immunity passports and contact tracing surveillance." *Stanford
Technology Law Review*, 24(2), 176–236.

Johnson, E. (2021, April 12). "School custodian refuses to download phone app that
monitors location, says it got her fired." CBC News. www.cbc.ca/news/gopublic/
tattleware-privacy-employment-1.5978337

Kampmark, B. (2020). "The pandemic surveillance state: An enduring legacy of
COVID-19." *Journal of Global Faultlines*, 7(1), 59–70.

Keane, M., & Su, G. (2019). "When push comes to nudge: A Chinese digital civilisa-
tion in-the-making." *Media International Australia*, 173(1), 3–16. https://doi.org/10
.1177/1329878X19876362

Kerr, I., Barrigar, J., Burkell, J., & Black, K. (2006, July). "Soft surveillance, hard
consent." www.researchgate.net/publication/228141180_Soft_Surveillance_Hard
_Consent

Khalil, L. (2020, November 2). "Digital authoritarianism, China and COVID." Lowy Institute. www.lowyinstitute.org/publications/digital-authoritarianism-china-and -covid

Kondor, D., Hashemian, B., de Montjoye, Y.-A., & Ratti, C. (2018). "Towards matching user mobility traces in large-scale datasets." *IEEE Transactions on Big Data*, 6(4), 714–726. https://doi.org/10.1109/TBDATA.2018.2871693

Kwet, M. (2019). "In stores, secret surveillance tracks your every move." *New York Times*. www.nytimes.com/interactive/2019/06/14/opinion/bluetooth-wireless -tracking-privacy.html

Levi, M., & Wall, D. (2004, June). "Technologies, security, and privacy in the post-9/11 European information society." *Journal of Law and Society*, 31(2), 194–220.

Li, C. (2018). "A repeated call for omnibus federal cybersecurity law." *Notre Dame Law Review*, 94, 2211.

Liang, F., Das, V., Kostyuk, N., & Hussain, M. M. (2018). "Constructing a data-driven society: China's social credit system as a state surveillance infrastructure." *Policy & Internet*, 10(4), 415–453. https://doi.org/10.1002/poi3.183

Mac Síthigh, D., & Siems, M. (2019). "The Chinese social credit system: A model for other countries?" *The Modern Law Review*, 82(6), 1034–1071.

Meaker, M. (2020, April 14). "Coronavirus tracing and the right to privacy in a pandemic." *World Politics Review*. www.worldpoliticsreview.com/articles/28682/ coronavirus-contact-tracing-and-the-right-to-privacy-in-a-pandemic

Morrison, S. (2020, April 16). "Apple and Google look like problematic heroes in the pandemic: New contact-tracing technology is supposed to go away after the pandemic. Privacy experts aren't so sure it will." Vox. www.vox.com/recode/2020/4/16/ 21221458/apple-google-contact-tracing-app-coronavirus-covid-privacy

Mozur, P. (2018). "Inside China's dystopian dreams: AI, shame and lots of cameras." *New York Times*. www.nytimes.com/2018/07/08/business/china-surveillance -technology.html

Mozur, P., Zhong, R., & Krolik, A. (2020). "In coronavirus fight, China gives citizens a color code, with red flags." *New York Times*, 1. www.nytimes.com/2020/03/01/ business/china-coronavirus-surveillance.html

Nellis, S., & Dave, P. (2020, May 4). "Apple, Google ban use of location tracking in contact tracing apps." Reuters. www.reuters.com/article/us-health-coronavirus -usa-apps/apple-google-ban-use-of-location-tracking-in-contact-tracing-apps -idUSKBN22G28W

Ng, A. (2020, April 14). "Apple, Google to terminate COVID-19 tracking tools once pandemic ends." CNET. www.cnet.com/tech/mobile/apple-and-google-say-they -will-shut-down-covid-19-tracking-tools-once-pandemic-ends/

Nicholas, G., & Shapiro, A. (2021). "Failed hybrids: The death and life of Bluetooth proximity marketing." *Mobile Media & Communication*, 9(3), 465–487.

Paul, K. (2020, May 20). "Apple and Google release phone technology to notify users of coronavirus exposure." *The Guardian*. www.theguardian.com/technology/2020/ may/20/apple-google-phone-app-trace-coronavirus

Poulos, J. (2021, September 15). "How bitcoin can immunize America from cancel culture." *New York Times*. www.nytimes.com/2021/09/15/opinion/cryptocurrency -americans-free.html

Ram, N., & Gray, D. (2020). "Mass surveillance in the age of COVID-19." *Journal of Law & the Biosciences*, 7(1).

Ratnam, G. (2020, May 20). "Apple, Google release template for COVID-19 contact tracing apps." Roll Call. www.rollcall.com/2020/05/20/apple-google-release -template-for-covid-19-contact-tracing-apps/

Reardon, J. (2021, April 27). "Why Google should stop logging contact-tracing data." AppCensus Blog. https://blog.appcensus.io/2021/04/27/why-google-should-stop -logging-contact-tracing-data/

Reilly, J., Lyu, M., & Robertson, M. (2021, March 30). "China's social credit system: Speculation vs. reality." *The Diplomat*. https://thediplomat.com/2021/03/chinas -social-credit-system-speculation-vs-reality/

Safdar, K., & Poulsen, K. (2020, June 5). "Google, Apple struggle to regulate Covid-19 tracing apps." *Wall Street Journal*. www.wsj.com/articles/why-google-and-apple -stores-had-a-covid-19-app-with-ads-11591365499

Schneier, B. (March 3, 2020). "Privacy vs. surveillance in the age of COVID-19." Schneier on Security. www.schneier.com/blog/archives/2020/03/privacy_vs_surv .html

Selinger, E., & Leong, B. (May 22, 2020). "The public is being misled by pandemic technology that won't keep them safe." OneZero by Medium. https://onezero .medium.com/the-public-is-being-misled-by-pandemic-technology-that-wont-keep -them-safe-1966ed740a87

Sharon, T. (2020). "Blind-sided by privacy? Digital contact tracing, the Apple/Google API and big tech's newfound role as global health policy makers." *Ethics and Information Technology*, 1–13. https://doi.org/10.1007/s10676-020-09547-x

Swire, P. (2020, March 24). "Security, privacy and the coronavirus: Lessons from 9/11." Lawfare Blog. www.lawfareblog.com/security-privacy-and-coronavirus -lessons-911

Tate, K. (2021, August 3). "Coming soon: America's own social credit system." The Hill. https://thehill.com/opinion/finance/565860-coming-soon-americas-own-social -credit-system

Thaler, R., & Sunstein, C. (2009). *Nudge: Improving Decisions About Health, Wealth, and Happiness*. Yale University Press.

Thompson, D. (2020, April 7). "The technology that could free America from quarantine." *The Atlantic*. www.theatlantic.com/ideas/archive/2020/04/contact-tracing -could-free-america-from-its-quarantine-nightmare/609577/

Thompson, S. A., & Warzel, C. (2019). "Twelve million phones, one dataset, zero privacy." *New York Times*. www.nytimes.com/interactive/2019/12/19/opinion/ location-tracking-cell-phone.html

Trauth-Goik, A. (2020, April 28). "How China is leveraging the social credit system in the fight against coronavirus." Medium. https://alexgoik.medium.com/ how-china-is-leveraging-the-social-credit-system-in-the-fight-against-coronavirus -a1a3e18530c6

Tufekci, Z. (2014). "Engineering the public: Big data, surveillance and computational politics." *First Monday*, 19(7). https://doi.org/10.5210/fm.v19i7.4901

Whittaker, Z. (2020, August. 19). "Fearing coronavirus, a Michigan college is tracking its students with a flawed app: And students have no way to opt out." TechCrunch. https://techcrunch.com/2020/08/19/coronavirus-albion-security-flaws-app/

Winder, D. (2020, June 28). "How to disable Apple and Google's COVID-19 notifications on your phone." Forbes. www.forbes.com/sites/daveywinder/2020/06/28/how -to-disable-apple-and-googles-covid-19-notifications-on-your-phone-coronavirus -tracking-and-contact-tracing-app/

Wong, K. L. X., & Dobson, A. S. (2019). "We're just data: Exploring China's social credit system in relation to digital platform ratings cultures in Westernised democracies." *Global Media and China*, 4(2), 220–232. https://journals.sagepub.com/doi/pdf/10.1177/2059436419856090

Woodhams, S. (2020, May 12). "COVID-19 digital rights tracker." Top10VPN. www.top10vpn.com/research/covid-19-digital-rights-tracker/

Xin, D. (2018, June 24). "Toward a reputation state: The social credit system project of China." SSRN. https://papers.ssrn.com/sol3/papers.cfm?abstract_id=3193577

Yang, Y., & Zhu, J. (February 7, 2020). "Coronavirus brings China's surveillance state out of the shadows." Reuters. www.reuters.com/article/us-china-health-surveillance/coronavirus-brings-chinas-surveillance-state-out-of-the-shadows-idUSKBN2011HO

Zastrow, M. (2020, May 19). "Coronavirus contact-tracing apps: Can they slow the spread of COVID-19?" *Nature*. https://doi.org/10.1038/d41586-020-01514-2

Zhang, B., Kreps, S., McMurry, N., & McCain, R. M. (2020, December 23). "Americans' perceptions of privacy and surveillance in the COVID-19 pandemic." *PLoS ONE*, 15(12): e0242652. https://doi.org/10.1371/journal.pone.0242652

Zuboff, S. (2019). *The Age of Surveillance Capitalism: The Fight for a Human Future at the New Frontier of Power*. Profile Books.

5. The developing narratives of pandemic surveillance

Joshua Fairfield

Inattention to both the mechanisms of narrative and the interaction between narrative and technology has left us incapable of crafting consensus on the meaning of the worldwide authoritarian moment as it relates to pandemic surveillance. This chapter examines why the path of pandemic surveillance narratives has been so hard to chart and predict, and why effective digital applications that help a population fight a deadly disease have been so difficult to deploy without furthering democratic decline amid a global techno-totalitarian trend.

In recent history there has been significant mission creep in technologies of surveillance (Mendelson, 2021, pp. 38–46). My theme is that narratives around surveillance are techno-social affordances, or features of the technology itself, and that we have insufficiently theorized how the loops between narrative and technology occur and how to leverage them to "authoritarian proof" pandemic surveillance technologies. This gap has left the democratic deliberative tradition unable to summon the political unity necessary to combat rising authoritarianism, even when nearly all members of a body politic believe COVID-19 has created an authoritarian moment and that the pandemic response is connected to an impermissible extension of government powers of surveillance.

Pandemic surveillance technologies have been deployed with varying success (Yang et al., 2020, pp. 188–194; Winkler, 2020). The fit between surveillance technology and the narratives around that technology impacts how well the technology works (e.g., dos Reis Peron et al., 2021, pp. 6–8). To give one example, the technical characteristics of different COVID tracing applications interact with the social contexts that interpret them (Vinuesa et al., 2020, pp. 2–3). Governments developed or sponsored smartphone apps to gather user information. Simultaneously, these apps produced data troves for use in policing or political suppression (deLisle & Kui, 2021, pp. 48–49). This mix of design decisions, social context, and social construction of technology is volatile. Some mixes of technological affordance and social meaning work better in fighting both the physical disease and the corrosive effects of surveillance on democratic norms—an attack on the body politic. Given these considerations, it is important to ask what future frameworks for the protection of privacy and security might look like.

THE TECHNO-SOCIAL LOOP

Technologists examine technology, and sociologists society, but the divisions between the fields are artificial (Latour, 1993). A network like that deployed to track the pandemic comprises human and non-human nodes, with multiple layers, from the operating system (for example, the Google Apple Exposure Notification framework, or GAEN, permits smartphones to pass on exposure notifications based on a common OS framework) to the networks of human trust in community.

Consider the primary surveillance apparatus: the smartphone. Smartphones are signifiers, a rich spot in a series of examples where we negotiate the boundary between citizen and state, private and public, natural and social. Despite academic movements that try to allocate the bulk of the heavy lifting to the realm of the "natural" (scientism) or the "social" (at its most concentrated in science and technology studies), or to undo the natural–social dichotomy (as Bruno Latour, Michel Callon, and other actor-network theorists attempt), what is certain is that neither the social nor the technological forces dominate (Latour, 2005). Rather, they form a loop, whereby social affordances blend into technological features, and vice versa.

Of course, a crude version of this is obvious: the technology used for pandemic surveillance is used for social ends like political suppression and policing (deLisle & Kui, 2021, pp. 48–49). While this represents a social–technical mix, it does so only at the most basic level: it is as if we posited the existence of both chicken and egg and left it at that, without acknowledging the millions of years of evolution that led to the present-day circumstances.

In the same way, we should consider how technological narratives around pandemic surveillance develop and what they are likely to mean, particularly for the affordances of the technology itself. Simply, technology works well given some narratives, works poorly given others, and the narratives change and iterate. For example, uptake of COVID tracing apps in the first week of their respective releases was 4% in my home state, Virginia, 20% in Germany, and 37% in Ireland, even when the underlying technology (GAEN) was functionally the same and greatly focused on protecting privacy. Design alone no longer serves—or at least, the behavior change campaign necessary to get a design to work must be part of the design decision. Now, as the world develops vaccines for COVID-19, the issue of insufficient (and often problematic) narratives about vaccines is a broader and more pressing issue than ever before.

What we need is a way of talking about the future, and particularly the kind of problems that require the full range of scientific and cultural resources found around the world. The COVID-19 pandemic has illuminated the fact that we do not have a way of speaking about complex, global, non-routine, innovation-based tasks that permits us to leverage the parallel thinking capacity of different cultures worldwide.

Here are some puzzles that stand in the way of tidy lessons learned about the crossover between the worldwide health crisis and what many have called the authoritarian moment, especially as regards surveillance. Why did quarantine measures that worked in New Zealand fail in the United States (Parker, 2021, pp. 78–80)? Why were some countries able to leverage COVID tracing apps with no rise in authoritarian practice (e.g., South Korea; Lee, 2020), whereas others gained next to no benefits from contact tracing but expanded authoritarian norms (e.g., various European countries; Eck & Hatz, 2020, pp. 607–608)? Why is vaccine hesitancy spreading virally even as more nation-states attempt to combat it (see, e.g., Hyatt et al., 2021)?

Particularly instructive is the wild rise in narratives of authoritarianism and surveillance in the context of COVID. Note that some narratives may be untrue but still powerful. Singapore repurposed contact tracing data for routine policing (Chandran, 2021). The US government continues to sweep up US persons' data under the FISA Section 702 program (Donohue, 2015, pp. 137–157). And conspiracy theories, which have now convinced a large percentage of Americans, place themes of COVID and surveillance in close proximity: people believe that the COVID vaccines include tracking implants (Reuters Staff, 2020b; Sherwin, 2021). Never mind the nonsense of the claim or the futility of worrying about such things instead of the suite of surveillance software built into every smartphone. The conspiracists are not wrong about the degree to which their privacy has been compromised; they simply pick bizarre, untrue, and society-damaging ways of expressing their sense of being watched.

Thus, we are presented with two narrative truths that explain the common understanding that COVID is connected with the worldwide rise of political authoritarianism (and note that this view is shared by cargo-cult conspiracist authoritarians): everyone agrees that COVID has provided the context for anti-democratic power grabs, but the narratives are framed using completely different languages that are unable to translate their common themes into political effectiveness. Consider, for example, the surprising bipartisan support for privacy bills in the United States despite the slow death of democracy in that country, and yet nothing can be done (see, e.g., Kern, 2021).

The United States and other states that waver between democratic traditions and a rising trend of conspiracist national authoritarianism have lost the ability to build common goals by developing meta-languages that permit translation of values into various other language frameworks. We are increasingly unable to talk to each other and draw on a common story to combat threats like COVID-19. The fissures are not merely between political spheres, nations, or cultures, but also between disciplines. Science's failed metanarratives of neutrality give credence to entirely false claims that the pandemic was socially engineered (Reuters Staff, 2020a). It wasn't, but enough else was, and the governments and private entities developing and deploying such technology have been dishonest enough about their own motivations—surveillance technology against civil society in particular—that the conspiracists are in good company not to believe a word they say (see, e.g., Shindelman, 2011). Have you ever rolled your eyes at yet another online pop-up claiming "We value your privacy" as the preface to a company's data use and exploitation policy? That is what I mean.

Similarly, those who study scientists continue methodological debates over whether one should study the macro patterns or the micro components of techno-social phenomena: actor-network theory versus the social construction of technology, for example. The dispute is akin to asking whether it is better to study ocean currents by looking at the characteristics of water molecules, or whether the characteristics of water molecules can best be determined by oceanographers studying ocean currents. It is useful to study patterns by looking at their constituent parts just as it is useful to study entities by how they behave in concert (whether molecules bouncing off one another or the spread of physical or disinformation viruses). But an insistence on studying phenomena at a level other than that at which they appear clouds already complex issues.

Consider a social media app that tracks proximity to other users and makes that data available to governments without serious legal constraint. Is it a product of social forces, patterns at the macro level that shape the use, effectiveness, and reception of the technology, a top-down move? The answer is indubitably yes. Are such social media apps (never mind smartphones themselves) *constitutive* of society, critical nodes in the communications networks that make up society, in a sense the building blocks of the society that creates their context and framing for use? The answer is also yes. Disciplines tend to use the social to explain the technological, or the technological to explain the social, without taking time to consider that social technology is a loop, a chicken-and-egg cycle, in which two definable and usefully describable phenomena are recursively and causally related to one another.

On the international stage, it is not enough to say that cultural differences drive differences in the costs (authoritarianism and dehumanization) and benefits (contact tracing and more rapid science) observed between various instantiations of COVID surveillance technologies. Rather, we must say something roughly like: the experience of COVID in some countries drove the techno-social loops of COVID surveillance onto different paths than in others. Sweden served to inspire the doomed UK herd immunity model and as fodder for US negligence (Orlowski & Goldsmith, 2020), and the sky-rocketing deaths in the United States and Brazil drove other countries (New Zealand, for example) into some of the world's harshest lockdown controls (Visual and Data Journalism Team, 2021), while other countries (South Korea and Taiwan come to mind) managed through free testing and robust social norms (Manantan, 2020). These solutions did not evolve in a vacuum. Countries watched each other carefully, and their practices evolved again by chicken-and-egg recursive loops.

COVID TRACING APPLICATIONS AS TECHNO-SOCIAL INSTALLATIONS

Compare two experiences with COVID tracer apps, one in New Zealand and one in Virginia, where I live and the first US state to adopt the GAEN framework. New Zealand has a population of 4.9 million people. There are 2.9 million registrations of the app for a country that, as of August 2021, has had close to 2,900 cases of COVID-19 and 26 deaths (Ministry of Health, 2021a; Ministry of Health, 2021b). The app relies on heavy manual input, making it quite difficult to use (Cumming, 2021; Ministry of Health, 2020). People scan QR codes when they enter an area or location, creating a digital diary. Until New Zealand added the Google/Apple Bluetooth framework in December 2020, this was not done by automatic Bluetooth tokenized processes that we've seen with other tracers, so there was significant investment by users and businesses in using the QR codes (Barbaschow, 2020; Macfarlane, 2020). The app data is centralized, directly communicated to the government, and acted upon. Tracers from the Ministry of Health contact users directly, because they believe that effective quarantines decline significantly when people aren't directly contacted for follow-up (Ministry of Health, 2021c).

Virginia, meanwhile, has 8.5 million citizens to New Zealand's 4.9 million. Virginia developed its own COVID app early and aggressively and is one of the leading states in the United States in terms of the percentage of citizens who had downloaded a state's COVID tracing app (Griset, 2020). It was tech-nologically designed for privacy and was the first state app to deploy under the open-source GAEN framework, meaning it is a decentralized, low-power Bluetooth program that generates dynamic tokens that then are compared to other people's dynamic tokens (O'Brien & Rankin, 2020; Cyphers & Gebhart, 2020). The app does not generate static identifiers, nor is data stored in central-ized servers. Yet despite having many more potential users, as of June 2021, Virginia's app had only two-thirds of the downloads of the New Zealand app (Virginia Department of Health, 2021a), approximately 25% of the population and 30% of Virginia smartphone users. This despite the fact that COVID has ravaged Virginia, with over 700,000 cases and 11,581 deaths as of August 2021 (Virginia Department of Health, 2021b), and is virtually nonexistent in New Zealand (Ministry of Health, 2021a).

These two examples show that strong pro-privacy design decisions did not drive uptake or engagement. The key difference is not technological, but techno-social. What is the social context that causes these applications to gain more pickup in one setting versus the other? Rather than simply saying these are different cultures, we should examine narratives that draw from the vocabularies of emergency, authority, disease, and surveillance to change our expectations around the narratives that will continue to emerge around COVID and surveillance.

We must ask why it is that when the New Zealand Ministry of Health says, for example, that data will never be used for enforcement purposes, the population seems to actively believe that statement—and has reason to do so within that legal and social framework—even though the technological affordances of the app are not remotely privacy protecting (Wilson, 2021; Goldfinch et al., 2021). Conversely, we must ask why apps deployed within the United States suffer low adoption despite being built from the ground up to preserve privacy and verifiably distance the ability of government to misuse the data. As laid out below, the answer is primarily the social technology of the application.

The GAEN framework is an open-source software layer within the Android and iOS operating systems that can compare proximity data between users. Public health apps then notify users of potential exposure. Within that framework, OS and app developers claim that they protect and respect privacy. Indeed, although apps vary within the framework, Google and Apple appear to be keeping their promises for once. The server framework source code is open (Google, n.d.). GAEN deploys a range of privacy-protective design measures, including using Bluetooth instead of GPS, using key servers and tokens, and retaining the information on the device itself (Sakin, 2021). If these privacy protection measures had been incorporated into much of the basic design of Internet of Things devices (which would not have been hard to do), it would have produced radically better outcomes for personal privacy in the United States.

That is the core of the issue. A well-designed app within an otherwise privacy-compromised technological, political, and social framework is rightfully discarded by recipients. After all, users have been reassured before that companies "care about their privacy" (Warzel & Thompson, 2019). Users do not have the informational wherewithal to determine that this time it looks as if Google was serious about the promise. So many promises have been broken for so long that trust fails, and so does the technological solution.

TRUST AS A TECHNOLOGICAL AFFORDANCE

Humans upgrade their social technology via language. We advance our social technology not by logical progression from preestablished factual premises, but instead by creating coordinating metaphors and narrative symbols like time, money, national and state laws, or religion. These tools let us cooperate at a massive scale with the potential to generate new economic systems, new political systems, and new ways of talking about problems that help us address the difficulties of the future. Language is generated by communities, grounded in context, and defined in the performance of a task.

Under these circumstances, it is easy to see how conversations about emergency, disease, privacy, authoritarianism, risk, and so on become fraught. Even where the words are the same, the context in which those words have been invoked are so different that they lend the words different meanings. And this effect is particularly pronounced between communities of meaning: one group uses words in one context to convey one meaning, which, to another group, conveys a different meaning. Consider the multiple ways a person can hear the phrase "I'm from the government and I'm here to help" merely within the US context and we begin to reach the root of the problem.

Let me give a concrete example that bears on the current questions of government surveillance power and the need to leverage the social network to fight disease. Consider how we talk about privacy and security. If, for example, we position "privacy" and "security" as words that are in opposition to each other, then we continue to discuss trade-offs. This has been the United States' conversation since long before 9/11, although the drive to dismantle privacy—not just practically but also as a concept—got a shot in the arm in the aftermath of those terrorist attacks (Mendelson, 2021, pp. 39–43). Now it bears fruit. Talking about privacy and security as a zero-sum game has direct, observable consequences for the ability of a democracy to fight off disease.

If, however, we talk about privacy as a security function, we obtain a different result. The New Zealand government defines security as the ability of the population to go about its daily life and regular business without undue interference. And this is borne out in a range of government practices, from actual restrictions on the New Zealand intelligence apparatus, which is not permitted to conduct mass surveillance, to effective practical experiences from citizens: a New Zealander submitting an Official Information Act request receives information and a response (Cullen & Reddy, 2016, pp. 43–45, 76–79). A US FOIA request brings a byzantine brush-off at best (Wasike, 2016; Editorial Board, 2020). Privacy statements made within a legal culture that has a history of effective restraints on government power are far different from statements made by the Russian, Chinese, or US governments, which, despite their vast differences, share an utter lack of credibility on questions of power and surveillance. Trust is a technological resource, and the technological design of an app has very little to do with its effectiveness as a disease-combating tool.

CONTINGENCY AND INCOMMENSURABILITY OF EVOLVING PANDEMIC SURVEILLANCE NARRATIVES

Humans find new ways of talking about problems by creating linguistic communities that use words differently. Consider the shifting associations and expectations of the silent generation, baby boomers, Generation X, millennials, and Generation Z with respect to government-based problem-solving. Words gain meaning through experience, and meanings shift as the way we talk about our problems evolves. Stories about pandemic surveillance are already entering common parlance: stories of children and workers surveilled at home by teachers and bosses; knowledge about the richer metadata sets gathered by sensors in the home when all of life was lived there for over a year; the shared sense of claustrophobia and lack of privacy because of being crammed together in quarantine; the wild claims of conspiracists. The pandemic and its attendant narratives of abuse of power came at a moment of worldwide decline in democracy (Ginsburg et al., 2018, pp. 244–245). It accompanied other strong techno-totalitarian capitalist trends, such as the evolution of the Chinese Social Credit System from a digital payment and service pricing system to a means of political control (Givens & Lam, 2020, pp. 863–865; Rettinger, 2021, pp. 20–27). Images of drones policing citizens are too visceral not to inform our debate.

The narratives that spring from this potent brew associate surveillance power with the spread of the disease in part by association, in part by real consequences. Mission creep over pandemic data is a vibrant story only because governments have proven untrustworthy; the thought of that data not being repurposed is incomprehensible to a citizenry that has heard every reuse of data supported in the name of security.

Pandemic surveillance narratives have two primary characteristics—contingency and incommensurability. The hope is that by identifying what these new narrative worlds of meaning look like, policymakers might understand the full impact of different interventions.

Contingency

Pandemic surveillance narratives do not survive and thrive by virtue of truth or falsity. Take, for example, the elaborate system of meaning woven by conspiracists, involving right-wing websites, Falun Gong-owned media, social media posts and threads, and constant reinforcement through YouTube and Parler text threads. Those are merely the means of (mis)communication: the facts themselves exist in a kind of techno-social Möbius strip, each providing support to the next. But the dangerous falseness of narrative does not stop there. Consider the set of claims that could be true or could come to be true now that the pandemic surveillance data exists. US states may well use data for purposes other than those for which it was gathered. Such repurposing is the primary theme of surveillance capitalism and its government hangers-on (Zuboff, 2019). It is not irrational to distrust such an app, given all the broken promises that have come before, even if trust is not presently being breached.

How can these false pandemic surveillance narratives exist? The most extreme thrive within a mutually reinforcing framework, within which scientific consensus is a network value that does not translate (Cichocka et al., 2016, pp. 571–572). From an outside perspective, experts are cast as enemies and elitists; their consensus reality matters not at all.

The key point here is to understand that these narratives are non-teleological. Consider Darwinian evolution: species evolve to survive adverse selection; they do not evolve upward to some higher form of complexity or intelligence. Likewise, narrative social technology does not evolve toward a goal (of truth, for example) but instead to survive certain problems—adverse selectors—for narrative speakers. Conspiracy narratives do not even serve the goals of the conspiracists, either those who are sucked into the conspiracy narrative, who feel sick and sad, or the originators and propagators, who just as often find themselves riding the tiger they created merely to stay in power. The narratives are *contingent* on what has come before, and form building blocks for the narratives of identity that come after. They do not make logical sense, but they do make historical sense.

Of course some pandemic surveillance narratives do value truth or falsity as determined by scientific consensus. Take, for example, the underlying narrative of academics weighing pandemic surveillance technology. The consensus seems to be that the pandemic is bad enough to warrant innovative technological approaches, and the risk of government overreach is enough to validate thoughtful criticism. A reasoned story—so why does it have such short legs in the global conversation?

What we must look out for is that future narratives which marry the pandemic to surveillance may not follow such careful, step-by-step logic. For example, both conspiracist and academic consensus narratives contain indicators of identity. Both groups' members signal their membership by calling on group authorities and reinforce those authorities as helping mark the boundaries of the group. This is not a process of determining fact, although some groups do value fact. This is a process of resonating with visceral commitments.

Consider the likely outcome of the binding of the stories of the pandemic to those of abusive surveillance as a node within language and culture. Many people around the world have felt hopeless and powerless, jobless and alone, subject to nagging fears yet unable to take immediate action. The lexical, the linguistic meanings of terms like "pandemic surveillance" are likely to become building blocks in further narratives about alienation and power, associated with other seminal historical and linguistic events in which surveillance played a role: Think, for example, of the relationship between the 9/11 terrorist attacks and the shifts in both popular acceptance of mass dragnet surveillance and profound and rising distrust of public service entities.

We must focus on the specific meanings that pandemic surveillance will evolve and the contingency of those meanings. Negotiating what happened— conducting studies, collecting stories and statistics—is a critical part of creating that meaning. But the process is more forward-looking than one might think. As Barack Obama, quoting Faulkner, said during his first candidacy for president, "The past isn't dead and buried. It isn't even past." The stories will fit into a new narrative somewhere and may well be less of a progression from current stories than a response to a new social landscape and new social needs.

The meaning of the pandemic has not yet been written, but when it is, the questions of techno-social surveillance will incorporate the stories of battered spouses whose attempts to vaccinate their children in secret open them to risks of abuse; of LGBTQIA youth whose views on vaccination may greatly differ from their parents because of a tangled mix of religious and political commitments; of Black, Indigenous, and people of color (BIPOC) communities that have legitimate reason to be concerned both about the commitment of public health agencies to the health of communities of color and about the potential misuse of any and all data by police forces eager to employ algorithms trained on racist data to target neighborhoods and individuals for increased scrutiny; of public school students who are subject to school rules in their bedrooms, taking one of the spaces least protective of student privacy and rights and overwriting it onto the most; and of individuals deeply identified with communities that have adopted anti-vaccination narratives as a litmus test of identity, so they hide and literally disguise themselves in order to be vaccinated. For these people, the prevailing narrative of government surveillance pales in comparison with the in- and out-group play of narrative and identity. The social trust they need as a technological affordance—the social gas that will make the apps work—is not technological proof of the difficulty of government repurposing of COVID tracing data, it is the reassurance that their neighbors, parents, local officials, local racists, church leadership, and so on, will not eject them from their narrative groups for taking health-promoting action.

Incommensurability

The philosophers Thomas Kuhn and Richard Rorty discussed the development of linguistic vocabularies as a core means of human negotiation of meaning. Kuhn did so for science: he argued that science is not the slow accumulation of facts that are indisputably true, but rather the replacement of one way of speaking about the model and core problems of a field (its "paradigm") with another (Kuhn, 1962). Scientific progress is linguistic; new paradigms take hold as the old ways of talking die out, and science progresses "one funeral at a time."

Rorty argued the same thing for other sorts of socially constructed meaning. Thus, for example, he discusses the importance of Freud not as establishing scientific principles of psychoanalysis—Freud was mostly wrong—but as changing the paradigm of how we look at people (Rorty, 1979). Before Freud, Rorty argued, humans were understood and measured against traits shared by all humans. After Freud, humans were understood as the result of a historical series of events.

Important to both Kuhn and Rorty was the idea that new narrative structures—a new paradigmatic scientific model, or a new system of meaning—are at least a little bit incommensurable with one another. Thus, the framework for understanding humans before Freud did not evolve into the Freudian framework; rather, it gave way to it. Similarly, new scientific paradigms did not iterate or improve on old ones, but rather developed a new set of problems that a different model could solve.

The result is lack of commensurability between linguistic communities, between systems of meaning. Take, for example, the question "How many angels can dance on the head of a pin?" or the illustration from scholar Shoshana Zuboff: How many hours a week is optimal for a child to work in a factory? (Naughton, 2019). A new system of meaning does not answer such questions, it un-asks them and replaces them with new meanings, new weightings of words within the language structure that a group uses to solve problems.

Consider the current state of affairs. Who could have predicted that an outcome of the pandemic as regards government and private surveillance would be narratives connecting the context and fact of the pandemic to the social reality of surveillance? With hindsight, we can say that one of the most disturbing trends to emerge from the pandemic context is the association of a context of claustrophobia, paranoia, and citizen observation via technology—to which private surveillance technologies have certainly contributed—with the vaccines that will end the pandemic (Troiano & Nardi, 2021, pp. 249–250). For example, the conspiracist association of 5G networks with COVID vaccination is utterly incomprehensible without an understanding of how and why socio-technological narratives evolve. We would have been better armed if, a year ago, we had developed tools and studies to address vaccine hesitancy as fallout from the United States' sordid recent history of warrantless dragnet surveillance. What a strange connection!

We cannot predict the exact paths that pandemic surveillance narratives will take. The very disruption and chaos that a black swan event like a pandemic works on global social structures makes attempting to reason from preexisting narratives an exercise in futility. But we can expect them to develop within incommensurable linguistic communities rather than progress by logical extension from present narratives. And while we cannot combat false pandemic surveillance narratives by presenting true ones, we can develop the kinds of linguistic communities that can heal from and fend off misinformation and assist in the organization of democratic resistance to behind-the-scenes power grabs that harm citizen freedoms.

REESTABLISHING A LANGUAGE OF TRUST

Language is our collective human superpower, our way of upgrading our social software rather than waiting for our hardware to upgrade. Law is a particular type of language; it encodes rules about how we've decided to work together. Given our growing inability to work together and draw on common narratives, we must find ways to generate better language around privacy and security going forward.

First of all, we need effective social technology of commitment. Right now, the legal language of the United States does not permit private companies or public entities to make committed statements around privacy. We don't believe Google and Apple when they make privacy-protective statements, and we're right not to: The legal framework does not provide for verification or vindication of those rights. At most, they disappear down the arbitration oubliette, or the Federal Trade Commission writes a sternly worded letter and issues fines that amount to a few days' profits (Samel & Beane, 2012; Preston, 2015; Kemp, 2019). There are neither repercussions nor enforcement or verification; there is no experience within society that companies like Google do anything other than exploit data at every level and for every use (Patel, 2019; Rosenberg & Hart, 2019).

US and EU citizens also don't believe the US government's statements around purpose-based restrictions on data use, and again, they're right not to. From Total Information Awareness to the abuses of the Terrorist Surveillance Program, through each iteration of the Patriot Act, the US government has systematically lied about and misdirected what it does with data gathered by third parties through personal technology (Samel & Beane, 2012, pp. 15, 28–30; Preston, 2015, p. 535; Kemp, 2019; Patel, 2019; Rosenberg & Hart, 2019). Positing that the intelligence community's goals are noble and their concern with security correct merely renders their statements on privacy and mission creep the more risible. This is the era of parallel construction, geo-fenced warrants, and algorithm-driven suspicionless mass surveillance (Babazadeh, 2018, pp. 8–14; "Geofence warrants," 2021, pp. 2512–2520; "Data mining," 2014, pp. 691–696). The US legal system has reduced security by destroying privacy and lying about it. The result is that the US body politic cannot fight disease, either physical or informational.

To rebuild immunity, democracies must develop diverse, non-hierarchical, and noncoercive communities that share common values while benefiting from widely divergent perspectives (Fairfield, 2021, pp. 251–277). Such communities are the antithesis of Facebook pages or Parler threads. Such communities are bound together by multiple ties, rather than a single obsessive focus or common interest. For that reason they are often local or at least grounded in physical reality, where the range of potential connectors is greater. Geography is a common one: we sometimes share space with people who share little else with us, forcing cooperation and communication orthogonal to our communities of interest. Studies have shown that engagement and access within close-knit communities by trusted figures within those communities is the key to shifting how a community talks about a given phenomenon (Dotson & Wilcox, 2016, pp. 528–29; Dotson, 2015, pp. 33–39). To strain the medical metaphor, robust communities are like B cells. They produce narratives that are more robust in the face of disinformation, as well as vectors for trust that permit healthy narratives to move throughout the body politic.

Finally, we need to amplify emerging privacy narratives. Privacy is not a term with a narrow definition, it is an action, a demand. Diverse communities benefit from the range of tools that community members bring to the table. The academic and technology communities are more than occasionally guilty of tunnel vision. For example, the threat that we have all been paying attention to, myself most certainly included, is the threat of mission creep and government misuse of pandemic surveillance data. Some voices are missing from that conversation, and that causes the thrust of our concerns to go astray. For example, consider teens and young adults. Many fear that their vaccination status or attempts to become vaccinated might be reported to parents who bring social, financial, and physical measures to bear (Smith, 2021). To them, surveillance and authority are local and have an immediate impact on their life. Further, many of the privacy safeguards built into the various notification apps do not guard against that source of harm. Limiting vaccine or exposure notifications to a teenager's smartphone does little if a parent has physical or software access to that device.

Relatedly, we must reinvigorate the transatlantic and worldwide privacy conversations. In particular, the characterization of privacy as opposed to security disserves both. We cannot afford to double down on the United States' definitions of privacy and security, which are characterized as opposing one another. Furthermore, we need to talk about the democratic norms of privacy. It's clear that democratic norms are having a rough year, and discussion that has traditionally occurred within the United States is increasingly shifting to Europe. It needs to shift further to become a conversation among people who are actively seeking to develop democratic norms around privacy and security.

THE WAY FORWARD

We expect narratives around pandemic surveillance to progress from current contexts, but that expectation is likely to be disappointed. Narratives evolve as new language communities spring up. The meaning of a global event like the pandemic serves a range of purposes within those contexts, some authoritarian and identarian, some factual and scientific. The lack of fit between technology and linguistic community—indeed, the location that technology takes within a cultural constellation of meanings—is as much a technological affordance necessary for the success of a pandemic intervention as is Bluetooth or decentralized tokenization.

The way forward is to address the generation of toxic narratives by building more robust and diverse communities of meaning, ones that focus on common values, diverse perspectives, and the inclusion of historically suppressed voices. Communities with those characteristics build better, life-giving narratives. Such communities have affordances, experiences of cooperation, and government restraint that permit them to use technologies not only to fight a global pandemic, but to do so while reaffirming democratic norms. Healthy democracies that can do so will be at a marked advantage over flawed democracies that can't.

BIBLIOGRAPHY

Babazadeh, N. (2018). Concealing evidence: "Parallel construction, federal investigations, and the Constitution." *Virginia Journal of Law and Technology*, 22, 1–57.

Barbaschow, A. (2020, December 8). "NZ adopts Google/Apple COVID-19 exposure notification tech for contact tracing." ZDNet. www.rnz.co.nz/news/national/432524/covid-19-contact-tracing-app-gets-bluetooth-upgrade

Bimber, B. (1998). "The internet and political transformation: Populism, community, and accelerated pluralism." *Polity*, 31(1), 133–160. https://doi.org/10.2307/3235370

Chandran, R. (2021, February 2). "Singapore to limit police access to COVID-19 contact-tracing data." Reuters. www.reuters.com/article/us-singapore-tech-lawmaking/singapore-to-limit-police-access-to-covid-19-contact-tracing-data-idUSKBN2A20ZI

Cichocka, A., Marchlewska, M., Golec de Zavala, A., & Olechowski, M. (2016). "'They will not control us': Ingroup positivity and belief in intergroup conspiracies." *British Journal of Psychology*, 107(3), 556–576. https://doi.org/10.1111/bjop.12158

Cullen, M., & Reddy, P. (2016, February 29). "Intelligence and security in a free society." Department of the Prime Minister and Cabinet.

Cumming, J. (2021, April). "COVID-19 health system response monitor New Zealand." World Health Organization. https://apps.who.int/iris/rest/bitstreams/1344244/retrieve

Cyphers, B., & Gebhart, G. (2020, April 28). "Apple and Google's COVID-19 exposure notification API: Questions and answers." EFF. www.eff.org/deeplinks/2020/04/apple-and-googles-covid-19-exposure-notification-api-questions-and-answers

"Data mining." (2014). "Data mining, dog sniffs, and the Fourth Amendment: A framework for evaluating suspicionless mass surveillance programs." *Harvard Law Review*, 128(2), 691–712.

deLisle, J., & Kui, S. (2021). "China's Response to COVID-19." *Administrative Law Review*, 73(1), 19–51.

Donohue, L. K. (2015). "Section 702 and the collection of international telephone and internet content." *Harvard Journal of Law and Public Policy*, 38, 117–265. https://doi.org/10.2139/SSRN.2436418

dos Reis Peron, A. E., Duarte, D. E., Simões-Gomes, L., & Nery, M. B. (2021). "Viral surveillance: Governing social isolation in Sao Paulo, Brazil, during the COVID-19 pandemic." *Social Sciences & Humanities Open*, 3(1), 1–10. https://doi.org/10.1016/j.ssaho.2021.100128

Dotson, T. C. (2015). "Communitarian technology: Realizing thicker communities within societies built for networked individualism" (Publication No. 10186405) [Doctoral dissertation, Rensselaer Polytechnic Institute]. ProQuest Dissertations Publishing.

Dotson, T. C., & Wilcox, J. E. (2016). "Generating community, generating justice? The production and circulation of value in community energy initiatives." *Revista Teknokultura*, 13(2), 511–540. https://doi.org/10.5209/rev_TEKN.2016.v13.n2.52840

Eck, K., & Hatz, S. (2020). "State surveillance and the COVID-19 crisis." *Journal of Human Rights*, 19(5), 603–612. https://doi.org/10.1080/14754835.2020.1816163

Editorial Board. (2020, May 12). "No, your FOIA request cannot wait 'until this emergency is over.'" *New York Times*. www.nytimes.com/2020/05/12/opinion/coronavirus-freedom-of-information.html

Fairfield, J. A. T. (2021). *Runaway Technology: Can Law Keep Up?* Cambridge University Press.

"Geofence warrants and the Fourth Amendment." (2021). *Harvard Law Review*, 134, 2508–2529.

Ginsburg, T., Huq, A. Z., & Versteeg, M. (2018). "The coming demise of liberal constitutionalism?" *University of Chicago Law Review*, 85(2), 239–255. www.jstor.org/stable/26455907

Givens, J. W., & Lam, D. (2020, June). "Smarter cities or bigger brother? How the race for smart cities could determine the future of China, democracy, and privacy." *Fordham Urban Law Journal*, 47, 829–881.

Goldfinch, S., Taplin, R., & Gauld, R. (2021). "Trust in government increased during the Covid-19 pandemic in Australia and New Zealand." *Australian Journal of Public Administration*, 80(1), 3–11. https://onlinelibrary.wiley.com/doi/10.1111/1467-8500.12459

Griset, R. (2020, December 11). "Virginia leads nation in COVID-19 app use." *Virginia Business.* www.virginiabusiness.com/article/virginia-leads-nation-in-covid-19-app-use/

Haggerty, K. D., & Gazso, A. (2005). "Seeing beyond the ruins: Surveillance as a response to terrorist threats." *Canadian Journal of Sociology*, 30(2), 169–187. https://doi.org/10.2307/4146129

Hyatt, J. M., Baćak, V., & Kerrison, E. M. (2021). "COVID-19 vaccine refusal and related factors: Preliminary findings from a system-wide survey of correctional staff." *Federal Sentencing Reporter*, 33(4), 272–277. https://doi.org/10.1525/fsr .2021.33.4.272

Kemp, K. (2019, August 11). "Here's how tech giants profit from invading our privacy, and how we can start taking it back." The Conversation. https://theconversation .com/heres-how-tech-giants-profit-from-invading-our-privacy-and-how-we-can -start-taking-it-back-120078

Kern, R. (2021, March 10). "Democrat renews data privacy effort with first bill of 2021." Bloomberg Law. https://news.bloomberglaw.com/tech-and-telecom-law/ democrat-renews-consumer-privacy-effort-with-first-bill-of-2021

Kuhn, T. S. (1962). *The Structure of Scientific Revolutions*. University of Chicago Press.

Latour, B. (1993). *We Have Never Been Modern*, trans. Catherine Porter. Harvard University Press.

Latour, B. (2001). *Down to Earth: Politics in the New Climactic Regime*. Polity.

Latour, B. (2005). *Reassembling the Social: An Introduction to Actor-Network Theory*. Oxford University Press.

Lee, H. (2020, July 25). "These elite contact tracers show the world how to beat Covid-19." Bloomberg. www.bloomberg.com/news/articles/20207–25/these-elite -contact-tracers-show-the-world-how-to-beat-covid-19

Macfarlane, A. (2020, December 8). "NZ Covid Tracer app gets major Bluetooth upgrade, to allow auto contact tracing." 1 News. https://web.archive.org/web/ 20201208210958/https://www.tvnz.co.nz/one-news/new-zealand/nz-covid-tracer -app-gets-major-bluetooth-upgrade-allow-auto-contact-tracing

Manantan, M. (2020, May 22). "Agile governance crushing COVID-19: Taiwan and South Korea." The Diplomat. https://thediplomat.com/2020/05/agile-governance -crushing-covid-19-taiwan-and-south-korea/

Mendelson, E. (2021). "How the fallout from post-9/11 surveillance programs can inform privacy protections for COVID-19 contact tracing programs." *City University of New York Law Review*, 24(1), 35–61.

Ministry of Health. (2020, May 20). "NZ COVID Tracer app released to support contact tracing." www.health.govt.nz/news-media/media-releases/nz-covid-tracer -app-released-support-contact-tracing

Ministry of Health. (2021a, June 16). "COVID-19: Current cases." www.health.govt .nz/our-work/diseases-and-conditions/covid-19-novel-coronavirus/covid-19-data -and-statistics/covid-19-current-cases

Ministry of Health. (2021b, June 16). "COVID-19: NZ COVID Tracer app data." www .health.govt.nz/our-work/diseases-and-conditions/covid-19-novel-coronavirus/ covid-19-data-and-statistics/covid-19-nz-covid-tracer-app-data

Ministry of Health. (2021c, June 24). "Contact tracing for COVID-19." www.health .govt.nz/our-work/diseases-and-conditions/covid-19-novel-coronavirus/covid-19 -health-advice-public/contact-tracing-covid-19

Naughton, J. (2019, January 20). "'The goal is to automate us': Welcome to the age of surveillance capitalism." *The Guardian*. www.theguardian.com/technology/2019/ jan/20/shoshana-zuboff-age-of-surveillance-capitalism-google-facebook

O'Brien, M., & Rankin, S. (2020, August 5). "Virginia first to roll out pandemic app from Apple, Google." AP News. https://apnews.com/article/virus-outbreak-ri-state-wire -smartphones-ca-state-wire-technology-46b54442d8faf71dab0a5c97b87374d7.

Orlowski, E. J., & Goldsmith, D. J. (2020). "Four months into the COVID-19 pandemic, Sweden's prized herd immunity is nowhere in sight." *Journal of the Royal Society of Medicine*, 113(8), 292–298. https://doi.org/10.1177/0141076820945282

Parker, R. W. (2021). "Why America's response to the COVID-19 pandemic failed: Lessons from New Zealand's success." *Administrative Law Review*, 73(1), 77–103. www.administrativelawreview.org/wp-content/uploads/2021/03/10.-ALR-73 .1_Parker-NZ_US_FINAL.pdf

Patel, N. (2019, July 12). "Facebook's $5 billion FTC fine is an embarrassing joke." The Verge. www.theverge.com/2019/7/12/20692524/facebook-five-billion-ftc-fine -embarrassing-joke

Preston, C. B. (2015). "'Please note: You have waived everything': Can notice redeem online contracts?" *American University Law Review*, 64(3), 535–590. https:// heinonline.org/HOL/P?h=hein.journals/aulr64&i=570

Rettinger, L. (2021). "The human rights implications of China's social credit system." *Journal of High Technology Law*, 21, 1–33.

Reuters Staff. (2020a, August 20). "Fact check: The coronavirus pandemic is not a hoax or a conspiracy to control the general public." www.reuters.com/article/uk-factcheck -hoax/fact-check-the-coronavirus-pandemic-is-not-a-hoax-or-a-conspiracy-to -control-the-general-public-idUSKBN25G2KM

Reuters Staff. (2020b, December 4). "Fact check: RFID microchips will not be injected with the COVID-19 vaccine, altered video features Bill and Melinda Gates and Jack Ma." www.reuters.com/article/uk-factcheck-vaccine-microchip-gates-ma/ fact-check-rfid-microchips-will-not-be-injected-with-the-covid-19-vaccine-altered -video-features-bill-and-melinda-gates-and-jack-ma-idUSKBN28E286

Rorty, R. (1979). *Philosophy and the Mirror of Nature*. Princeton University Press.

Rosenberg, S., & Hart, K. (2019, March 29). "For tech giants, profits far outweigh fines." Axios. www.axios.com/google-facebook-fines-profits--134d3567-1052-4d9d-aa70 -dc7c25ed4ebf.html

Sakin, N. (2021, February 1). "Google and Apple's joint COVID-19 exposure notifications system shows privacy is important to consumers and marketers." IAPP. https:// iapp.org/news/a/google-and-apples-joint-covid-19-exposure-notification-system -shows-privacy-continues-to-be-important-to-consumers-and-marketers/

Samel, C. H., & Beane, A. J. (2012). "Closing the courthouse doors to consumer class actions? What recent case law reveals about successful enforcement of arbitration agreements and class action waivers." *Competition Journal of the Antitrust and Unfair Competition Law Section of the State Bar of California*, 21(1), 15–30.

Sherwin, B. (2021). "Anatomy of a conspiracy theory: Law, politics, and science denialism in the era of COVID-19." *Texas A&M Law Review*, 8(3), 537–581. https://doi .org/10.37419/LR.V8.I3.3

Shindelman, E. R. (2011). "Time for the court to become 'intimate' with surveillance technology." *Boston College Law Review*, 52(5), 1909–1943. https:// lawdigitalcommons.bc.edu/bclr/vol52/iss5/8

Smith, H. (2021, May 17). 2For teenagers, vaccinations are a ticket to freedom. Some parents still not sure." *Los Angeles Times*. www.latimes.com/california/story/ 20215-17/as-california-expands-vaccine-eligibility-to-adolescents-parents-weigh -the-risks

Troiano, G., & Nardi, A. (2021). "Vaccine hesitancy in the era of COVID-19." *Public Health*, 194, 245–251.

Vinuesa, R., Theodorou, A., Battaglini, M., & Dignum, V. (2020). "A socio-technical framework for digital contact tracing." *Results in Engineering*, 8, 100163. https://doi.org/10.1016/j.rineng.2020.100163

Virginia Department of Health (2021a, June 8). "Virginia's Covidwise Exposure Notification app campaign is honored with a Telly Award and two Emmy nominations." www.vdh.virginia.gov/news/6860-2/

Virginia Department of Health (2021b, August 11). "COVID-19 in Virginia." www.vdh.virginia.gov/coronavirus/covid-19-in-virginia/

Visual and Data Journalism Team. (2021, June 14). "Covid map: Coronavirus cases, deaths, vaccinations by country." BBC. www.bbc.com/news/world-51235105

Warzel, C., & Thompson, S. A. (2019, August 10). "Tech companies say they care." *New York Times*. www.nytimes.com/interactive/2019/04/10/opinion/tech-companies-privacy.html

Wasike, B. (2016, July). "FoIA in the age of 'Open. Gov': An analysis of the performance of the Freedom of Information Act under the Obama and Bush administrations." *Government Information Quarterly*, 33(3), 417–426.https://doi.org/10.1016/j.giq.2016.05.001

Wilson, E. (2021, May 31). "Trust in government and Covid-19." Office of the Privacy Commissioner. www.privacy.org.nz/blog/trust-in-government-and-covid-19/

Winkler, R. (2020, November 21). "More states offer Covid-19 contact-tracing apps, but adoption is uneven." *Wall Street Journal*. www.wsj.com/articles/more-states-offer-covid-1-contact-tracing-apps-but-adoption-is-uneven-1160597440

Yang, F., Heemsbergen, L., & Fordyce, R. (2021). "Comparative analysis of China's Health Code, Australia's COVIDSafe and New Zealand's COVID Tracer surveillance apps: A new corona of public health governmentality?" *Media International Australia*, 178(1), 182–197. https://doi.org/10.1177/1329878X20968277

Zuboff, S. (2019). *The Age of Surveillance Capitalism: The Fight for a Human Future at the New Frontier of Power*. PublicAffairs.

PART II

Contextualizing challenges in regulating
pandemic surveillance

6. Pandemic surveillance and US foreign surveillance

Peter Margulies

The severity of the COVID-19 pandemic has led experts to characterize it as a national security threat that justifies greater state control and expanded surveillance (see, e.g., Wright, 2020; R. E. Hamilton, 2020). The United States and other countries have deployed sophisticated pandemic surveillance methods, including smartphone and geolocational tracking that are more often associated with foreign intelligence. The compulsory nature of some surveillance policies deployed during the pandemic increased fear about lasting data privacy harms (see I. A. Hamilton, 2020). While countries may implement these emergency surveillance measures solely for use during the pandemic, there is a risk that some countries will continue to use them after the pandemic ends (see I. A. Hamilton, 2020). The blurring between data collection for epidemiological purposes and national security purposes poses unique challenges in US law, especially in the context of foreign intelligence.

US federal law provides legal oversight for foreign intelligence gathering. However, in the context of pandemic surveillance where the surveillance falls outside the justification of foreign intelligence, the surveillance boundaries may be less clear. The Snowden disclosures revealed deep cooperation between some technology companies and the intelligence community, causing concern that COVID-19 tracking technologies, driven by Big Tech innovation, may also feed information to the intelligence community (Romm et al., 2020). The Snowden revelations led to a concern that mass surveillance and corporate spying could be justified under a pretext of national security (Glanz & Lehren, 2013, reported that the NSA performed economic spying in the interest of national security in addition to other espionage activities). For example, the accusations include that of the National Security Agency (NSA) spying on Petrobras, the largest Brazilian oil company at the time, through network exploitation (Watts, 2013). Additionally, reports from the NSA and the UK's Government Communications Headquarters (GCHQ) revealed that the United States had conducted surveillance on Total, a French oil and gas company (Glanz & Lehren, 2013). Framing COVID-19 as a national security threat, therefore, according to some critics, will facilitate the threat of mass surveillance expansion by the intelligence community.

Although surveillance powers granted to US intelligence agencies had been set to lapse during the pandemic, Congress pushed to reinstate tools under the Foreign Intelligence Surveillance Act (FISA) as a temporary measure, citing a lack of time to revise the foreign surveillance power during the chaos of the pandemic crisis (Fandos & Savage, 2020; Ewing, 2020). FISA is a federal statute enacted in 1978 in the wake of widespread revelations of the US government spying on its citizens. In the 1960s, for example, the discovery that the FBI conducted surveillance of Dr. Martin Luther King Jr., approved by the then Attorney General Robert Kennedy, sparked national outrage (Boykoff, 2007; Giorgis, 2021). FISA was passed in reaction to that and other concerns of surveillance abuses domestically in the United States, allowing for surveillance upon a court order granted if an individual was an agent of a foreign power or if the court was shown probable cause establishing someone as an agent of a foreign power (Foreign Surveillance Intelligence Act, 2006). These court orders are issued by the Foreign Intelligence Surveillance Court, or FISC. The FISC comprises life-tenured, lifetime appointee federal judges who have the requisite independence to adequately assess government requests for surveillance.

After 9/11, the United States broadened the scope of surveillance beyond FISA. The first expansion was through the Terrorist Surveillance Program, run solely by the George W. Bush administration (see Yoo, 2007, pp. 566–568). After the public became aware of that program, there was outrage over its lack of legal authority under FISA. As a result, Congress enacted Section 702 of FISA, part of the FISA Amendments Act of 2008. That Act grants the government the ability to target both individuals and data abroad, which could include email addresses, websites, and other forms of digital information to gather foreign intelligence. Foreign intelligence often includes information about espionage, sabotage, or territorial attacks on the United States with respect to a foreign power or foreign territory. Critics have expressed concern that the authorization to conduct surveillance with respect to a foreign power is a category that is unduly broad under Section 702 of the Act (see Margulies, 2015, pp. 1294–1295). Warrants are not required under Section 702 (see Clarke et al., 2013, p. 135; as cited in Margulies, 2015, p. 1288, fn. 17).[1]

---

[1]   As I wrote previously in Margulies (2015, p. 1288, fn. 17), the report of the President's Review Group on Intelligence and Communications Technologies explains when the government need not obtain an individual warrant from the FISC. The lack of a requirement for FISC approval of individual targeting choices under Section 702 stems from the constitutional status of foreign surveillance and the path to enactment of Section 702. The Supreme Court held in *United States v. Verdugo-Urquidez*

Instead, the FISC only approves an annual certification of targeting procedures to ensure that the US agencies are not targeting US persons who are citizens, lawful residents, or people located in the United States (see Margulies, 2015, pp. 1287–1288; *United States v. Hasbajrami*, 2019, pp. 649–658). Although the digital surveillance targets people abroad, the US intelligence community can incidentally sweep in communications with people residing within the United States. This situation occurs when a recipient is located abroad but another party is in the United States. This issue involving the legality of incidental collection of data of US persons formed the basis of a recent decision by the Second Circuit US Court of Appeals. In *United States v. Hasbajrami* (2019), the court held that queries on US persons in the 702 database—that is, searching the database for information about US persons in these one-end foreign communications—constituted a search under the Fourth Amendment, which bars unreasonable searches and seizures.

The *Hasbajrami* case illustrates that federal courts in the United States have appeared to be more responsive to the surveillance concerns of US citizens in the wake of the Snowden disclosures. After the Snowden revelations of 2013, the US intelligence community posted opinions of the Foreign Intelligence Surveillance Court online, pivoting from a prior neglect of transparency. At earlier points in time, the NSA was humorously referred to as "Never Say Anything" or "No Such Agency" (Gearan, 2013; "Who's reading your emails?" 2013). In the wake of Snowden, the NSA has become better known. US intelligence agencies now provide a great deal of very useful information about US intelligence practices and surveillance through agency websites and other attempts to demonstrate fuller transparency.

At the same time, there is concern that pandemic surveillance technologies, primarily developed through the innovation of US tech companies, also pose unprecedented threats to data privacy on the global stage. The initial talks between tech giants and the US government to build coronavirus information databases, as well as location tracking systems for contact tracing, have created international fears of surveillance mission creep, despite assurances that any such collaboration would only use anonymized data (Romm et al., 2020). Suspicion of US companies working hand in hand with US government spying agencies, for instance, appears to have motivated the Court of Justice of the European Union (CJEU) decision in *Schrems II* to rule that data protection in the United States was inadequate for data transfers between the United States

---

(1990) that non-US persons (defined as those not citizens, lawful permanent residents, or located in the territorial United States) do not enjoy the protections of the Fourth Amendment (265; cf. Kerr, 2015, pp. 291–294, discussing reasons for not extending Fourth Amendment protections to communications between non-US persons abroad).

and the European Union, heightening the difficulty of international collaboration during the pandemic as it related to data flows (see, e.g., Rubinstein &
Margulies, 2022).

In *Data Protection Commissioner v. Facebook Ireland, Ltd. and Maximilian
Schrems* (2020; hereafter *Schrems II*), the CJEU held that the EU–US Privacy
Shield Framework was inadequate in protecting EU persons' data. The
July 2020 decision immediately posed significant obstacles to international
trade. This sweeping nature of US foreign intelligence was cited as a concern
by the *Schrems II* court. There is now ongoing dialogue between the European
Union and the United States on how best to protect data privacy and data
transfers. The European Commission—the EU's executive arm—and the
United States have expressed a commitment to a resolution after the finding
that the Privacy Shield agreement on transatlantic data transfers violated the
European Union's privacy law, the General Data Protection Regulation, or
GDPR (Regulation [EU] 2016/679, 2016).

In *Schrems II* (2020), the CJEU followed in broad terms the outline that it
had first used in *Schrems I*, suggesting that a company doing business in the
European Union had to ascertain that protections for the data were "adequate"
under EU law in the country that would ultimately receive the data (para. 186).
Under *Schrems II*, transfer of data to a third country is always appropriate
so long as the third country "ensures an adequate level of protection" for
the privacy of the data (see Regulation [EU] 2016/679, 2016, Art. 45[1]).[2]
However, as the following paragraphs explore, transfers in the absence of
an adequacy finding or appropriate safeguards under GDPR Article 46 may
be unlawful, unless they meet the conditions for derogation under GDPR
Article 49.

According to the *Schrems II* (2020) court, an adequacy finding hinges on
two conditions. First, the protections in the third country must be "essentially
equivalent" to EU law (para. 105).[3] EU law is highly protective of individual
data, although those protections do not always extend to the national security
surveillance conducted by EU member states (see Regulation [EU] 2016/679,
2016, Art. 2[2]). In addition, the legal system of the third country must fit
the factors laid out in Article 45(2), including the rule of law, independent
review of government decisions affecting privacy, and "effective" recourse
for persons or entities ("data subjects") who assert that the third country has
wrongly obtained or used their personal data. This provision of the GDPR also
considers whether the third country has entered into international agreements

---

[2]   A third country refers to any country outside the European Union or that does not
enjoy the EU right to free movement.
[3]   For a valuable analysis, see Kuner (2020).

that further bolster privacy (*Schrems II*, 2020, paras. 104–105). In the absence of an adequacy decision, the company seeking to transfer data must show that appropriate safeguards ensure the data's protection after it enters the third country.

In addressing who makes that decision about "essential equivalence" and adequacy of protection, the *Schrems II* court emphasized that ultimate authority resided with the court itself. The court is at the apex of a pyramid that includes other EU bodies and member states. The European Commission has an initial, provisional role. The Commission determines whether a particular third country—such as the United States—has ensured an adequate level of protection of personal data (*Schrems II*, 2020, paras. 117–118). If nationals of EU member states are dissatisfied with the Commission's stance, those individuals can file complaints with their own national data protection authority (*Schrems II*, 2020, para. 120). Those authorities have a mechanism for seeking CJEU review. The national authorities can bring a lawsuit in a national court, arguing that protections are not adequate in a third state. The national court may then refer the matter to the CJEU, which makes the ultimate determination (*Schrems II*, 2020, para. 120). The European Commission's initial decision, under both *Schrems I* and *Schrems II*, received little if any deference from the court.

The *Schrems II* court also raised questions about the use of so-called standard contractual clauses (SCCs)—private agreements to supply additional safeguards for data transfer against government surveillance—as a workaround for failures in adequacy. The court did not opine definitively on such clauses (*Schrems II*, 2020, paras. 143–146). In theory, parties to data transfer may be able to craft SCCs that largely obviate the risk of surveillance from the United States or other third states. To give a stylized example, parties may agree to share data through shipment of a portable hard drive.[4] The hard drive containing this data is an inanimate object without an internet link or other communications capability. Upon receipt, the contents of the hard drive could then be downloaded onto a computer that was also "air gapped" to disable all internet connectivity.

This cumbersome process would not, at least in theory, be subject to US surveillance. However, for any less elaborately contrived transfer, some risk of internet connectivity remains. In those situations, the court said that the most important provision of an SCC would be a provision that requires suspension of the data transfer if compliance with protections is impossible (*Schrems II*, 2020, para. 137).

---

[4]   Ira Rubinstein and I are indebted to privacy lawyer David Kessler of Norton Rose Fulbright for this example.

In terms of US law, the court stressed the importance of independent review and suggested that US law was lacking both in this respect and in the proportionality of surveillance under Section 702 and Exec. Order No. 12333 (*Schrems II*, 2020, paras. 177–178). In addition, painting with too broad a brush, the court stated that the FISC never addressed whether individual selectors under Section 702 are "'properly targeted to acquire foreign intelligence information'" (*Schrems II*, 2020, para. 179). This description is unduly stark. Both the European Commission and the *Schrems II* court conflated the nature of the procedures that the FISC follows in its Section 702 review and the substantive standard that the FISC employs.

The *Schrems II* (2020) court conceded that FISC review was "designed to verify whether … surveillance programmes relate to the objective of acquiring foreign intelligence information" (para. 179). Moreover, the court was correct in its analysis of procedure, since the FISC does not review each possible selector to determine its fit with Section 702's substantive criteria, such as detection of threats against the United States.

That said, the FISC has the ability to consider selectors and determine whether the criteria that US intelligence agencies apply in choosing selectors are consistent with statutory purposes. FISC review is not limited to the written submissions of the US Department of Justice in its certification. Indeed, as recent FISC decisions have shown, the FISC regularly reviews the querying practices of the FBI and other agencies (see *In re Section 702 2018 Certification*, 2018, pp. 68–75). It does so because if implementation of the statute fails to fit the guidance that US officials supply in their certification, that failure undermines the statutory scheme. Some FISC review of individual selectors is necessary to find that US officials have implemented the statute correctly.

The perception of the *Schrems II* (2020) court that FISA "does not indicate any limitations on the power it confers to implement government surveillance" (para. 180) is thus a needlessly sweeping generality. The court's failure to acknowledge the actual scope of the FISC's review is problematic (see "Comment, recent case," 2021; Rubinstein & Margulies, 2022, fn. 66). However, the *Schrems II* court was correct in two important respects.

First, the court's sound descriptions outweighed its passing exaggerations. The CJEU accurately observed that the FISC does not review each and every selector that US surveillance officials target. That lack of comprehensive individualized review poses a problem under EU law, although post-*Schrems II* decisions such as *Quadrature du Net* and *Privacy International* suggest that states may have a measure of flexibility in determining the targets of national security surveillance and the means of collecting data on those targets (Rubinstein & Margulies, 2022, fn. 67). Second, the *Schrems II* (2020) court was correct in stating that neither Section 702 nor Exec. Order No. 12333 gives individual data subjects an avenue for seeking recourse against US officials for surveillance abuses (paras. 181–182). Moreover, the court found that US bulk collection was not necessary or proportionate (*Schrems II*, 2020, paras. 183–184).

In addition, the *Schrems II* court found that the US mode of review of EU persons' complaints under Privacy Shield lacked independence from executive branch influence. Under Privacy Shield, the United States had tasked an ombudsperson at the State Department with fielding EU persons' privacy complaints. In assessing whether the State Department ombudsperson post was a sufficient privacy fix, the court found that the ombudsperson could not be sufficiently independent, since that official reported to the US Secretary of State and lacked any protection against dismissal (*Schrems II*, 2020, paras. 195–196). Moreover, the ombudsperson lacked binding power over US intelligence agencies conducting surveillance. Fortified by this conclusion, the court found that Privacy Shield was "incompatible" with Article 45 of the GDPR (*Schrems II*, 2020, para. 199).

This conclusion put the onus on standard contractual clauses to protect data. However, as the CJEU noted, SCCs may not be a sufficient safeguard against the broad surveillance efforts of a country like the United States (*Schrems II*, 2020, paras. 141–142). When a party recognizes the failure of SCCs to protect data, the most drastic option under SCCs kicks in: suspension of data transfers (*Schrems II*, 2020, para. 142). That harsh alternative would undermine the functioning of US companies with EU offices, holdings, or interests.

The United States has a lot of work to do if it wants to meet the requirements of the GDPR and the CJEU's expectations of privacy. If the United States attempts to renegotiate another transatlantic data-sharing agreement with the European Union, it must adopt a more formal and independent procedure for accountability. These considerations must be front and center when weighing the objectives and consequences of US foreign surveillance and the possible ramifications of pandemic surveillance. Data flows between the United States and the European Union can serve important public health goals during the pandemic. However, concern about the overreach of US surveillance after the Snowden disclosures may make data sharing between the United States and the European Union more difficult. In that fashion, fear occasioned by the broad scope of US foreign surveillance may impair legitimate and necessary data-sharing in global public health crises.

NOTE

Portions of this chapter are excerpted and adapted, with permission, from Ira Rubinstein and Peter Margulies (2022). "Risk and rights in transatlantic data transfers: EU privacy law, U.S. surveillance, and the search for common ground." *Connecticut Law Review*, 54(2), 391–456. http://dx.doi.org/10.2139/ssrn.3786415

REFERENCES

Boykoff, J. (2007). "Surveillance, spatial compression, and scale: The FBI and Martin Luther King Jr." *Antipode*, 39(4), 729–756.

Clarke, R., Morell, M., Stone, G., Sunstein, C., & Swire, P. (2013, December 12). "Liberty and security in a changing world: Report and recommendations of the President's Review Group on Intelligence and Communications Technologies. President's Review Group on Intelligence and Communications Technologies." https://obamawhitehouse.archives.gov/sites/default/files/docs/2013-12-12_rg_final_report.pdf

"Comment, recent case: National Security Law—surveillance—Court of Justice of the European Union invalidates EU–U.S. Privacy Shield." (2021). *Harvard Law Review*, 134(1567), 1571–1573.

Data Protection Commissioner v. Facebook Ireland, Ltd. and Maximilian Schrems, C-311/18 (2020).

Ewing, P. (2020, May 14). "Senate passes surveillance bill with new protections, but political fate uncertain." NPR. www.npr.org/2020/05/14/856362998/senate-passes-surveillance-bill-with-new-protections-but-political-fate-uncertai

Fandos, N., & Savage, C. (2020, March 16). "Senate, bidding for time, tries to temporarily revive spy tools." *New York Times*. www.nytimes.com/2020/03/16/us/politics/surveillance-laws-fisa-senate.html

Foreign Surveillance Intelligence Act of 1978, 50 U.S.C. § 1804(a)(3) (2006).

Gearan, A. (2013, November 9). "'No Such Agency' spies on the communications of the world." *Washington Post*. www.washingtonpost.com/world/national-security/no-such-agency-spies-on-the-communications-of-the-world/2013/06/06/5bcd46a6-ceb9-11e2-8845-d970ccb04497_story.html

Giorgis, H. (2021, January 18). "When the FBI spied on MLK." *The Atlantic*. www.theatlantic.com/culture/archive/2021/01/mlk-fbi-surveillance/617719/

Glanz, J., & Lehren, A. W. (2013, December 20). "N.S.A. spied on allies, aid groups and businesses." *New York Times*. www.nytimes.com/2013/12/21/world/nsa-dragnet-included-allies-aid-groups-and-business-elite.html

Hamilton, I. A. (2020, April 14). "Compulsory selfies and contact-tracing: Authorities everywhere are using smartphones to track the coronavirus, and it's part of a massive increase in global surveillance." Business Insider. www.businessinsider.com/countries-tracking-citizens-phones-coronavirus-2020-3

Hamilton, R. E. (2020, July 9). "COVID-19 and pandemics: The greatest national security threat of 2020 and beyond." Foreign Policy Research Institute. www.fpri.org/article/2020/07/covid-19-and-pandemics-the-greatest-national-security-threat-of-2020-and-beyond/

In re Section 702 2018 Certification, Foreign Intelligence Surveillance Court. (2018, October 18). www.intelligence.gov/assets/documents/702%20Documents/declassified/2018_Cert_FISC_Opin_18Oct18.pdf

Kerr, O. S. (2015). "The Fourth Amendment and the global internet." *Stanford Law Review*, 67(2), 285–329.

Kuner, C. (2020, August 25). "Schrems II re-examined." Verfassungsblog. https://verfassungsblog.de/schrems-ii-re-examined

Margulies, P. (2015). "Defining 'foreign affairs' in Section 702 of the FISA Amendments Act: The virtues and deficits of post-Snowden dialogue on U.S. surveillance policy." *Washington and Lee Law Review*, 72, 1283–1306.

Regulation (EU) 2016/679 of the European Parliament and of the Council of 27 April 2016 on the protection of natural persons with regard to the processing of personal data and on the free movement of such data and repealing Directive 95/36/EC (General Data Protection Regulation). 2016 O.J. (L 119). https://gdpr-info.eu/

Romm, T., Dwoskin, E., & Timberg, C. (2020, May 17). "US government, tech industry discussing ways to use smartphone location data to combat coronavirus." *Washington Post*. www.washingtonpost.com/technology/2020/03/17/white-house -location-data-coronavirus/

Rubinstein, I., & Margulies, P. (2022). "Risk and rights in transatlantic data transfers: EU privacy law, U.S. surveillance, and the search for common ground." *Connecticut Law Review*, 54(2), 391–456. http://dx.doi.org/10.2139/ssrn.3786415

United States v. Hasbajrami, 945 F.3d 641 (2019).

United States v. Verdugo-Urquidez, 494 U.S. 259 (1990).Watts, J. (2013, September 9). "NSA accused of spying on Brazilian oil company Petrobras." *The Guardian*. www.theguardian.com/world/2013/sep/09/nsa-spying-brazil-oil-petrobras

"Who's reading your emails?" (2013, June 9). *Sunday Times*. www.thetimes.co.uk/ article/whos-reading-your-emails-g0dsqlfxsds

Wright, R. (2020, October 7). "The coronavirus pandemic is now a threat to national security." *The New Yorker*. www.newyorker.com/news/our-columnists/america-the -infected-and-vulnerable

Yoo, J. (2007). "The terrorist surveillance program and the constitution." *George Mason Law Review*, 14, 565–604.

7. Regulating privacy and data ethics in the context of the UK's contact tracing apps

Ian Brown

As a highly connected global travel hub, the United Kingdom saw COVID-19 cases arriving from China and then neighboring European countries from mid January 2020, with over 1,000 separate arrivals, later identified by genomic analysis, before the national lockdown (du Plessis et al., 2021). As the number of cases started to soar in March 2020, the UK government downplayed the effects of the virus, with an initial response based on plans for an influenza pandemic (Helm et al., 2020). Prime Minister Boris Johnson engaged with the public, visiting hospital patients and shaking their hands, then found himself infected with the virus and nearly died during two weeks in hospital (Landler, 2020).

Inspired by Singapore's TraceTogether tracing app and recent modeling by a team at Oxford University (Ferretti et al. 2020), UK government advisers (responsible for English healthcare) identified the production of a smartphone app as a potential response to reduce transmission of the coronavirus (as did the three other UK nations: Scotland, Wales, and Northern Ireland; Cellan-Jones, 2020a). NHSX, a "digital transformation" unit of the government's Department of Health and Social Care, commissioned a private software company to produce a centralized contact tracing app (Kelion, 2020c) with data about individuals' encounters held centrally by the government (Lomas, 2020), and an academic-commercial team to model its deployment (Hinch et al., 2020).

By contrast, in a decentralized technology model, such as that announced on 10 April 2020 by Apple and Google, which many countries adopted (Wang, 2021), contact information is held on the user's own device under their control. The differences in privacy and security of these models would be important in the discussions in the United Kingdom about which system to adopt.

The production of version 1 of the centralized tracing app took many months. It was announced to great fanfare in March 2020 and was still being developed and tested when it was abandoned in June 2020 (Sabbagh & Hern,

2020). While the epidemiologists at Oxford University advising the government suggested that a centralized model would allow better top-level monitoring of the pandemic, technical experts and the media had loudly criticized the delay in producing the app and questioned why it was not developed using the Apple and Google system for reasons of simplicity, effectiveness, and privacy protection (Cellan-Jones, 2020a). This pressure increased as other governments announced they were switching to a decentralized model, particularly the Republic of Ireland at the end of April 2020 (Kitchin, 2020).

Another initial driver for the centralized model—to enable detection of malicious self-notification of infection—dissipated as the UK government dramatically increased its COVID testing capability and hence was able to add a requirement that test results be authenticated using a government-issued code before notifications were sent to individuals who had been in sustained close contact with a confirmed-positive user.

Once the centralized NHSX app entered testing in the summer, the fears voiced by technical experts proved well founded. The app did not integrate well with Google's and particularly Apple's smartphone operating systems (Android and iOS) or hardware (Sabbagh & Hern, 2020; Hern & Sabbagh, 2020). Its functionality relied on frequently sending Bluetooth signals to other phones to help those phones measure and track contact with individuals (Cellan-Jones, 2020a; Vincent, 2020). A large-scale trial on the Isle of Wight (IoW), a small island off the south coast of England, found that 96% of iPhones were not detectable by the app, because the iPhones frequently put the app to sleep to save energy (Cellan-Jones, 2020a; Sabbagh & Hern, 2020).

Trials also took place in the London Borough of Newham and with National Health Service Volunteer Responders (NHSV). An evaluation found most users were most concerned about knowing when they had been at risk, as shown in Figure 7.1.

Additional reasons that users gave for downloading the app included the following:

- Access to useful information (that is, local risk level) which some groups felt gave them an increased level of confidence and greater sense of safety
- Having the opportunity to identify as an "early-adopter"
- Supporting a return to "normal life" by facilitating visiting venues and travelling on public transport [and]
- A sense of civic, public or social responsibility or obligation to help society and protect loved ones. (Department of Health and Social Care [DHSC], 2021b)

The impact on privacy was the most significant reason given for not downloading the app, with others including concerns about the effectiveness of the app; the impact on phone battery life, security, and storage capacity; and the impos-

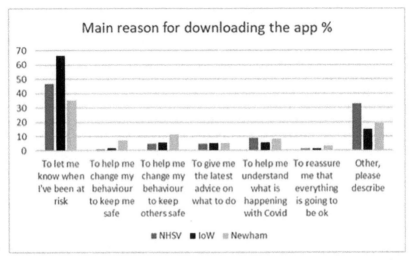

Source: Department of Health and Social Care. (2021b, April 8). "NHS COVID-19 app: Early adopter evaluation report," p. 15 (https://assets.publishing.service.gov.uk/government/uploads/ system/uploads/attachment_data/file/976862/EA_report_April_2020.pdf). © Crown copyright 2021. Licensed under the Open Government License v3.0.

Figure 7.1   Main reason that pilot users downloaded the tracing app

sibility of self-isolating after an exposure notification for non-home workers and those with low incomes or precarious jobs, as shown in Figure 7.2.

Apple and Google's own system had the great advantage of those companies' control over their operating systems, enabling them to selectively lift the background processing restriction on apps and then move the Bluetooth signaling into the operating system. The English, French, and German governments all encountered this problem when trying to develop their own apps, and all failed to persuade Apple to change the functionality of its operating system (Scott et al., 2020). Apple was adamant it was protecting user privacy, while several senior government figures in these countries criticized Apple's decision as anti-democratic (Kelion, 2020b).

The Isle of Wight trial figures were the final straw, and the BBC reported on 18 June that the government was switching to an app built on the Apple and Google technology. A week later, the government in Northern Ireland announced its own Apple/Google-based app, which would be compatible with the Republic of Ireland's (Cellan-Jones, 2020b)—a critical consideration given the tens of thousands of people crossing the border daily (FactCheckNI, 2017). And on 31 July, the Scottish government announced it was developing a separate Apple/Google-based version of the app that would be based on the

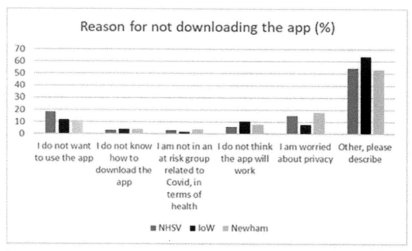

Source: Department of Health and Social Care. (2021b, April 8). "NHS COVID-19 app: Early adopter evaluation report," p. 17 (https://assets.publishing.service.gov.uk/government/uploads/system/uploads/attachment_data/file/976862/EA_report_April_2020.pdf). © Crown copyright 2021. Licensed under the Open Government License v3.0.

Figure 7.2   *Reasons pilot users gave against downloading the tracing app*

open-source software released by Ireland (Wise, 2020). This timeline is summarized in Figure 7.3.

The second version of the NHSX app proved reasonably popular, with over 10 million downloads in the first three days of availability and 21 million downloads by the end of 2020, with usage between November and December 2020 equating to roughly 28% of the total population of England and Wales (DHSC, 2020; Wang, 2021).

After the launch, there was further media criticism over feature functionality issues such as a failure of older phones to properly log test results (Mageit, 2020), while improvements to the reliability of the underlying Apple/Google proximity detection algorithm allowed more exposure notifications to be sent by the app starting in the end of October (Kelion, 2020d). Seven months after its launch, the app had 16 million users (DHSC, 2021c).

One positive consequence of the switch to the Apple/Google system by the entire United Kingdom (as well as the Crown Dependencies of Jersey, Guernsey and the Isle of Man, and the British Overseas Territory of Gibraltar) was the ease with which the systems could be made interoperable to better cover users traveling between these areas (Burke, 2020). Unfortunately, however, the United Kingdom was not able to participate in a cross-EU

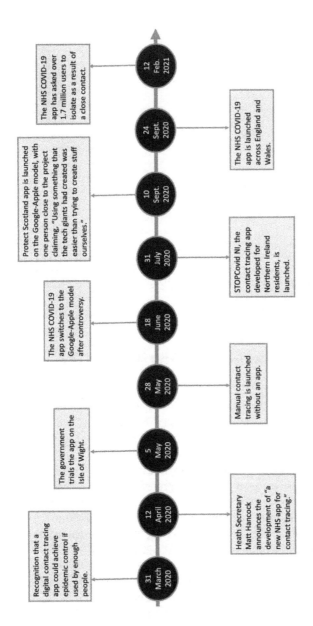

Source: Adapted from Dawda, S., Allsopp, R., Bessant, C., Emmett, C., Higgs, M., Janjeva, A., Oswald, M., Li, G., Sutton, S., & Warner, M. (2021, May 18). "Snapshot report 2: Tech-driven approaches to public health," p. 3, Observatory for Monitoring Data-Driving Approaches to COVID-19 (www.omddac.org.uk/wp-content/uploads/2021/05/OMDDAC-Snapshot-Report-2-Tech-Driven-Approaches-to-Public-Health.pdf). © 2021 OMDDAC. Reproduced and adapted with authors' permission. CCBY 2.0.

Figure 7.3   COVID tracing app timeline

interoperability system after Brexit, because of the lack of an agreement on sharing health data and the continued tension between the United Kingdom and European Union over the withdrawal process (Scott, 2020).

INSTITUTIONAL MECHANISMS FOR OVERSIGHT AND REGULATION

There are two important background issues to consider when discussing the UK regulation of privacy and data ethics in the context of pandemic surveillance. Despite the United Kingdom's withdrawal from the European Union in 2020, the provisions of the European Union's General Data Protection Regulation (GDPR) were brought into UK domestic law after the separation (Information Commissioner's Office, 2020). Second, the United Kingdom's government-provided National Health Service, which is free at the point of use for everyone ordinarily resident in the United Kingdom and is paid for out of taxation, is one of the most trusted institutions in the United Kingdom (DHSC, 2021a; Mintel Press Office, 2018).

Health is a "devolved" policy area, with the governments of Scotland, Wales, and Northern Ireland responsible in those nations, and four separate NHS organizations provide healthcare there and in England. Some of the tensions discussed in this chapter result from the split of responsibilities for operational and policy matters between the NHS and the four governments (Hammond et al., 2018).

During the initial development of the contact tracing app, the United Kingdom's data protection authority, the Information Commissioner's Office, provided advice to NHSX on ensuring compliance with data protection law in its app design and operation (Denham, 2020). However, it can be difficult for regulators intimately involved in the production of a system to take enforcement action against its use if they assess that the responsible organization is not obeying data protection laws—and other types of regulatory capture may occur if the relationship becomes too close. This criticism was made by several members of Parliament's Joint Committee on Human Rights, although it was rejected by the Information Commissioner (Joint Committee on Human Rights, 2020).

NHSX also created an independent ethics advisory board "to ensure that the development of the NHS App helped to control the COVID-19 epidemic and return people to normal life more rapidly whilst operating in line with ethical requirements, and in a manner that was transparent and open to public scrutiny" (Ethics Advisory Board, 2020, p. 4). Unpaid members were appointed from existing oversight bodies, academia, and civil society. The board participated in roundtables with epidemiological, privacy, and technical experts;

consulted officials; and organized focus groups with members of the public (Ethics Advisory Board, 2020, pp. 5–6).

To encourage use of tools like contact tracing apps, data protection regulators, ethics boards, and other institutional mechanisms play an important role in assuring members of the public that their privacy is being protected. Neither the UK government nor any other European government mandated people to download and run these apps, making voluntary adoption key.

As Yeung (2020) noted, "Without sufficient transparency and accountability in the exercise of decision-making authority, those in government will not sustain the trust, cooperation, and solidarity of citizens" needed for pandemic management (p. 56). Mollicchi et al. (2020) similarly noted, "Transparency, accountability, oversight and responsible use of data are central to earning public trust" (p. 280). A citizen jury exercise commissioned by NHS organizations regarding data sharing during the COVID pandemic similarly found that transparency and independent oversight were critical to public support (Oswald & Laverty, 2021).

In its final report, the Ethics Advisory Board (2020) for the NHSX app noted that the speed of app development made it difficult "to explore the ethical implications of the technical choices and tests that were being undertaken to evaluate the effectiveness of the app" (p. 8). The board expressed frustration at the quality of information it was given to conduct its work, and "did not always feel that suitably comprehensive or final answers were supplied to their questions" (Ethics Advisory Board, 2020, p. 8). The board further noted that "journalists had received briefings that appeared to be at variance with those being presented to the board. Sometimes technical information that we regarded as ethically significant, and had requested, was not available to us at the point when we needed to crystallise advice" (Ethics Advisory Board, 2020, pp. 15–16).

It turned out that the Ethics Advisory Board members were too critical of the contact tracing system for the government's liking, leading it to scrap the board (Field, 2020). However, the government committed to making use of the ethical framework developed by the board in its broader test and trace program (based on previous work by the government's Centre for Data Ethics and Innovation), whose principles are quoted in Table 7.1.

The final report of the Ethics Advisory Board (2020) noted:

> Lack of support and advice may have contributed to the fact that media interest in the EAB was limited to whether there were frustrations within the group and suspicions of tensions between it and NHSX or the Secretary of State. We were disappointed that there was no media coverage of the ethical principles set out in our advice, despite having presented a summary at a press briefing at the Science Media Centre. However, as our letter setting them out was not publicly available until some weeks after the briefing this was understandable. (p. 15)

Table 7.1   *Ethics Advisory Board Principles*

Value	There must be good reason to believe that the app will provide sufficient net-value back to the citizen or society as a whole so as to justify its introduction and any adverse consequences for individuals.
Impact	There must be good reason to believe the app will be an effective tool in controlling the outbreak of COVID-19.
Security and privacy	Data sharing and storage should be secure. The data collected should be minimised and protected as much as possible, so users' privacy is preserved.
Accountability	There must be a reliable and understandable decision-making process in place to manage the app—with clear democratic accountability, particularly with regard to introducing new functionality, data collection or use cases.
Transparency	Details on what data is gathered and why, as well as the app's code and underlying algorithms, must be available publicly to enable scrutiny and give people the ability to object to decisions.
Control	Users should be able to see what kinds of data are held about them so that they can understand how it is impacting on decisions.

Source: From Ethics Advisory Board. (2020, August 25). "Report on the work of the Ethics Advisory Group to NHSX on the COVID-19 contact tracing app," National Health Service, pp. 30–31 (https://covid19.nhs.uk/pdf/ethic-advisory-group-report.pdf).

The second version of England and Wales's contact tracing app, which uses the Apple/Google system, integrated data privacy in its design from the start (Sabbagh & Hern, 2020). Even additional features, such as the ability for users to "check in" to public locations such as bars and cafes using a QR code, were required by Apple and Google's technical and contractual constraints to be privacy-protective (such as blocking tracing apps from accessing the phone's location.)

This is a good example of the GDPR's requirement for data protection by design, where technology should be designed to enforce the rights in the GDPR (Bradford et al., 2020, p. 14). But curiously, when marketing the second version of the app, the UK government was coy about mentioning the United Kingdom's rigorous Data Protection Act 2018; nor did it promote the role of the UK privacy regulator, the Information Commissioner's Office. Advertising focused on the technical protections.

The government rejected calls from experts and Parliament's Joint Committee on Human Rights for legislation providing specific limits on how contact tracing-related personal data could be processed, stating, "The Government agrees that privacy with regard to data collection is important and feels there are sufficient measures in place for this not to require legislation" (Secretary of State for Health and Social Care, 2020, p. 42).

CONTROVERSY OVER OTHER ORGANIZATIONS INVOLVED

Other organizations in the United Kingdom were sometimes given access to contact tracing data and were sometimes barred from access. In October 2020, the government announced that the police would not be given access to contact tracing app data but would be given access to other test and trace data that the government held. The police would be able to use this data to check whether people diagnosed with COVID-19 were self-isolating for 14 days as legally required (Kleinman, 2020; BBC, 2020b). Violations came with significant penalties of up to £10,000 (around $12,500 in US dollars; BBC, 2020a). A revised memorandum of understanding between the Department of Health and Social Care and police forces on "Sharing of data to enable self-isolation enforcement" came into effect on 19 March 2021 (DHSC & National Police Chiefs' Council, 2021).

The possible fines led to concerns that the contact tracing app data would be used to help identify violators, causing many to question their decision to download and use the app, even though technical experts were able to explain that the government could not give police access to contact tracing app data, because of the decentralized nature of the system (Gross & Parker, 2020).

The UK Government Communications Headquarters (GCHQ), its largest intelligence agency, was involved in checking the security of access to NHS information systems during the pandemic, as well as the design of the app (and was even potentially a joint controller for data protection law purposes; Carding, 2020; Rapson, 2020). Interestingly, GCHQ's involvement did not seem to raise broad public concerns, even though one study found that UK residents expressed privacy concerns and government misuse as one of their top fears about contact tracing apps (Williams et al., 2021). The notion of an intelligence agency interacting with a contact tracing app might have caused significant concern in some countries, particularly after the Snowden revelations. However, there was no substantial outcry in the UK media.

Palantir, a well-known US company that develops database tools for intelligence and security agencies to integrate their databases, which more recently have been used by a number of governments for immigration enforcement, was also involved in the behind-the-scenes infrastructure for the UK government (Kelion, 2020a; BBC, 2021). The company's work did not deal with the tracing app, but rather involved other elements of the government's COVID response (BBC, 2021). Palantir's involvement caused some controversy in the United Kingdom, as well as that of other private sector companies (BBC, 2021).

A complex web of large and small outsourcing companies worked with the UK Department of Health and Social Care on the overall tracking and tracing program, with disappointing results (Wood, 2021). The House of Commons Public Accounts Committee (2021) concluded of the program: "It is unclear whether its specific contribution to reducing infection levels, as opposed to the other measures introduced to tackle the pandemic[,] has justified its costs" (p. 3). While compliance was high for those who received self-isolation instructions directly from NHS Test and Trace, surveys of the wider population found self-isolation compliance to range between 43% and 62% (Comptroller & Auditor General, 2021, p. 60).

BROADER QUESTIONS RAISED

The United Kingdom's experience since March 2020 with contact tracing apps raises broader questions for privacy and security governance. The first is practical: How well do they work, since this is crucial for their proportionality? In early 2020, governments were looking for any tools available to deal with a rapidly spreading novel virus, with very limited information. But as the pandemic wore on, many government critics became more cynical, seeing the app as an example of Sean McDonald's "technology theatre," used to distract attention from a litany of errors made in the first few months of the crisis (after which it was demoted to the "cherry on top" of a still-dysfunctional tracing system; McDonald, 2020, pp. 20–27).

Since the Apple/Google system is designed to minimize the amount of personal data collected and made available centrally, its public health efficacy is more difficult to assess. With the benefit of more than a year's experience, some empirical evidence is available. In an early four-week controlled experiment on the Spanish island of La Gomera, Rodríguez et al. (2021) found that the Spanish government's tracing app (Radar COVID) identified about 6.3 close contacts per primary simulated infection. Many of these contacts were strangers who would have been less likely to be detected using manual contact tracing. However, when these contacts were notified, only about 10% of these potential cases followed up with primary care.

A much-larger-scale study of the NHS tracing app in England and Wales found that it was used regularly by 16.5 million people (28% of the population), sending roughly 1.7 million exposure notifications, equivalent to 4.2 per index case (Wymant et al., 2021, p. 408). Roughly 6% of those individuals tested positive for COVID. The study's authors used two methods to estimate the number of COVID cases averted by the app, giving a modeling estimate of 284,000, and 594,000 by comparing matched neighboring local areas. For each percentage point increase in app uptake, 0.8% (estimated using modeling) or 2.3% (using statistical analysis) of cases could be reduced (Wymant et al., 2021). However, as a more infectious variant (Delta) spread through the UK population, which itself received three types of vaccinations (Oxford/ AstraZeneca, Pfizer/BioNTech, and Moderna) throughout 2021, it became less clear that the policy of exposure notification followed by self-isolation would be cost-effective, as "only a few of 100 vaccinated contacts would be expected to become cases" (Spiegelhalter and Masters, 2021).

As with previous pandemics, COVID-19 has had a disparate impact on different social groups (Bambra et al., 2020). There were concerns in the United Kingdom that spending on a contact tracing app could exacerbate this. A nationally representative survey found 19% of respondents did not have access to a smartphone, which was particularly acute for those with disabilities and those on the lowest household incomes. These groups were also less likely to feel that health apps would be effective (Ada Lovelace Institute, 2021). Older individuals, who are particularly vulnerable to COVID, have generally lower levels of internet usage (see Figure 7.4), as do disabled individuals (Office for National Statistics, 2021). And in three tracing app "early adopter" groups, a survey found significant differences in the level of downloads between white (51%) and BAME (Black and Minority Ethnic; 33%) respondents. These sampling effects in app usage are likely to contribute to increased disparate consequences of the pandemic, to the extent that direct comparison of rate of attack on notified cases through digital and manual contact tracing could be misleading as to its true impact (Mancastroppa et al., 2021).

In one of these early adopter groups (residents of Newham, which has a significantly higher BAME population), there were higher concerns about privacy, including concern about being monitored or having smartphones hacked when Bluetooth was switched on (DHSC, 2021a, p. 19).

The pandemic will likely retreat somewhat and become endemic thanks to global vaccination programs (despite the shamefully slow progress in the Global South and significant vaccine reticence in parts of the Global North, such as the United States). But pandemic surveillance will remain in ways it did not before the emergence of COVID-19. McDonald (2020) notes, "There will be an enormous number of individual contexts and outcomes when we start trying to force biosurveillance and proximity tracking apps back out of our lives" (p. 25).

When Apple and Google first announced their API system, their "Exposure Notification: Frequently Asked Questions" document stated that they "will disable the exposure notification system on a regional basis when it is no longer needed" (Apple & Google, 2020, p. 5). Since at the time of this writing in mid 2021 no region using their system had yet reached this state, the speed at which this will happen, as well as the potential pressures the companies will come under from governments to leave the system enabled, remains unclear. A significant benefit of decentralized tracing systems is that such disabling can

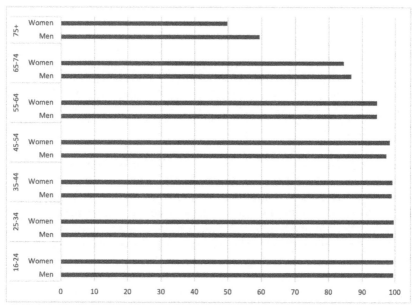

Source: Office for National Statistics. (2021, April 6). "Internet Users, 2020" [Data set]. UK Statistics Authority (www.ons.gov.uk/businessindustryandtrade/itandinternetindustry/datasets/internetusers). Licensed under the Open Government License v3.0.

Figure 7.4   *Percentage of UK residents who used the internet in the past three months, by age group (years) and sex, 2020*

be done effectively, without the risks caused by potentially leaving in place indefinitely a large volume of very sensitive personal data (McDonald, 2020), especially if data breaches occur.

Longer term, how could governments better prepare for future emergencies by improving governance frameworks for technological tools that protect privacy and public health and other important societal values? Early in the COVID crisis, Marda (2020) found a prevalence of "opaque processes that concern governments and private actors alone, and do not lend themselves to transparency, accountability, public consultation, and legal oversight" (p. 30).

In the context of the Ebola crisis in Liberia in 2014/15, McDonald (2016) found that "the governance of emergency powers over digital systems remain[s] poorly defined and badly regulated, and lack[s] the basic due process checks and balances that exist for nearly every other kind of government emergency authority" (p. 2), and found a lack of "critical discussion that acknowledges the experimental nature of data modeling in emergency response and social engineering, with a primary emphasis on quality control, public understanding, and human rights" (p. 27). He concluded:

> Even in places where there are regulatory institutions to fill the gap, emergency contexts often cause disruption or suspension of the safeguarding processes required to protect human rights. Without these processes—or any other form of public oversight—digitizing humanitarian systems can add layers of opacity to the already complex data models, implementation approaches, or intended outcomes of the response, further crippling tenuous public trust and good governance. (McDonald, 2016, p. 2)

The United Kingdom initially performed poorly in protecting fundamental rights in producing the England and Wales tracing app, with Health Secretary Matt Hancock dismissing the legally required Data Protection Impact Assessment (DPIA) for the Track and Trace program as mere "bureaucracy." A DPIA for the Isle of Wight trial was criticized as omitting key technical and legal information (Veale, 2020a). The Ethics Advisory Board (2020) for the NHSX app noted, "What was initially envisaged as a tech project is now a large-scale health project, in which tens of thousands of people are employed. This will require a different form of ethics advice and governance to that set up for an independent App" (p.15).

The government has continued to resist publication of COVID-related DPIAs, even via statutory mechanisms such as parliamentary oversight and freedom of information laws. Oswald and Grace (2021) argue that in such situations, governments should pay careful attention to human rights legal requirements "combined with a robust and rolling oversight function," to ensure the "experimental proportionality" of novel technologies (p. 27).

The long delay in developing and releasing the tracing app also raises questions about the United Kingdom's system for scientific foresight and governance advice (in mid 2021, the Prime Minister established a new ministerial council and an Office of Science and Technology Strategy within the Cabinet Office and appointed a National Technology Adviser; Prime Minister's Office, 2021). A respiratory pandemic had been the highest impact/likelihood event on the UK government's national risk register since it was created in 2008 (Cabinet Office, 2008, p. 5). A large-scale pandemic response exercise in 2016 showed the potential for many deaths (Public Health England, 2017). Government-funded academic research into computing tools for monitoring epidemics had been underway since 2007, with the first prototype shown in Figure 7.5 (Yoneki, 2011). Yet while NHSX consulted some of those researchers starting in late March 2020, prior to the pandemic, the government had not taken any further actions to enable the much more streamlined production of such tools.

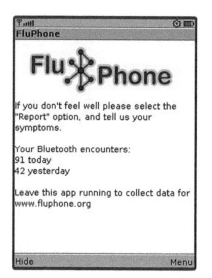
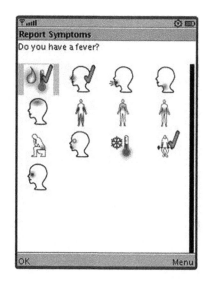
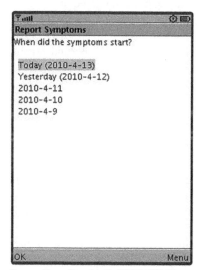
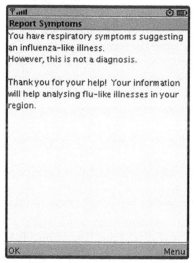

Source: From Yoneki, E. (2011). "FluPhone, study: virtual disease spread using haggle." In *CHANTS '11: Proceedings of the 6th ACM Workshop on Challenged Networks*, p. 65. (https://doi.org/10.1145/2030652.2030672). © 2001 by the Association for Computing Machinery, Inc. (AMC). Reproduced with author's permission.

Figure 7.5   FluPhone screenshots for influenza symptom reporting

A remaining overarching question raised widely in 2020 is whether governments should have stronger legal powers to compel technology companies to change the designs of their systems to assist with public health emergencies. Should the UK, French, German, and other governments who initially wished to operate centralized apps have been able to compel Apple to modify iOS so they could run their own apps? Cohen (2020) notes, "Without question, responding to the COVID-19 pandemic requires mobilizing the resources and expertise of information technology firms. … Equally without question, allowing those processes to unfold in ways superintended by the firms themselves and structured by their economic interests threatens important public values" (p. 290).

Veale (2020b) notes, "To change the status quo of global systems governed by global firms is to open Pandora's box" (p. 38). National governments could have attempted to pass laws compelling this assistance within their own borders, but the United Kingdom made no such attempt. Notably, while some European governments called loudly for such powers, they are not contained in the comprehensive legislation proposed at the end of 2020 by the European Commission to regulate digital platforms (the Digital Services Act and Digital Markets Act).

Would most smartphone users have trusted such a centralized app if governments had compelled technology companies to do this? Given the significant privacy concerns noted earlier, there is a strong argument to be made that maintaining a "separation of powers" between government and private sector infrastructure providers can contribute to public trust. It may be that in countries such as the United Kingdom, where public sector health agencies are strongly trusted by the public, governance models can be designed in the future where such agencies play a stronger role.

POSTSCRIPT

As this chapter was finalized in early July 2021, the United Kingdom suffered a third wave, propelled by the highly infectious COVID-19 Delta variant, of tens of thousands of daily infections even as vaccination coverage and post-infection immunity reached very high levels. This coincided with government determination to lift all legal requirements in England on 19 July for social distancing, mask wearing, self-isolation after a positive test result or an in-person notification by the NHS Test and Trace service, and other non-pharmaceutical interventions (Allegretti & Geddes, 2021).

Such conditions would be ideal for an automated contact tracing system to demonstrate its advantages over a manual contact tracing program, which, even with a total government budget of £13.5 billion spent by NHS Test and Trace in 2020–21, could not remotely cope with this projected number of cases in the United Kingdom. During the second wave of infections in

December 2020, timely test results, which test-and-isolate systems rely on, fell to 17% received within 24 hours (Torjesen, 2021).

However, the soaring number of third-wave exposure notifications instead provoked media calls to "ping off," with complaints of "house arrest" and cynicism about compliance rates (understandable given the extremely limited financial support given to those self-isolating), alongside politicians apparently determined to demonstrate they made these laws for others to follow (Purves, 2021). As fears grew that the NHS and the hospitality industry would be crippled by this level of self-isolation, the government agreed to "tune the app to ensure that it is appropriate to the risk" in anticipation of removing the legal requirement on 16 August 2021 for fully vaccinated individuals to quarantine after sustained contact with a confirmed case (Bowden & Lee, 2021).

As in the United States, although to a lesser degree, UK mask wearing became significantly politicized during the pandemic, with government ministers declaring they could barely wait to stop wearing them after "freedom day" on 19 July 2021. A tracing app widely seen to be inaccurate and opaque, advising hundreds of thousands of individuals to self-isolate, and from an increasingly distrusted government (Purves, 2021), runs a significant risk of becoming similarly politicized and ignored.

Exposure notifications do not include information on the context in which sustained contact with a case occurred. These privacy constraints significantly limit the ability of recipients to evaluate the risk. Was the contact inside or outside? (As a mainly airborne virus, the risk of COVID infection is around 19 times higher indoors; Bulfone et al., 2021.) Was an indoor venue well-ventilated? (Environmental engineers have suggested using ambient carbon dioxide levels as a proxy for ventilation; Peng and Jiminez, 2021.) Was the notification source or the recipient (or both) wearing a mask; were they separated by plexiglass screens or other forms of protective equipment; and were their phones out on a shared table, in pockets, or buried in bags?

Given the changing risk parameters of multiple COVID variants spreading throughout the United Kingdom in late 2020 and 2021, it was therefore particularly alarming that the tracing app's designers struggled to update the software, or even to update the app to adjust these parameters for vaccinated users (both their own reduced risk of infection and their reduced risk of infecting others). One academic adviser to the program worried that "the people who actually built the serious risk model in the successful app have left … so the team may not have the skills to update the system to include other risk factors (new variant & vaccination)" (J. Crowcroft, personal communication, 5 July 2021).

As always, maintaining a clear understanding of the sociotechnical environment in which a technology is deployed—alongside social and economic interventions essential to its success, such as financially supporting those who cannot otherwise afford to self-isolate—is critical if it is to have any hope of achieving its goals.

ACKNOWLEDGMENTS

The author thanks Jon Crowcroft, Paul-Olivier Dehaye, Lilian Edwards, Marion Oswald, Michael Veale, and Eiko Yoneki for their helpful feedback.

REFERENCES

Ada Lovelace Institute. (2021, March). "The data divide: Public attitudes to tackling social and health inequalities in the COVID-19 pandemic and beyond." www.adalovelac einstitute.org/wp-content/uploads/2021/03/The-data-divide_25March_final-1.pdf

Allegretti, A. & Geddes, L. (2021, July 4). "PM to confirm 19 July end to COVID rules despite scientists' warnings." *The Guardian.* www.theguardian.com/politics/2021/jul/04/pm-confirm-19-july-end-covid-restrictions-scientists-warnings-england

Apple & Google. (2020, May). "Exposure notification: Frequently asked questions, v1.1." https://covid19-static.cdn-apple.com/applications/covid19/current/static/contact-tracing/pdf/ExposureNotification-FAQv1.0.pdf

Bambra, C., Riordan, R., Ford, J., & Matthews, F. (2020). "The COVID-19 pandemic and health inequalities." *Journal of Epidemiology & Community Health*, 74(11), 964–968. https://doi.org/10.1136/jech-2020-214401

BBC. (2020a, September 28). "COVID-19: Up to £10,000 fine for failure to self-isolate in England." www.bbc.com/news/uk-54320482

BBC. (2020b, October 18). "Coronavirus: Police get access to NHS Test and Trace self-isolation data." www.bbc.com/news/uk-54586897

BBC. (2021, March 31). "Palantir: NHS says future deals 'will be transparent.'" www.bbc.com/news/technology-56590249

Bowden, G., & Lee, J. (2021, July 9). "NHS COVID app may change as rules change, Grant Shapps says." BBC News. www.bbc.com/news/uk-57772515.amp

Bradford, L., Aboy, M., & Liddell, K. (2020). "COVID-19 contact tracing apps: A stress test for privacy, the GDPR, and data protection regimes." *Journal of Law and the Biosciences*, 7(1), 1–21. https://academic.oup.com/jlb/article/7/1/lsaa034/5848138

Bulfone, T. C., Malekinejad, M., Rutherford, G. W., & Razani, N. (2021). "Outdoor transmission of SARS-CoV-2 and other respiratory viruses: A systematic review." *Journal of Infectious Diseases*, 223(4), 550–561. https://doi.org/10.1093/infdis/jiaa742

Burke, E. (2020, November 5). "Cross-border contact tracing now possible across all UK apps." Silicon Republic. www.siliconrepublic.com/enterprise/uk-contact-tracing-covid-tracking-apps-nearform

Cabinet Office. (2008). "National risk register" (Ref: 289116/0708). https://assets.publishing.service.gov.uk/government/uploads/system/uploads/attachment_data/file/969213/20210310_2008-NRR-Title-Page_UPDATED-merged-1-2.pdf

Carding, N. (2020, April 29). "Hancock grants GCHQ powers over NHS IT systems." *Health Service Journal.* www.hsj.co.uk/technology-and-innovation/hancock-grants-gchq-powers-over-nhs-it-systems/7027528.article

Cellan-Jones, R. (2020a, June 20). "Coronavirus: What went wrong with the UK's contact tracing app?" BBC. www.bbc.com/news/technology-53114251

Cellan-Jones, R. (2020b, June 26). "Northern Ireland to launch separate contact-tracing app." BBC. www.bbc.com/news/technology-53200521

Cohen, J. E. (2020). "United States: Capitalising on crisis." In L. Taylor, G. Sharma, A. Martin, & S. Jameson (eds.), *Data Justice and COVID-19: Global Perspectives* (pp. 284–291). Meatspace Press.

Comptroller & Auditor General. (2021). "Test and trace in England—progress update" (HC 295). National Audit Office. www.nao.org.uk/wp-content/uploads/2021/06/Test-and-trace-in-England-progress-update.pdf

Dawda, S., Allsopp, R., Bessant, C., Emmett, C., Higgs, M., Janjeva, A., Oswald, M., Li, G., Sutton, S., & Warner, M. (2021, May 18). "Snapshot report 2: Tech-driven approaches to public health." Observatory for Monitoring Data-Driven Approaches to COVID-19. www.omddac.org.uk/wp-content/uploads/2021/05/OMDDAC-Snapshot-Report-2-Tech-Driven-Approaches-to-Public-Health.pdf

Denham, E. (2020, April 17). "Blog: Combatting COVID-19 through data: Some considerations for privacy." Information Commissioner's Office. https://ico.org.uk/about-the-ico/news-and-events/news-and-blogs/2020/04/combatting-covid-19-through-data-some-considerations-for-privacy/

Department of Health and Social Care. (2020, September 27). "NHS COVID-19 app has been downloaded over 10 million times." www.gov.uk/government/news/nhs-covid-19-app-has-been-downloaded-over-10-million-times

Department of Health and Social Care. (2021a, January 1). "Introduction to the NHS Constitution." Retrieved from www.gov.uk/government/publications/the-nhs-constitution-for-england/the-nhs-constitution-for-england

Department of Health and Social Care. (2021b, April 8). "NHS COVID-19 app: Early adopter evaluation report." https://assets.publishing.service.gov.uk/government/uploads/system/uploads/attachment_data/file/976862/EA_report_April_2020.pdf

Department of Health and Social Care. (2021c, June 24). "Management information on NHS Test and Trace: 24 June 2021." www.gov.uk/government/publications/management-information-on-nhs-test-and-trace-24-june-2021/management-information-on-nhs-test-and-trace-24-june-2021

Department of Health and Social Care & National Police Chiefs' Council. (2021, March 19). "Sharing of data to enable self-isolation enforcement process." Process Level Memorandum of Understanding between NPCC and Department of Health and Social Care. https://assets.publishing.service.gov.uk/government/uploads/system/uploads/attachment_data/file/972961/umbrella-memorandum-of-understanding-between-DHSC-and-NPCC-March-2021.pdf

du Plessis, L., McCrone, J. T., Zarebski, A. E., Hill, V., Ruis, C., Gutierrez, et al. (2021). "Establishment and lineage dynamics of the SARS-CoV-2 epidemic in the UK." *Science*, 371(6530), 708–712. https://doi.org/10.1126/science.abf2946

Ethics Advisory Board. (2020, August 25). "Report on the work of the Ethics Advisory Group to NHSX on the COVID-19 contact tracing app." National Health Service. https://covid19.nhs.uk/pdf/ethic-advisory-group-report.pdf

FactCheckNI. (2017, April 27). "Do 30,000 people cross Ireland-Northern Ireland border daily?" https://factcheckni.org/articles/do-30000-people-cross-ireland-northern-ireland-border-daily/

Ferretti, L., Wymant, C., Kendall, M., Zhao, L., Nurtay, N., Abeler-Dörner, L., Parker, M., Bonsall, D., & Fraser, C. (2020). "Quantifying SARS-CoV-2 transmission sug-

gests epidemic control with digital contact tracing." *Science*, 368(6491). https://doi
.org/10.1126/science.abb6936

Field, M. (2020, July 23). "NHS contact-tracing app ethics board scrapped." *The
Telegraph*. www.telegraph.co.uk/technology/2020/07/23/nhs-contact-tracing-app
-ethics-board-scrapped/

Gross, A., & Parker, G. (2020, October 18). "Experts decry move to share Covid test
and trace data with police." *Financial Times*. www.ft.com/content/d508d917-065c
-448e-8232-416510592dd1

Hammond, J., Speed, E., Allen, P., McDermott, I., Coleman, A., & Checkland, K.
(2018). "Autonomy, accountability, and ambiguity in arm's-length meta-governance:
The case of NHS England." *Public Management Review*, 21(8), 1148–1169. https://
doi.org/10.1080/14719037.2018.1544660

Helm, T., Graham-Harrison, E., & McKie, R. (2020, April 19). "How did Britain get
its coronavirus response so wrong?" *The Guardian*. www.theguardian.com/world/
2020/apr/18/how-did-britain-get-its-response-to-coronavirus-so-wrong

Hern, A., & Sabbagh, D. (2020, May 6). "Critical mass of Android users crucial for
NHS contact-tracing app." *The Guardian*. www.theguardian.com/world/2020/may/
06/critical-mass-of-android-users-needed-for-success-of-nhs-coronavirus-contact
-tracing-app

Hinch, R., Probert, W., Nurtay, A., Kendall, M., Wymant, C., Hall, M., et al. (2020).
"Effective configurations of a digital contact tracing app: A report to NHSX."
https://cdn.theconversation.com/static_files/files/1009/Report_-_Effective_App
_Configurations.pdf

Information Commissioner's Office. (2020, July 10). "Information rights at the end
of the transition period frequently asked questions." https://ico.org.uk/media/for
-organisations/documents/brexit/2617110/information-rights-and-brexit-faqs-v2_3
.pdf

Joint Committee on Human Rights. (2020, May 4). "Oral evidence (virtual proceeding):
The government's response to COVID-19: Human rights implications" (HC 265).
UK Houses of Parliament. https://committees.parliament.uk/oralevidence/334/html/

Kelion, L. (2020a, March 28). "Coronavirus: NHS turns to big tech to tackle COVID-19
hot spots." BBC. www.bbc.com/news/technology-52079287

Kelion, L. (2020b, April 21). "Coronavirus: Apple and France in stand-off over
contact-tracing app." BBC. www.bbc.com/news/technology-52366129

Kelion, L. (2020c, April 27). "NHS rejects Apple-Google coronavirus app plan." BBC.
www.bbc.com/news/technology-52441428

Kelion, L. (2020d, October 29). "NHS COVID-19 app to issue more self-isolate alerts."
BBC. www.bbc.com/news/technology-54733534

Kitchin, R. (2020). "Ireland: A marginal contribution to the pandemic response?" In L.
Taylor, G. Sharma, A. Martin, & S. Jameson (eds.), *Data Justice and COVID-19:
Global Perspectives* (pp. 154–159). Meatspace Press.

Kleinman, Z. (2020, October 19). "COVID contact-tracing app not sharing data with
police." BBC. www.bbc.com/news/technology-54599320

Landler, M. (2020, April 12). "Boris Johnson leaves U.K. hospital after coronavirus
treatment." *New York Times*. www.nytimes.com/2020/04/12/world/europe/boris
-johnson-coronavirus.html

Lomas, N. (2020, April 28). "UK's coronavirus tracing app could ask users to share
location data." TechCrunch. https://techcrunch.com/2020/04/28/uks-coronavirus
-contacts-tracing-app-could-ask-users-to-share-location-data/

Mageit, S. (2020, September 28). "NHS contact tracing app downloaded 10 million times despite glitch." Healthcare IT News. www.healthcareitnews.com/news/emea/nhs-contact-tracing-app-downloaded-10-million-times-despite-glitch

Mancastroppa, M., Castellano, C., Vezzani, A., & Burioni, R. (2021). "Stochastic sampling effects favor manual over digital contact tracing." *Nature Communications*, 12(1919), 1–9. https://doi.org/10.1038/s41467-021-22082-7

Marda, V. (2020). "Papering over the cracks: On privacy versus health." In L. Taylor, G. Sharma, A. Martin, & S. Jameson (eds.), *Data Justice and COVID-19: Global Perspectives* (pp. 28–33). Meatspace Press.

McDonald, S. (2016, March). "Ebola: A big data disaster." Centre for Internet and Society. https://cis-india.org/papers/ebola-a-big-data-disaster

McDonald, S. (2020). "Technology theatre and seizure." In L. Taylor, G. Sharma, A. Martin, & S. Jameson (eds.), *Data Justice and COVID-19: Global Perspectives* (pp. 20–27). Meatspace Press.

Mintel Press Office. (2018, June 7). "British lifestyles: The NHS tops list of UK's most cherished institutions." Mintel. www.mintel.com/press-centre/social-and-lifestyle/british-lifestyles-the-nhs-tops-list-of-uks-most-cherished-institutions

Mollicchi, S., Peppin, A., Safak, C., & Walker, T. (2020). "United Kingdom: Pandemics, power, and publics: Trends in post-crisis health technology." In L. Taylor, G. Sharma, A. Martin, & S. Jameson (eds.), *Data Justice and COVID-19: Global Perspectives* (pp. 276–283). Meatspace Press.

Office for National Statistics. (April 6, 2021). "Internet users, 2020" [Data set]. UK Statistics Authority. www.ons.gov.uk/businessindustryandtrade/itandinternetindustry/datasets/internetusers

Oswald, M., & Grace, J. (2021). "The COVID-19 contact tracing app in England and 'experimental proportionality.'" *Public Law*, 2021(Jan.), 27–36. http://dx.doi.org/10.2139/ssrn.3632870

Oswald, M., & Laverty, L. (2021). "Data sharing in a pandemic: Three citizen's juries—Juries report." National Institute for Health Research. www.arc-gm.nihr.ac.uk/media/Resources/ARC/Digital%20Health/Citizen%20Juries/12621_NIHR_Juries_Report_ELECTRONIC.pdf

Peng, Z. & Jiminez, J. L. (2021). "Exhaled CO_2 as a COVID-19 infection risk proxy for different indoor environments and activities." *Environmental Science & Technology Letters*, 8(5), 392–397. https://doi.org/10.1021/acs.estlett.1c00183

Prime Minister's Office. (2021, June 21). "Press release: Prime Minister sets out plans to realise and maximise the opportunities of scientific and technological breakthroughs." www.gov.uk/government/news/prime-minister-sets-out-plans-to-realise-and-maximise-the-opportunities-of-scientific-and-technological-breakthroughs

Public Accounts Committee. (2021, March 10). "COVID-19: Test, track and trace (part 1)" (HC 932). House of Commons. https://committees.parliament.uk/publications/4976/documents/50058/default/

Public Health England. (2017). "Exercise Cygnus Report: Tier one command post exercise pandemic influenza 18 to 20 October 2016." Department of Health. https://assets.publishing.service.gov.uk/government/uploads/system/uploads/attachment_data/file/927770/exercise-cygnus-report.pdf

Purves, L. (2021, July 5). "It's time for NHS contact tracing to ping off." *The Times*. www.thetimes.co.uk/article/its-time-for-nhs-contact-tracing-to-ping-off-dwf7wrjtd

Rapson, J. (2020, March 18). "NHS developing coronavirus contact tracking app." *Health Service Journal*. www.hsj.co.uk/free-for-non-subscribers/nhs-developing-coronavirus-contact-tracking-app/7027163.article

Rodríguez, P., Graña, S., Alvarez-León, E. E., Battaglini, M., Darias, F. J., Hernán, M.
    A., López, R., Llaneza, P., Martín, M. C., RadarCOVIDPilot Group, Ramirez-Rubio,
    O., Romaní, A., Suárez-Rodríguez, B., Sánchez-Monedero, J., Arenas, A., & Lacasa,
    L. (2021). "A population-based controlled experiment assessing the epidemiological
    impact of digital contact tracing." *Nature Communications*, 12, Article 587. https ://
    doi.org/10.1038/s41467-020-20817-6
Sabbagh, D., & Hern, A. (2020, June 18). "UK abandons contact-tracing app for Apple
    and Google model." *The Guardian*. www.theguardian.com/world/2020/jun/18/uk
    -poised-to-abandon-coronavirus-app-in-favour-of-apple-and-google-models
Scott, M. (2020, September 30). "UK coronavirus app to miss out on EU-wide
    contact-tracing scheme." Politico. www.politico.eu/article/uk-coronavirus-app-to
    -miss-out-on-eu-wide-contact-tracing-scheme/
Scott, M., Braun, E., Delcker, J., & Manancourt, V. (2020, May 15). "How Google and
    Apple outflanked governments in the race to build coronavirus apps." Politico. www
    .politico.eu/article/google-apple-coronavirus-app-privacy-uk-france-germany/
Secretary of State for Health and Social Care. (2020, December). "The government's
    response to the Joint Committee on Human Rights report: The government's
    response to COVID-19: Human rights implications." CM335. HMSO. https://assets
    .publishing.service.gov.uk/government/uploads/system/uploads/attachment_data/
    file/944103/The_Government_s_Response_to_the_Joint_Committee_on_Human
    _Rights_Report_The_Government_s_Response_to_COVID-19_Human_Rights
    Implications-_CP_335_pdf.pdf
Spiegelhalter, D., & Masters, A. (2021, July 11). "Should all contacts of COVID
    cases go into self-isolation?" *The Guardian*. www.theguardian.com/theobserver/
    commentisfree/2021/jul/11/should-all-contacts-of-covid-cases-go-into-self
    -isolation
Torjesen, I. (2021). "NHS Test and Trace: Lack of progress is 'deeply disappointing.'"
    British Medical Journal, 373, Article 1636. https://doi.org/10.1136/bmj.n1636
Veale, M. (2020a). "Analysis of the NHSX contact tracing app 'Isle of Wight' data
    protection impact assessment." https://doi.org/10.31228/osf.io/6fvgh
Veale, M. (2020b). "Sovereignty, privacy and contact tracing protocols." In L. Taylor,
    G. Sharma, A. Martin, & S. Jameson (eds.), *Data Justice and COVID-19: Global
    Perspectives* (pp. 34–39). Meatspace Press.
Vincent, J. (2020, May 5). "Without Apple and Google, the UK's contact-tracing app
    is in trouble." Verge. www.theverge.com/2020/5/5/21248288/uk-covid-19-contact
    -tracing-app-bluetooth-restrictions-apple-google
Wang, C. J. (2021, May 25). "Contact-tracing app curbed the spread of COVID in
    England and Wales." *Nature*. www.nature.com/articles/d41586-021-01354-8
Williams, S. N., Armitage, C. J., Tampe, T., & Dienes, K. (2021). "Public attitudes
    towards COVID-19 contact tracing apps: A UK-based focus group study." *Health
    Expectations*, 24(2), 377–385. https://doi.org/10.1111/hex.13179
Wise, J. (2020). "COVID-19: Scotland launches contact tracing app with England and
    Wales to follow." *British Medical Journal*, 370(8260). https://doi.org/10.1136/bmj
    .m3566
Wood, P. (2021, February 21). "Opinion: We need to stop calling it 'NHS' Test and
    Trace." City A.M. www.cityam.com/opinion-we-need-to-stop-calling-it-nhs-test
    -and-trace/
Wymant, C., Ferretti, L., Tsallis, D., Charalambides, M., Abeler-Dörner, L., Bonsall,
    D., Hinch, R., Kendall, M., Milsom, L., Ayres, M., Holmes, C., Briers, M., & Fraser,

C. (2021). "The epidemiological impact of the NHS COVID-19 app." *Nature*, 584, 408–412. www.nature.com/articles/s41586-021-03606-z

Yeung, K. (2020). "Instruments for pandemic governance." In L. Taylor, G. Sharma, A. Martin, & S. Jameson (eds.), *Data Justice and COVID-19: Global Perspectives* (pp. 50–57). Meatspace Press.

Yoneki, E. (2011). "FluPhone study: Virtual disease spread using haggle." *CHANTS '11: Proceedings of the 6th ACM workshop on Challenged networks*, pp. 65–66. https://doi.org/10.1145/2030652.2030672

8. Privacy and pandemic surveillance apps in Latin America

María Soledad Segura

The new needs and problems posed by the advance of the first global coronavirus (COVID-19) pandemic, as well as the exceptional isolation measures adopted in many countries of the world, renewed debates about digital rights in general, and privacy in particular. In addition, these debates have moved from the narrow circle of specialists to the broader realm of social, media, and political discussion. While these new challenges go beyond national borders, they have taken on specific features in each region and country.

Contact tracing is the process of detecting, evaluating, and deciding what to do with individuals exposed to a certain contagious disease in order to prevent the spread of transmission. The response time of governments to an emergency like the current one is vital for the containment and protection of lives. However, the COVID-19 pandemic has overwhelmed the capacity of the teams dedicated to this task. Faced with this, new technical tools were sought to assist in the fight against this infectious disease.

In Latin America, as in other regions of the world, governments adopted measures to use information from mobile phones and their apps to control the spread of COVID-19. As the pandemic has advanced in Latin America, there are discussions concerning the use of personal data for surveillance and population control to monitor the transmission of the virus.

This chapter analyzes strategies, conditions, debates, and disputes about privacy during the advance of the pandemic and the various measures of isolation taken in Latin American countries between March 2020 (when most governments dictated confinement with different levels of restriction) and October 2020 (when this chapter was finished). It addresses the following questions: How is privacy affected by digital technologies that governments implemented during the health emergency in Latin America? How do civil society organizations and international organizations position themselves? What safeguards stand in the way of massive surveillance during the pandemic? What precedents do these strategies—developed in an exceptional context—set for the post-crisis scenario?

I approached these questions from the theoretical perspective of privacy and data protection as fundamental human rights. The information analyzed and evaluated is taken from studies of national and international public organizations as well as from private companies.

My argument is as follows: In Latin America, and probably also in other peripheral countries, the privacy problems aroused by the implementation of COVID-19 apps are not as accentuated as in higher-income countries. Nonetheless, this is not because of the governments' decisions to protect personal data, but because of their restricted capacity for massive technological surveillance. In Latin America, geolocalization and contact tracing technologies for epidemiological surveillance present limitations and risks inherent to the limited technological development in this region of the world (Waisbord & Segura, 2021). In addition, these technologies present another kind of risk linked to political or business objectives and uses, especially within the context and the history of the political and health systems of Latin American countries.

In the following pages, I present the theoretical and methodological approach I used to assess digital COVID apps in various Latin American countries. I describe the apps' features, privacy vulnerabilities, and penetration levels and discuss the reasons why these technologies have had limited use in the region.

THEORETICAL AND METHODOLOGICAL APPROACH

In general, as I have written elsewhere,

> digital rights imply the protection and realization of existing rights, such as the right to privacy, access to information, or freedom of expression in the context of new digital and connectivity technologies. They are the rights to access, use, create, and publish by digital means as well as access, use, manufacture, and manage electronic devices and telecommunications networks. (Segura & Bizberge, 2021, p. 122)

In particular, the civil right to privacy is asserted against the control of states and the commercial use of personal data: digital surveillance is linked to the cost-free use of behavioral data, partly to improve products or services, but also to anticipate and control what people will do in the future (Zuboff, 2019, p. 8). The definitions of privacy as human rights used here are those of multilateral organizations, especially the Organization of American States (OAS) and the United Nations (UN). International human rights standards overcome the statist and mercantilist approaches, because these standards seek to curb the power of both the market and the state (Segura & Waisbord, 2016, p. 58).

The principle of progressiveness for the protection of human rights is enshrined in the American Convention on Human Rights (ACHR), in the Universal Declaration of Human Rights, and in documents of the Inter-American Commission on Human Rights (IACHR, 2020) of the OAS. This principle establishes that states must guarantee, at the national and international level, the exercise of the rights recognized in the Universal Declaration of Human Rights (1948). Progressiveness refers to the implementation of measures to achieve the effectiveness of these rights. It also "implies its opposite, non-regressiveness, which prevents States from adopting measures that worsen the situation of rights enjoyed by the population" (Segura & Bizberge, 2021, p. 123).

For this study, I conducted a comparative analysis of the adopted public app policies using a theoretical-normative approach to the implications in terms of progression or regression of rights according to the international standards mentioned above. I also analyzed the causal factors that explain the impact of these apps and the policy dilemmas presented in this context.

This study draws on public documents, regulations, declarations, and recommendations from international organizations, as well as articles from the mass media and specialized press. The information collected by national governments, international organizations, and private companies is evaluated in relation to human rights standards.

APP CHARACTERISTICS

In 2020, Latin America turned into an epicenter of the COVID-19 pandemic. Most Latin American countries deployed digital technologies to control the transmission of the virus. Civic and academic initiatives offered their expertise. In countries such as Argentina, public universities offered to help develop COVID apps (Segura & Bizberge, 2021, pp. 126–127). Surveillance technology companies such as the NSO Group saw a huge business opportunity. As was recently revealed in Mexico and Guatemala, the governments had used the company's technologies to spy on journalists and activists in the region (Rodríguez, 2018). Fourteen governments—those of Argentina, Uruguay, Chile, Brazil, Paraguay, Bolivia, Peru, Ecuador, Colombia, Panama, Costa Rica, Honduras, Guatemala, and Mexico—collaborated with national (e.g., Argentina) or transnational (e.g., Uruguay) private companies and universities to set up mobile apps (Economic Commission for Latin America and the Caribbean [ECLAC], 2020, p. 13; International Association of Privacy Professionals [IAPP], 2020; Mejía, 2020). As in many other countries of the world, digital technologies appeared as magical and essential instruments to control the spread of the virus. Techno-optimism had returned.

Most of the apps implemented nationally by the governments include information and prevention features such as auto-test systems, information and maps to prevent infections and directions to follow during quarantine, and for confirmed or suspected infections, official data and maps about the COVID-19 situation in the country (ECLAC, 2020, p. 13; IAPP, 2020).

A third of the 14 national mobile apps are of two types that are sometimes combined: geolocation and contact tracing (ECLAC, 2020, p. 13; IAPP, 2020). They are used to locate people who are possibly infected or to track people with whom a symptomatic person may have had contact. Five of the apps have geolocalization, and four of them perform contact tracing by Bluetooth and require contact information (ECLAC, 2020; IAPP, 2020).

In addition, some of the national apps present distinctive features. The Chilean CoronApp and the Mexican COVID-19MX allow monitoring of the symptoms of select individuals (such as family members; IAPP, 2020). The Ecuadorian SaludEC, CovidEC, and Así Ecuador and the Peruvian PerúEnTusManos schedule medical appointments (ECLAC, 2020, p. 13). The Argentine CuidAr and the Colombian CoronApp provide a "permission to circulate" function while circulation is restricted during quarantine. At the beginning of the pandemic, the Argentine app was also implemented to monitor compliance with the mandatory quarantine for those who arrived in the country from abroad (Dirección Nacional de Migraciones, 2020; ECLAC, 2020, pp. 12–13, 17). The Chilean CoronApp allows users to report risky conduct by others (IAPP, 2020). The Panamanian Protégete has a bot called ROSA that makes a pre-diagnosis and can connect with a medical call center (IAPP, 2020).

Every app is voluntary and asks for informed consent. No app is mandatory for users. Nonetheless, most of the privacy policies are not clear about who has access to the data, how they obtain it, or for how long access to the collected data lasts, as well as the anonymization technique or for how long the information will be stored. Even worse, the apps of Guatemala and Paraguay—the countries that do not have personal data protection laws—do not have any privacy policies (IAPP, 2020). In addition, the Brazilian Coronavírus SUS received criticism from civil society organizations that raised issues of transparency and security, and to a lesser extent, consent (Gomes et al., 2020).

There are two models of information storage with different epidemiological and privacy implications. Some of the proposed protocols and apps in the region, such as the Argentine one, store all user data on government servers, which perform the data analytics and contact tracing (Zastrow, 2020). Advocates of this "centralized" approach explain that it "allows health authorities to use the database to piece together a view of the network of contacts, enabling further epidemiological insights such as revealing clusters and superspreaders" (Zastrow, 2020). However, with these additional insights come higher risks. As Zastrow writes, "If the database is hacked, the anonymity provided by rotating pseudonyms is nullified, and individuals can be more easily tracked." Experts worry about the inevitability of state surveillance and the likelihood of a data breach.

In contrast, other Latin American countries, like Uruguay, use the platform launched on April 10, 2020, by Apple and Google, for apps to allow effective Bluetooth-driven contact tracing (Zastrow, 2020; Ministerio de Salud Pública, 2020). The companies altered the operating system of their respective phones, iPhones and Androids, to allow app developers battery-efficient and continuous access to Bluetooth. In response to privacy concerns raised by the collection of large amounts of personal data in databases, Apple and Google emphasized that their new platform spearheaded an international effort to "decentralize" contact tracing efforts (Criddle & Kelion, 2020). To better protect users' privacy and data, Apple and Google announced that any and all data collected by tracing apps built on their platform would be kept on the user's individual phone instead of in a central database (Criddle & Kelion, 2020; Apple & Google, 2021, p. 1).

On the side of good data protection practices, the Argentine app has anonymous and optional geolocalization, and its code is open source (Repositorio oficial del Gobierno de la República Argentina, 2020). These improvements were made after civil society organizations raised concerns about how the use of personal data, especially geolocalization, could endanger the privacy of the population (Muro, 2020). Digital rights organizations argued that the purpose of the app was not clear, since it generated uncertainty about what other functions it might include in the future. At first the code was private. Then the government became receptive to critics and implemented adjustments to the app such as opening the source code, making geolocalization optional, and restricting storage of the data to the duration of the pandemic (Infobae, 2020).

On other side, that is, of poor data protection practices, the Guatemalan app Alerta Guate leaked data, leading many people to uninstall it, and now it is no longer available to download for Apple or Android (IAPP, 2020). These differences in app security levels show that the technology is not inherently bad, but it requires high design standards to meet the aim of controlling the pandemic while not violating the right to privacy.

CONCERNS ABOUT SURVEILLANCE

These problems have predictably raised concerns about the negative impact of massive surveillance, especially in a region where police, military, and intelligence services have historically developed technologies to control populations, as I have written elsewhere (Segura & Bizberge, 2021; Waisbord & Segura, 2021, p. 30). The Rapporteurs for Freedom of Expression of the UN, the OAS, and the European Union asked governments to limit the use of surveillance technologies for tracking the spread of the virus. The IACHR (2020) also recommended the preservation of privacy and the protection of personal data of patients and individuals who are examined during the pandemic (p. 15).

In addition, to ensure that implemented digital technologies respect human rights, regional civil societies have urged governments to limit the use of surveillance technologies that track the spread of the virus. The coalition of Latin American civil society organizations, Al Sur, and more than 100 organizations around the world urged governments to ensure that the development of digital technologies that use sensitive data and location information in this context respect human rights (Derechos Digitales, 2020; Amnesty International, 2020). As I have written elsewhere,

> Such organizations also alerted about the possible irreversibility of measures implemented during the pandemic. The regional organization Derechos Digitales warns that the use of these technologies poses countless doubts: "how the information will be anonymized and aggregated so as not to identify individuals, who has access to the information, how it will be used (and in contrast to what other data), for how long and under what conditions it will be stored, etc. … (while) its usefulness in relation to its penetration levels, meanwhile, are still a mystery." (Segura & Bizberge, 2021, p. 135, quoting Lara, 2020, para. 4)

Moreover, some national governmental agencies also expressed their concerns. Cases like the Brazilian one demonstrate that government administrations are not monolithic and that there are internal disputes.

> Once the Brazilian press released information on projects for the collection and digital processing of mobility data of users of telecommunications services for health and security purposes, Agência Nacional de Telecomunicações … warned that this must be subject to current legislation and, above all, to the Federal Constitution. It pointed out as well that "the balance of protection between health and privacy is at the highest level of our normative hierarchy"; and that even in the current crisis, "reconciling both legal rights" is possible. … The agency also argued that, since individual rights can be affected, the "proportionality" of the judgment, the cost-benefit relationship, the possibility of less invasive alternatives and individual consensus must be observed. (Segura & Bizberge, 2021, p. 134, quoting Agência Nacional de Telecomunicações [Anatel], 2020, para. 3)

IMPACT OF COVID-19 APPS

Nonetheless, these digital technologies have had weak impact. Initially, specialists said that to provide significant results, an app should be adopted by at least 60% of the population. Recent analyses have concluded that an app is useful even with much lower levels of adoption, but the adoption rate should still be significant (Cerrato et al., 2020, p. 12).

As of October 2020, the most popular digital COVID-19 apps in Latin America were the Brazilian and the Argentine apps, downloaded by more than five million people, followed by the Colombian app, downloaded by more than three million people. The apps from Peru, Mexico, and Ecuador were downloaded by fewer than one million people, and other apps were downloaded by fewer than 100,000 people (Pasquali, 2020). Comparing the downloads of these apps and the number of cell phones available in each country (Turner, 2021), the Argentine app has the most use (14% of cell phone owners), followed by the Colombian app (5% usage), and the Brazilian app (4% usage). Given that the penetration of app usage is not significant, the apps' usefulness to control the pandemic is extremely limited.

Why are the Latin American COVID-19 apps rarely used? As I have written elsewhere, institutional, technological, and sociological problems discourage their widespread use (Waisbord & Segura, 2021, pp. 29–30). The collection and use of personal data depends on several factors: the objective of governments; their order or disorder; their transparency with citizens when taking, using, and analyzing information; the functionality of the app (while setting it up is relatively easy, sustaining it is not); and the state of the epidemiological surveillance system by country (without functional systems, an app cannot solve anything—or worse, it could cause unexpected privacy problems).

In general, in comparison with core countries, there is a state incapacity thanks to economic precariousness, little technological training, and a bureaucracy without experience or expertise in collecting and processing large amounts of data (Segura & Waisbord, 2019, p. 417; Waisbord & Segura, 2021, p. 29). In addition, in some countries, there is a lack of interest in public health (as in Brazil or Nicaragua), a lack of interest in conducting epidemiological research and recording data on sick and deceased people (as in Peru), or at least, a greater interest in investing resources in controlling opponents than in public health (such as in Mexico or Guatemala, which as noted earlier, have used spyware on opponents).

REASONS FOR LIMITED APP USE

First, most national health systems in Latin America suffer severe deficits. They historically underserve large swathes of the population and are underfunded and inequitable. They also lack effective administrative systems to set up, conduct, and maintain health monitoring on a massive scale. As I have written previously, "The spotty record of health systems in the region in responding to dengue, zika, chagas and other infectious disease outbreaks in recent years" indicates that state limitations are not conducive to deploying widespread digital-based monitoring and interventions (Waisbord & Segura, 2021, p. 31). In fact, the Brazilian president, Jair Bolsonaro,

> rescinded an agreement between telecommunication companies and the Ministry of Science, Technology, Innovation and Communication that was intended to provide information on mobile phones related to geographic location and mobilization. The decision was more connected with a reckless policy regarding the pandemic than to the protection of personal data. However, state authorities have the power to implement them. (Lara, 2020, as cited in Segura & Bizberge, 2021, p. 134)

Second, as stated above, digital technologies do not provide significant results without high adoption rates for cell phone contact tracing and geolocalization apps. But app adoption has been limited and restricted because of technological limitations of the apps themselves, and because of the unequal access to technology in the region.

The apps have several technical limitations. For apps that locate where people's cell phones are, the phone's GPS does not provide the location with precision in closed environments, because it cannot correctly distinguish between floors in the same building. Meanwhile, the contact tracing system measures the proximity between cell phones that people carry by sensing the strength of the Bluetooth signal. These apps are not sufficiently accurate. They have technical limitations that give false positives and false negatives, the risk for privacy is great, and their functions must necessarily be complemented with intensive groundwork by social or health workers. Therefore, the benefits are not as high as the costs (see, e.g., Haskins et al., 2020).

Furthermore, in Latin American countries, contact tracing technologies are even less useful thanks to the limited technological development in the region. The availability of high-end cell phone equipment with Bluetooth and GPS in the region is limited, and the infrastructure of cell coverage is unevenly distributed.

Besides, although 89% of Latin Americans own a cell phone (Latinobarómetro, 2018, p. 76), most use prepaid plans, which offer the most expensive and lowest-quality service (the higher-quality subscription services are less expensive overall but require regular payments). In some cases, to overcome the limitations due to the costs of the technology use, the national regulatory authority on telecommunications made agreements with mobile operators. In Brazil, for example, the Coronavírus SUS app does not use consumers' data (Segura & Bizberge, 2021, p. 132). In addition, consumers in Mexico, Argentina, Brazil, Colombia, and Venezuela often complain about poor-quality cellular services (Pardo, 2013). Moreover, many health apps use considerable battery power and memory space, which would reduce people's willingness to use them (Waisbord & Segura, 2021, p. 31).

The availability of technology, the level of battery consumption required, and the willingness of people to use it (download the app, open it, and have Bluetooth turned on all the time) are key conditions to reaching a high rate of adoption and providing significant results (Schapachnik, 2020).

Finally, app malfunctions during the launch of COVID-19 apps in several countries have discouraged people from using them. Because of poor design, the apps had many vulnerabilities. This was the case, for example, in Guatemala, as discussed earlier. Because of the limited technological training of software developers, apps with many vulnerabilities are produced, as happened in the Argentine provinces of San Juan, where all the identity documents of Argentine citizens were leaked (including the authentication factor processing code and photo), and Buenos Aires, where it was possible to access citizens' dates of birth and addresses (see, e.g., Bischoff, 2020). The massive data breaches that these vulnerabilities allow are exploitable by private actors with commercial interests.

Therefore, governments in the region face significant problems when launching and maintaining large-scale digital surveillance apparatuses to contain the pandemic. The main reasons are not a "firm official commitment to protecting personal data or balancing public health objectives and democratic rights," but a "poor reach and limited effectiveness of digital and mobile technologies, as well as the inability of the Latin American state to govern and provision health services" (Waisbord & Segura, 2021, pp. 29–30).

CONCLUSIONS

In summary, in Latin America, as in other areas of the world, governments have adopted measures to use information from mobile phones and their apps to control the spread of COVID-19, but human rights are not always protected to a satisfactory extent. There are doubts about whether these pandemic surveillance measures are absolutely necessary. Less-intrusive methodologies, such as human contact tracing, have been successful at preventing the spread of other infectious diseases around the world. Moreover, it is unclear whether these measures can be discontinued once the exceptional situation has ended, and it is not clear that they will achieve the expected results.

In Latin America during the COVID-19 pandemic thus far, there have been no developments or implementations of mass control and surveillance technologies of the population for health reasons. This is so not because governments are interested in protecting the personal data and privacy of the population, even when this ends up being the consequence. The obstacle is not a strong culture of privacy and data protection, but rather problems in government agencies to ensure that health systems have ample and quality coverage, coupled with disproportionate commitments to addressing the pandemic. It is better that this is the case, given the older history (of dictatorships and civil wars) and more recent history (of espionage and persecution of social and political leaders) of the authoritarian and repressive states in the region.

In situations of emergency and risk, exceptional measures can set adverse precedents, such as surveillance practices. However, these measures also provide the opportunity to build progressive, viable, and sustainable alternatives. The crisis is also fertile ground for debating digital rights from a participatory approach that considers inputs from all the players involved with a much broader social scope, and to extend these debates from the specialists' circle to social, media, and political discussions. It is up to social activism, the cooperation of private companies, and state decisions to transform this unfortunate situation into a window of opportunity to guarantee and exercise broader and better rights.

REFERENCES

Agência Nacional de Telecomunicações. (2020, April 15). "Posicionamento da Anatel a respeito da utilização de rastreamento de usuários de telecomunicações no âmbito de medidas no combate à pandemia de Covid-19" [Anatel's position regarding the use of tracking of telecommunications users within the scope of measures to combat the Covid-19 pandemic]. www.gov.br/anatel/pt-br/assuntos/noticias/ posicionamento-da-anatel-a-respeito-da-utilizacao-de-rastreamento-de-usuarios-de -telecomunicacoes-no-ambito-de-medidas-no-combate-a-pandemia-de-covid-19

Amnesty International. (2020, April 2). "Digital surveillance to fight COVID-19 can only be justified if it respects human rights." www.amnesty.org/en/latest/news/2020/ 04/covid19-digital-surveillance-ngo/

Apple & Google. (2021, April). "Exposure Notification Privacy-preserving Analytics" (ENPA) [White Paper]. https://covid19-static.cdn-apple.com/applications/covid19/ current/static/contact-tracing/pdf/ENPA_White_Paper.pdf

Bischoff, P. (2002, July 30). "Argentina health officials expose personal data on 115,000 COVID-19 quarantine exemption applicants." Comparitech. www.comparitech .com/blog/information-security/argentina-covid-permit-data-leak/

Cerrato, I., D'Agostino, M., Galdon Clavell, G., Pombo, C., & Tejerina, L. (2020, December). "Tecnologías digitales para la notificación de exposición en época de pandemia" [Digital technologies for exposure notifications in times of pandemic]. Inter-American Development Bank. https://publications.iadb.org/publications/ spanish/document/Tecnologias-digitales-para-la-notificacion-de-exposicion-en -epoca-de-pandemia.pdf

Criddle, C., & Kelion, L. (2020, May 7). "Coronavirus contact-tracing: World split between two types of app." BBC. www.bbc.com/news/technology-52355028

Derechos Digitales. (2020, March 19). "Civil society from Latin America and the Caribbean demands to respect human rights when governments deploy digital technologies to fight against COVID-19." www.derechosdigitales.org/14301/civil -society-from-latin-america-and-the-caribbean-demands-to-respect-human-rights -when-governments-deploy-digital-technologies-to-fight-against-covid-19/

Dirección Nacional de Migraciones. (2020, September 7). "Medidas vigentes para el ingreso y el egreso al territorio nacional" [Measures in force for entry and exit

to the national territory]. Ministerio del Interior. www.argentina.gob.ar/interior/
migraciones/ddjj-migraciones

Economic Commission for Latin America and the Caribbean (ECLAC). (2020, August
26). "Universalizar el acceso a las tecnologías digitales para enfrentar los efectos
del COVID-19" [Universalizing access to digital technologies to address the consequences of COVID-19]. United Nations Economic and Social Council. https://
repositorio.cepal.org/bitstream/handle/11362/45938/4/S2000550_es.pdf

Gomes, A., Luciano, M., Fragoso, N., & Pavarin V. (2020, April 30). "COVID-19:
Apps do governo e seus riscos à privacidade" [COVID-19: Government apps
and their privacy risks]. InternetLab. www.internetlab.org.br/pt/privacidade-e
-vigilancia/covid-19-apps-do-governo-e-seus-riscos/

Haskins, C., Lee, S. M., Rajagopalan, M., & Dixit, P. (2020, April 29). "We need an
'army' of contact tracers to safely reopen the country. We might get apps instead."
Buzzfeed   News.   www.buzzfeednews.com/article/carolinehaskins1/coronavirus
-contact-tracing-google-apple

Infobae. (2020, May 16). "Coronavirus en Argentina: El Gobierno modificará la
app CuidAR para reforzar la protección de los datos personales" [Coronavirus in
Argentina: The government will modify the CuidAR app to reinforce the protection
of personal data]. www.infobae.com/politica/2020/05/16/coronavirus-en-argentina
-el-gobierno-modificara-la-app-cuidar-para-reforzar-la-proteccion-de-los-datos
-personales/

Inter-American Commission on Human Rights. (2020) "Pandemia y derechos humanos
en las Américas" [Pandemic and human rights in the Americas]. Organization of
American States. www.oas.org/es/cidh/decisiones/pdf/Resolucion-1-20-es.pdf

International Association of Privacy Professionals. (2020, June 3). "Algunas apli-
caciones que están siendo utilizadas en América Latina para tratar de controlar
la propagación del Covid-19" [Some applications that are being used in Latin
America to try to control the spread of COVID-19]. https://iapp.org/news/a/
algunas-aplicaciones-que-estan-siendo-utilizadas-en-america-latina-para-tratar-de
-controlar-la-propagacion-del-covid-19/

Lara, C. (2020, May 1). "La pandemia de COVID-19 y la pulsión por la vigilancia
estatal" [The COVID-19 pandemic and the drive for state surveillance]. Derechos
Digitales. www.derechosdigitales.org/14411/la-pandemia-de-covid-19-y-la-pulsion
-por-la-vigilancia-estatal/

Latinobarómetro.   (2018).   "Informe   2018."   www.latinobarometro.org/latdocs/
INFORME_2018_LATINOBAROMETRO.pdf

Mejía, A. (2020, May 22) "Polémica por app para Covid-19 que según sectores vulnera
privacidad" [Controversy over app for Covid-19 that according to sectors violates
privacy]. *El Heraldo.* www.elheraldo.hn/pais/1381469-466/polémica-por-app-para
-covid-19-que-según-sectores-vulnera-privacidad

Ministerio de Salud Pública. (2020, June 15). "Información sobre la aplicación
Coronavirus UY" [Information on the Coronavirus UY app]. www.gub.uy/ministerio
-salud-publica/politicas-y-gestion/informacion-sobre-aplicacion-coronavirus

Muro, V. (2020, May 11). "App CuidAR: Los expertos piden cambios y más control
sobre el destino de los datos" [CuidAR app: Experts ask for changes and more control
over the destination of the data]. *La Nación.* www.lanacion.com.ar/tecnologia/app
-cuidar-expertos-reclaman-cambios-mas-controles-nid2364104

Pardo, D. (2013, July 1). "Por qué los latinoamericanos se quejan tanto de los celulares"
(Why do Latin Americans complain so much about cell phones). BBC. www.bbc

.com/mundo/noticias/2013/07/130701_tecnologia_celulares_latinoamerica_quejas
_dp

Pasquali, M. (2020, September 24). "Las apps de movilidad aliadas en la lucha contra el coronavirus en Latinoamérica" [Mobility apps, allies in the fight against coronavirus in Latin America]. Statista. https://es.statista.com/grafico/23026/apps-de-covid-19 -mas-descargadas-en-latinoamerica/

Repositorio oficial del Gobierno de la República Argentina (Argob). (2020, September 30). "Cuidar Android." https://github.com/argob/cuidar-android

Rodríguez, K. (2018, December 30). "Where governments hack their own people and people fight back: 2018 in review." Electronic Frontier Foundation. www.eff.org/ es/deeplinks/2018/12/where-government-hack-their-own-people-and-people-fight -back-latin-american

Schapachnik, F. (2020, May 8). "Apps para contact tracing, ¿ahora?" [Apps for contact tracing, now?]. Medium. https://medium.com/@fernando_36842

Segura, M. S., & Bizberge, A. (2021). "Direitos digitais durante a pandemia de Covid-19 na América Latina" [Digital rights during the COVID-19 pandemic in Latin America]. *Comunicação e Sociedade*, 39, 119–144. https://doi.org/10.17231/ comsoc.39(2021).2852

Segura, M. S., & Waisbord, S. (2016). *Media Movements: Civil Society and Media Policy Reform in Latin America.* Zed Books.

Segura, M. S., & Waisbord, S. (2019). "Between data capitalism and data citizenship." *Television & New Media*, 20(4), 1–8. https://doi.org/10.1177%2F1527476419834519

Turner, A. (2021, July). "How many smartphones are in the world?" BankMyCell. www.bankmycell.com/blog/how-many-phones-are-in-the-world#sources

Waisbord, S., & Segura, M. S. (2021). "COVID-19 pandemic and biopolitics in Latin America." In S. Milan, E. Treré, & S. Masiero (eds.), *COVID-19 from the Margins: Pandemic Invisibilities, Policies and Resistance in the Datafied Society* (pp. 29–32). Institute of Network Cultures. https://networkcultures.org/blog/publication/covid-19 -from-the-margins-pandemic-invisibilities-policies-and-resistance-in-the-datafied -society/

Zastrow, M. (2020, May 19). "Coronavirus contact-tracing apps: Can they slow the spread of COVID-19?" *Nature.* https://doi.org/10.1038/d41586-020-01514-2

Zuboff, S. (2019). *The Age of Surveillance Capitalism: The Fight for a Human Future at the New Frontier of Power.* PublicAffairs.

9. Implementing effective digital privacy policy: the road ahead in post-pandemic times

Stuart N. Brotman

THE PANDEMIC EXPERIENCE

In the United States, the sudden nationwide lockdown in March 2020 due to COVID-19 brought dramatic changes in how we work, live, and interact with digital media. Although there will be no certain date when the pandemic finally ends conclusively, there seems to be a growing consensus that the United States was entering a post-pandemic period in 2021.

COVID-19 has had a profound impact on the central role of digital media in our everyday lives. According to the research firm NPD (2021), between February 2020 and February 2021, an additional 100 million TV-connected and mobile devices were installed in U.S. households. Internet-connected homes averaged 9.5 networked digital devices in February 2021, compared to an average of 8.5 devices just before the pandemic became widespread in the United States (NPD, 2021).

The range of these digital devices in homes is broad, from internet-connected televisions to streaming media players to laptops, tablets, and smartphones. As Bill Demas, CEO of the streaming media intelligence company Conviva, noted, "The way consumers view content fundamentally changed in 2020 with the launch of smart TVs and connected devices and changing social behavior" ("Conviva Q4 2020 Data," 2021).

Smartphones in particular have emerged as ubiquitous digital devices. According to Edison Research (2021), 85% of Americans aged 12 and older own a smartphone. Additionally, data from Global Wireless Solutions (2021) indicate that daily smartphone use averaged four hours a day during COVID-19, an increase of ten minutes per day compared to before the pandemic.

There has also been an increased reliance on digital devices for both professional and personal use. WARC, an international marketing intelligence service, reports that digital media consumption rose by over 30% during the pandemic (Clapp, 2021). And as many workplaces shifted online, many workers recouped time once spent commuting. According to MIDiA Research, "overall consumption time [went] up by 12%," including consumption of digital entertainment by the average working consumer (Mulligan, 2021).

Notably, the increase in ecommerce transactions and personal data shared with streaming media and other digital service providers during the pandemic also heightened consumer concerns over how their personal data is stored and shared. A 2020 survey of U.S. consumers by KPMG found that data privacy is important to 97% of respondents, and that 56% want more control over their personal data.

There are real gaps in digital trust, too. According to the KMPG survey, more than 90% want companies to establish data privacy guidelines and be held responsible for corporate data breaches. The majority also don't trust companies to ethically handle the sale of personal data (68%), or even to ethically use personal data internally (54%; KMPG, 2020).

PANDEMIC SURVEILLANCE PERSPECTIVES

The pandemic created public health demands for COVID tracking. Digital technologies were seen as critical to stop the spread of the virus. There was an urgency to understand the greater potential and need for data to be collected and shared by private internet and telecommunications companies. Such data was seen as invaluable to government agencies involved in public health planning and implementation during the pandemic.

Other democratic countries, such as Israel, established government orders requiring companies to provide location tracking and to turn data over for public health analysis. The United States did not pursue this course. Rather, it remained in active discussions regarding why and how such data could and should be made available to relevant government agencies.

Despite expectations formed early in the pandemic, cooperation between the public and private sectors has not always been strong. Even with strong government pressure, major companies that collected this information and developed exposure-tracking processes, particularly as seen in the collaboration between Google and Apple, were wary of providing full access to consumer data, even if doing so would be more efficacious in slowing the pandemic (Scott et al., 2020).

That's why the pandemic created a key opportunity for the government and the private sector to develop clear transparency rules for such data transfers. Transparency in general is a cornerstone for gaining public confidence during such a crisis. This confidence eroded when individuals felt that the nation was becoming a surveillance state.

Location-tracking data, while collected individually, has value only if it is compiled in the aggregate so that trends can be mapped in determining public health recommendations and outcomes. This has already been useful in collecting cell tower pings in Kenya to predict the spread of malaria. In the United States, even more precise ways to track locations based on apps and telecommunications operating systems have been developed and implemented, with varying degrees of success (Smith-Spark, 2012).

But users need to be assured that these aggregate practices do not fall into the category of personally identifiable information, which current and impending privacy laws are intended to protect. Typical users are often unaware of this distinction. As of June 2020, for example, only 29% of Americans planned to use contact tracing apps; the majority who did not cited digital privacy as a primary concern for their hesitancy (Avira, 2020). This placed the burden on the government and the private sector to provide details about the collection and dissemination of anonymous, aggregated data. Similar projects in the future should communicate this clearly and quickly.

As a practical matter, transparency should also include a requirement that companies that provide location-tracking data modify their user agreements, as needed, to reflect this practice. Additionally, these companies and all involved government agencies—whether federal, state, or local—should be required to visibly post these disclosures on websites, apps, and social media.

Digital transparency was important during the pandemic, but it may still require additional measures that have not yet been created in the United States to dissuade bad actors from reverse engineering this aggregated data to discover individual identities for exploitation directly or through third parties (Newlands et al., 2020). This may call for accompanying tighter controls for transferring the data between companies and government agencies, and possible criminal or civil penalties for those involved in malicious reverse engineering.

The emergency circumstances at play required marshaling all resources to help fight the pandemic. Yet even here, informing the public about the limited use of collected digital data for aggregated analysis reflected both good policy and good sense (Brotman, 2020).

THE POST-PANDEMIC DIGITAL NATION

We are now in a historic transition; from a nation organized for pandemic response to a nation organized for recovery that surely will create a "new normal." Kara Swisher (2021), technology columnist for the *New York Times*, noted that "people will surely do more in-person purchasing as the pandemic fades. But online commerce might now be ingrained as a daily practice and innovations related to it are sure to make it even more powerful."

Post pandemic, digital media writ large will be shaped by larger social forces. What the "new normal" work environment will look like is at the top of the mind for many Americans. This will influence digital media habits, including how much and how frequently consumers will provide personally identifiable information online.

Microsoft CEO Satya Nadella observed, "Over the past year, no area has undergone more rapid transformation than the way we work. Employee expectations are changing, and we will need to define productivity much more broadly. ... This needs to be done with flexibility in when, where, and how people work" (Microsoft, 2021, p. 4).

From an employer perspective, data shows that this new normal will take hold. In a 2021 survey by ResetWork, of respondents who had finalized their post-pandemic workplace models, 86% plan to adopt a hybrid model of a home/office mix (pp. 4–5). Less than 6% expect employees to revert to a traditional five days in the office workweek (pp. 4–5).

Further, Microsoft's 2021 "Work Trend Index" notes, "Employees are at an inflection point. The way companies approach the next phase of work— embracing the flexibility people want to retain and learning from the challenges of the past year—will impact who stays, who goes, and who ultimately seeks to join your company" (p. 22).

McKinsey Global Institute (2021) has concluded that 20–25% of the workforce in advanced economies could work remotely three to five days a week as effectively as in the office. This data may perhaps apply even more so to digital media companies, because many of their employees have the ability to work remotely and may in fact prefer a more flexible work environment between home and office.

Microsoft's perspective may set the standard for corporate America. "The data is clear. Extreme flexibility and hybrid work will define the post-pandemic workplace. The decisions business leaders make in the coming months to enable flexible work will impact everything from culture and innovation to how organizations attract and retain top talent" (Microsoft, 2021, p. 4).

Already, for example, GM has announced that it will give its 155,000 global office-based employees the flexibility to choose between working from home or in the office (Wayland, 2021). And from the perspective of employees, a February 2021 Gallup survey showed that 23% of U.S. workers prefer working remotely some or all of the time (Saad & Hickman, 2021).

Put simply, we can expect that remote work will be the norm rather than an exception for the foreseeable future. The blurred lines between home and work use of digital devices in residential settings will persist. This will perpetuate the habit of consumers providing their personally identifiable information to a wide range of commercial providers, who in turn will have various levels of digital privacy protection in place—often with little or no government guidance or oversight.

ROUTES FOR POST-PANDEMIC GOVERNMENT DIGITAL PRIVACY POLICY INITIATIVES

The Biden administration's legislative agenda for post-pandemic voting rights, infrastructure, immigration reform, and job creation in advance of the election of the 118th Congress in 2022 makes it unlikely that there will be any White House initiative to advance comprehensive privacy legislation before 2023, if at all (Levine, 2021). This would follow the record of inaction in this area during President Trump's four years in office (McCabe, 2019; McIntosh, 2020).

It is also possible that the Republicans could gain control of the House of Representatives in the 2022 election. Additionally, there may be some or no action regarding reform because of the filibuster rules in the U.S. Senate, which make it difficult for any legislation to receive the necessary 60 votes. This is very difficult to accomplish under the current 50-50 party split in the Senate (Montanaro, 2021). The continuing lack of a bipartisan consensus on privacy legislation reflects the continuing political division on both sides of the aisle, which is another formidable barrier to any federal privacy legislation gaining momentum (Fazlioglu, 2019).

Another barrier was demonstrated by the 116th Congress, which had a lot of legislative activity but no resolution in the area of digital privacy protection (McCabe, 2019). The Democrats and Republicans separately drafted multiple pieces of legislation rather than bipartisan bills aimed at achieving a successful consensus (Gaffney, 2020, p. 1).

Although the 117th Congress has at last produced significant draft bipartisan legislation that bridges current political divides, as of June 2022, nothing has been passed by either the House of Representatives or the Senate. The short legislative calendar leading up to the 2022 midterm elections, along with no legislative push from the White House, suggests that this promising development will not result in any federal law being enacted during this congressional session.

Moreover, on a policy level, two continuing issues can be characterized as major sticking points that would need to be resolved in order to break the current political stalemate. The first sticking point is federal preemption—whether and how any federal digital privacy law would override any current or future state law. This issue is especially important after November 2020, when California voters went to the ballot box to enact Proposition 24, the California Privacy Rights Act (Lazzarotti et al., 2020).

This new law will essentially strengthen the extant California Consumer Privacy Act, which took effect on January 1, 2020 (Lazzarotti et al., 2020). As a ballot measure, the California Privacy Rights Act cannot be rescinded or repealed by statute, which means that the bar on digital privacy protection in California has been raised (Cal. Const. art. II, § 10). Furthermore, it likely will be more difficult for the federal government to step in and say, "We're going to ignore the will of millions of voters in California" by enacting a new federal law that overrides, but is less robust than, the state law. As explained by Xavier Becerra (2020), then attorney general of California, "I am optimistic Congress will be able to craft a proposal ... looking to state law as providing a floor for privacy protections, rather than a ceiling."

The second sticking point is whether federal law should permit or prohibit private rights of action against digital privacy violators (Kerry & Morris, 2020). Recent years have seen a lot of litigation in this area, leading to large monetary damages awards that companies seek to avoid in the future by vesting enforcement authority solely with the federal government (Stegmaier & Fisher, 2020; Geetter & Zacharias, 2020). The Republicans support this approach—namely, that enforcement by the Federal Trade Commission with expanded legal authority would be sufficient.

In contrast, the Democrats argue that the possibility of civil lawsuits adds an extra layer of deterrence and can thus serve as an incentive for full compliance. The history of private rights of action that are permitted under the federal antitrust laws supports their argument for a "belt and suspenders" approach. Additionally, in an era of tight or shrinking federal budgets, there is no assurance that government enforcement alone will be provided with the necessary financial resources for investigating and prosecuting multiple digital privacy law violations.

Yet even with these unlikely federal prospects, digital privacy protection is a significant concern at the state legislative level in post-pandemic times. As of June 2022, only California, as noted, and more recently Virginia, Colorado, Utah, and Connecticut have enacted state privacy legislation. Several other states had active privacy bills under consideration during the prior year: Alabama, Alaska, Illinois, Massachusetts, Minnesota, New Jersey, New York, and Texas (Rippy, 2021).

The significant number of these states and their aggregate populations represent another political obstacle for federal privacy legislation. If all the bills under consideration as of June 2021 were enacted, over 130 million Americans would be covered by state privacy legislation. If Congress moved ahead to preempt those state privacy legislative actions, especially with less stringent federal requirements, it would surely generate enormous political blowback for elected officials in Washington, D.C.

On the other hand, at least ten states introduced privacy bills that did not gain necessary legislative traction, including Arizona, Florida, Kentucky, Maryland, Mississippi, North Dakota, Oklahoma, Utah, Washington, and West Virginia (Rippy, 2021). These failed attempts advance the argument that state legislators are unwilling or unable to act unless they receive a strong signal about whether the federal government intends to assert its preemption authority for digital privacy protection.

Digital companies also continue to argue that a fully federal approach would obviate a crazy-quilt situation where compliance is structured state by state rather than nationally (Kang, 2018). After all, digital data is not confined to state geographic borders, so a law that covered the entire United States would better conform to the realities of digital technology.

Viewed broadly, state privacy legislation—whether successful, pending, or unsuccessful—will focus on guaranteeing a set of consumer rights and imposing business obligations for those serving the residents of a particular state.

The consumer rights include (1) a right of access to personally identifiable information; (2) a right of information rectification; (3) a right of deletion; (4) a right of restriction; (5) a right of portability; (6) a right to opt out; (7) a right against automated decision-making; and (8) a private right to pursue civil litigation against violators (Rustad & Koenig, 2019).

Business obligations include (1) establishing age-based rules to require opt-in consent; (2) notice and transparency requirements; (3) mandatory requirements to perform privacy risk assessments; (4) prohibiting discrimination against consumers exercising their privacy rights; and (5) limiting the processing of personal information to specific necessary purposes (Marini et al., 2019; Macenaite & Kosta, 2017, pp. 147–197; Matheson, 2018; Costigan, 2021; California Consumer Privacy Act [CCPA], 2018, § 1798.125; Regulation [EU]) 2016/679, 2016, Art. 5).

The more likely route of state legislative action can also have the benefit that states have often played in other areas—as policy laboratories that are useful for comparative analysis (Volden, 2006, p. 294) and for the White House and Congress when they are in a better political position to exercise federal leadership in this area. Given the dynamic technological forces at play, having states rather than the federal government involved at the outset might provide a necessary time buffer so that federal digital policy better reflects our post-pandemic times as well.

In any event, the post-pandemic digital privacy policy front seems destined to reflect its own sense of a "new normal." There must be both focus and resolve throughout the government to provide workable approaches that enhance digital trust and responsible business practices.

REFERENCES

Avira. (2020). "Majority of Americans say they won't use COVID contact tracing apps." www.avira.com/en/covid-contact-tracing-app-report

Becerra, X. (2020, February 25). "Letter to the Honorable Roger Wicker (R-Miss.), Chairman, US Senate Committee on Commerce, Science, and Transportation, et al., The California Consumer Privacy Act and Federal Privacy Legislation. State of California, Office of the Attorney General." https://oag.ca.gov/system/files/attachments/press-docs/Letter to Congress on CCPA preemption.pdf

Brotman, S. N. (2020, March 25). "Stuart N. Brotman: Thinking about digital privacy protection in pandemic times." *Post-Gazette*. www.post-gazette.com/opinion/Op-Ed/2020/03/25/Stuart-N-Brotman-Thinking-about-digital-privacy-protection-in-pandemic-times/stories/202003250017

Cal. Const. art. II, § 10.

California Consumer Privacy Act of 2018. (2018). https://leginfo.legislature.ca.gov/faces/codes_displayText.xhtml?division=3.&part=4.&lawCode=CIV&title=1.81.5

Clapp, R. (2021, April 30). "COVID-19 causes digital consumption to rise by over 30%, forming new and lasting consumer habits." WARC. www.warc.com/newsandopinion/opinion/covid-19-causes-digital-consumption-to-rise-by-over-30-forming-new-and-lasting-consumer-habits/4209

"Conviva Q4 2020 data caps off momentous year for streaming as smart TV market explodes and big screens dominate." (2021, January 28). BusinessWire. www.businesswire.com/news/home/20210128005280/en/

Costigan, M. T. (2021). "CPRA series: The CPRA and risk assessments." *National Law Review*, 11(123). www.natlawreview.com/article/cpra-series-cpra-and-risk-assessments

Edison Research. (2021, March 11). "The infinite dial 2021." www.edisonresearch.com/the-infinite-dial-2021-2/

Fazlioglu, M. (2019, December 3). "Tracking the politics of US privacy legislation." IAPP. https://iapp.org/news/a/tracking-the-politics-of-federal-us-privacy-legislation/

Gaffney, J. M. (2020, April 3). "Watching the watchers: A comparison of privacy bills in the 116th Congress." Congressional Research Service. https://crsreports.congress.gov/product/pdf/LSB/LSB10441

Geetter, J., & Zacharias, E. (2020, March 31). "Republicans and Democrats introduce competing privacy bills to protect consumers' health information related to the COVID-19 pandemic." JD Supra. www.jdsupra.com/legalnews/republicans-and-democrats-introduce-58345/

Global Wireless Solutions. (2021, March 23). "Gen Z doubles times spent on finance/trading apps during pandemic year; Phone use among all consumers up more than an hour per week led by finance and social media app growth." https://news.gwsolutions.com/2021/03/23/gen-z-doubles-time-spent-on-financetrading-apps-during-pandemic-year-phone-use-among-all-consumers-up-more-than-an-hour-per-week-led-by-finance-and-social-media-app-growth/

Kang, C. (2018, August 26). "Tech companies pursue a federal privacy law, on its own terms." *New York Times*. www.nytimes.com/2018/08/26/technology/tech-industry-federal-privacy-law.html

Kerry, C. F., & Morris, J. B., Jr. (2020, July 7). "In privacy legislation, a private right of action is not an all-or-nothing proposition." Brookings. www.brookings.edu/blog/

techtank/2020/07/07/in-privacy-legislation-a-private-right-of-action-is-not-an-all-or
-nothing-proposition/#cancel

KMPG. (2020, July 29). "KMPG survey: American consumers want more control, visibility into how companies use their personal data." https://home.kpmg/us/en/home/media/press-releases/2020/07/kpmg-survey-american-consumers-want-more-control-visibility-into-how-companies-use-their-personal-data.html

Lazzarotti, J. J., Gavejian, J. C., & Attrakchi, M. (2020, November 5). "California passes Prop 24: Here comes CCPA 2.0." *National Law Review*. www.natlawreview.com/article/california-passes-prop-24-here-comes-ccpa-20

Levine, A. S. (2021, June 1). "A U.S. privacy law seemed possible this Congress. Now, prospects are fading fast." Politico. www.politico.com/news/2021/06/01/washington-plan-protect-american-data-silicon-valley-491405

Macenaite, M., & Kosta, E. (2017). "Consent for processing children's personal data in the EU: Following in US footsteps?" *Information & Communications Technology Law*, 26(2), 146–197.

Marini, A., Kateifides, A., Papageorgiou, N., Bates, J., Ashcroft, V., Zanfir-Fortuna, G., Bae, M., Gray, S., Greenberg, J., & Sen, G. (2019). "Comparing privacy laws: GDPR v. CCPA." Future of Privacy Forum. https://fpf.org/wp-content/uploads/2019/12/ComparingPrivacyLaws_GDPR_CCPA.pdf

Matheson, L. (2018, February 28). "Top operational responses to the GDPR–part 6: Transparency and privacy notice." IAPP. https://iapp.org/news/a/top-10-operational-responses-to-the-gdpr-part-6-transparency-and-privacy-notices/

McCabe, D. (2019, October 1). "Congress and Trump want a national privacy law. It is nowhere in sight." *New York Times*. www.nytimes.com/2019/10/01/technology/national-privacy-law.html

McIntosh, V. (2020, October 21). "Looking at the Trump administration's impact on privacy." Comparitech. www.comparitech.com/blog/vpn-privacy/internet-privacy-trump/

McKinsey Global Institute. (2021, February 18). "The future of work after COVID-19." McKinsey & Company. www.mckinsey.com/featured-insights/future-of-work/the-future-of-work-after-covid-19

Microsoft. (2021, March 22). "2021 Work trend index: Annual report." https://ms-worklab.azureedge.net/files/reports/hybridWork/pdf/2021_Microsoft_WTI_Report_March.pdf

Montanaro, D. (2021, March 20). "The democratic push for filibuster reform." NPR. www.npr.org/2021/03/20/979594965/the-democratic-push-for-filibuster-reform

Mulligan, M. (2021, February 19). "The COVID bounce and the coming attention recession." MIDiA Research. www.midiaresearch.com/blog/the-covid-bounce-and-the-coming-attention-recession

Newlands, G., Lutz, C., Tamò-Larrieux, A., Villaronga, E. F., Harasgama, R., & Scheitlin, G. (2020). "Innovation under pressure: Implications for data privacy during the Covid-19 pandemic." *Big Data & Society*, 7(2). https://doi.org/10.1177/2053951720976680

NPD. (2021, April 26). "U.S. households now have over one billion computers, mobile, and tv-connected devices." www.npd.com/news/press-releases/2021/us-households-now-have-over-one-billion-computers-mobile-and-tv-connected-devices/

Regulation (EU) 2016/679 of the European Parliament and of the Council of 27 April 2016 on the protection of natural persons with regard to the processing of personal data and on the free movement of such data and repealing Directive 95/36/EC (General Data Protection Regulation). 2016 O.J. (L 119). https://gdpr-info.eu/

ResetWork. (2021, April 30). "Survey of return-to-office decision makers highlights uncertain road ahead and need for increased support for managers." www.resetwork .co/return-to-office-survey-results-hybrid-workplace-concerns-managers/

Rippy, S. (2021, June 11). "US state privacy legislation tracker." IAPP. https://iapp .org/resources/article/us-state-privacy-legislation-tracker/

Rustad, M. L., & Koenig, T. H. (2019). "Towards a global data privacy standard." *Florida Law Review*, 71(2), 365–452. https://scholarship.law.ufl.edu/cgi/ viewcontent.cgi?article=1446&context=flr

Saad, L., & Hickman, A. (2021, February 12). "Majority of U.S. workers continue to punch in virtually." Gallup. https://news.gallup.com/poll/329501/majority-workers -continue-punch-virtually.aspx

Scott, M., Braun, E., Delcker, J., & Manancourt, V. (2020, May 15). "How Google and Apple outflanked governments in the race to build coronavirus apps." Politico. www .politico.eu/article/google-apple-coronavirus-app-privacy-uk-france-germany/

Smith-Spark, L. (2012, September 13). "Tracking a killer: Cell phones aid pioneering malaria study in Kenya." CNN. www.cnn.com/2012/10/13/health/kenya-malaria/ index.html

Stegmaier, G. M., & Fisher, C. E. (2020). "Caveat director: Analyzing cybersecurity challenges in corporate governance." *Delaware Law Review*, 38(2), 14–25.

Swisher, K. (2021, April 20). "Tech in the post-pandemic world." *New York Times*. www.nytimes.com/2021/04/20/opinion/tech-covid-future.html

Volden, C. (2006). "States as policy laboratories: Emulating success in the children's health insurance program." *American Journal of Political Science*, 50(2), 294–312. https://doi.org/10.1111/j.1540-5907.2006.00185.x

Wayland, M. (2021, April 20). "GM's new remote work plan for employees is ambiguous, yet surprisingly simple: 'Work appropriately.'" CNBC. www.cnbc.com/2021/ 04/20/gms-simple-message-to-employees-about-return-to-work-work-appropriately .html

10. Tracing the invisible: information fiduciaries and the pandemic

Anne L. Washington and Lauren Rhue

INTRODUCTION

The global pandemic that spread an infectious respiratory disease beginning in 2019 was unlike earlier pandemics (Centers for Disease Control and Prevention [CDC], 2020a; see generally Rosenwald, 2021; Sauer, 2021). Other public health emergencies occurred within a concentrated geographic region (CDC, 2013; CDC, 2020b) or before the digital era (see Rosenwald, 2021). Most importantly, past emergencies rarely impacted Silicon Valley organizations building digital platforms and data technology. Major technology companies turned their attention to data innovations that could help to ameliorate the pandemic (see, e.g., Sato, 2020). The personal experiences of people designing the newest mobile phone technology motivated innovative data solutions; however, this may have obscured the visibility of other populations ("Design bias," 2021).

Interpreting data has been essential to understanding the progression of the deadly pandemic's spread. Daily analysis of the number of cases, hospital capacity, and deaths were part of regular media reports (see Johns Hopkins Coronavirus Resource Center, 2021; see also Farzan et al., 2020). Interest in COVID-19 data was not a matter of idle curiosity; rather, the data directly impacted behavior, and fear of contracting the virus controlled the economy (Barua & Levin, 2020). Everyone eagerly consumed data to grapple with the risk of infection. Conflicting advice and contradictory regulatory guidance across regional and local authorities, coupled with a decentralized federal response, further contributed to the need for data and research across the United States (see Alter & Villa, 2020; Lipton et al., 2020). As fear spread and the economy slowed, businesses (Smialek, 2020), schools (see Natanson & Strauss, 2020), municipalities (see Alter & Villa, 2020), and other organizations were left on their own to combat the pandemic's effects. Many were looking for an easy solution and a savior.

At first glance, the technology industry was an ideal hero for managing public health problems. The industry can deliver solutions at scale and reach millions of people simultaneously. Technological solutions began to surface: websites to triage patients for testing (Verily, 2021; see Wakabayashi & Singer, 2020), mobile device applications ("apps") for contact tracing (see Apple, 2020), and smart medical devices for monitoring symptoms (see, e.g., McNeil, 2020). Readily available mobile phone technology (see Rhue & Sundararajan, 2014) is similar around the globe, and apps can be easily delivered anywhere (see Sato, 2020). The reuse of existing devices solves a critical logistics problem with relatively little effort. The technology industry, which dominates worldwide markets (see generally Ventura, 2020), already has the physical infrastructure to deploy solutions through software and firmware updates to billions of devices (see Harpaz, 2020). Because of the ubiquity of mobile technology, data from consumer devices could easily generate population-level public health statistics.

The benefits of offering solutions at scale come with a cost: a diminished ability to respond to individual experiences and preferences. As much as data collection may contribute to solving public health crises, it may also provoke personal privacy concerns (see Perrigo, 2020). This places the onus on individuals to determine whether they feel comfortable downloading an app or sharing information through digital contact tracing (cf. Timberg et al., 2020). Regulatory systems around sensitive data, outside of the tech industry, generally provide guidelines on maintaining privacy. For example, medical organizations that share health data must protect patient privacy under the Health Insurance Portability and Accountability Act of 1996 (HIPAA). Given the fragmented regulatory structure across industries, however, HIPAA's privacy rules that govern medical organizations do not apply to many tech companies (Tovino, 2020, p. 282).

Considering the great extent to which large companies already reuse data they collect, privacy concerns may hamper widespread use of the tools that these companies provide. It is reasonable to presume that enough individuals would hesitate to opt in, limiting the ultimate usefulness of these tools. If organizations building pandemic data technology were required to act as fiduciaries for this information, then the organizations, not the individuals, would bear the consequences for data misuse (see Scholz, 2020, pp. 144, 145).

This chapter reviews the viability of using mobile technology and data in the COVID-19 pandemic. The technology solutions we discuss include mobile phone call records, smartphone applications, Bluetooth proximity data, and third-party health applications such as smart thermometers. Two primary issues with these technology solutions exist. First, these solutions are based on inaccurate assumptions and thus do not fulfill the technology's intended purpose. Specifically, the solutions rely upon broad participation, but pandemic technology only operates under rigid technical and social conditions that thwart participation from all population groups. Second, the entities behind these technology solutions, including digital technology companies and private hospitals, have financial incentives that are inherent conflicts of interest, which may further compromise public health goals.

More robust solutions are necessary if pandemic technology is to provide the universal coverage that a public health emergency demands. For instance, one privacy-related challenge facing individuals is the perceived infallibility of data organizations' proprietary algorithms, which makes it difficult for individuals to challenge the legality of the use of their data (see Washington, 2019, pp. 133–134, 145). Further complicating this is the "third-party doctrine," which dictates that information shared with a third party is discoverable by law enforcement (Brennan-Marquez, 2015, pp. 614–614). If organizations currently collecting data refuse to exercise a duty of care over the information they collect, then the data steward should be another entity that is able to perform information fiduciary responsibilities (see Borgman, 2018, pp. 370–371, 375). The current technology solutions provide individuals little insight into what happens to their health data and even less recourse if something goes wrong. We consider whether these realities support an alternative policy response.

This chapter evaluates current legal scholarship on the concept of an information fiduciary and argues that it may be a better model for deploying pandemic data technology. We conclude our analysis with tangible policy suggestions, such as conflict-of-interest notices and the creation of new public health information fiduciary organizations that maintain pandemic data, have long-term fiduciary responsibilities, and provide just-in-time access to data for medical or public health reasons.

Data technology could play a vital role in resolving the pandemic if the technology were in the hands of an information fiduciary responsible for gathering accurate information across all populations without penalty. Technology should be part of the public health solution; however, pandemic data technology should not be driven by the desire to reach a niche group of consumers or extend digital business models. Investing in an entity with fiduciary responsibility for pandemic information would support a faster reduction in the spread of the virus. An information fiduciary would limit the reuse of data for purposes beyond public health ones and would be loyal both to individuals and to whole communities, thereby instilling greater confidence in and adoption of data technology solutions to the pandemic.

I   PANDEMIC DATA TECHNOLOGY

During a public health crisis, trust is essential, and those tasked with ameliorating the crisis must earn the trust of millions with life-or-death consequences.

However, large technology companies, colloquially known as Big Tech, have a track record of squandering trust for profit (e.g., Waters, 2019). This pattern of behavior may limit the effectiveness of data technology in lessening the pandemic's spread and diminishing its negative consequences. Given the realities of public health emergencies, the pandemic data technology solutions emerging from Big Tech may not meet their most altruistic goals.

A   The Public Health Crisis

Containing the spread of an infectious disease is always the central goal of fighting a pandemic, and the coronavirus pandemic has been no different. Because a respiratory virus easily transmits between people, understanding who is in contact with whom is important for anticipating future spread and providing early warning to those at risk (CDC, 2020c; see World Health Organization [WHO], 2020). The goal of many non-pharmaceutical interventions ("NPIs"), such as social distancing, is to stop disease spread by reducing contact between infected and non-infected people (CDC, 2019). By acquiring population-level views of positive cases and potential spread, pandemic data technology seeks to illuminate the effectiveness of NPIs.

Technology enables organizations and societies to handle problems at scale, and the scale of the pandemic within the United States reached across all states, communities, and populations (see Johns Hopkins Coronavirus Resource Center, 2021). As of January 1, 2021, the United States had suffered 350,000 deaths (Kornfield & Jacobs, 2021). A population of approximately 330 million people had 29 million diagnosed cases by March 2021 (*New York Times*, n.d.; Bureau of the Census, n.d.). As the coronavirus situation has worsened, the U.S. federal, state, and local governments adopted guidelines to prevent the virus's spread, such as mask-wearing mandates. Businesses, if they were allowed to open, operated at reduced capacity and enforced social distancing measures requiring a six-foot distance between people within the physical space (see, e.g., CDC, 2020d).

Advances in technology drove hopes for eradicating the virus quickly. Biomedical advances made it possible to produce vaccines within 12 months instead of multiple years (U.S. Food and Drug Administration, 2021). Supply chain and production expertise facilitated distribution of vaccines as soon as regulatory authorities approved them (see Johnson, 2020). School robotics clubs turned their 3D printers to making protective equipment for hospitals (Borchert, 2020). Publishers that normally keep academic articles behind paywalls released works for free to the public to increase the speed of scientific discovery (Hoban, 2020). A collaborative and open environment made it possible to more efficiently solve new logistics and medical problems with technology.

Big Tech has notable advantages for managing public health issues. Its products are ubiquitous. Its solutions require little overhead for implementation. An ethos of universal design facilitates quick distribution across geographies and languages. Big Tech envisioned that data technology could easily calculate population-level statistics across local and regional areas, track adherence to medical guidelines, observe the existence of symptoms and spread of the virus through communities, and predict the places where medical equipment is needed (see Grantz et al., 2020; Warzel, 2020). Entrepreneurs located in Silicon Valley—in a state among the most negatively impacted by the pandemic in a country that also struggled at the national level—were ready to lead the charge (see Elflein, 2021; Karlamangla et al., 2020).

Although Big Tech may assume that it has the solution to all problems, the industry, and the governments that demand its solutions, have a checkered record of gaining the public's trust.[1] Instead of relying on medical, public health, logistics, or economics expertise, Silicon Valley relied on its expertise in delivering data technology (see Anderson, 2008; Coveney et al., 2016; Mazzocchi, 2015, pp. 1250–1251). The industry assumes that any data-driven response delivered at scale is the solution even in the absence of subject-matter expertise or theory (see Coveney et al., 2016, p. 1250). The assumption that technology is the solution to the public health crisis is no different; however, the public health crisis has aspects that the current landscape of data-driven technology cannot sufficiently address.

B   Individual Mobility Data

Mobile phones have the ability to track one person through multiple related sources (see Nield, 2018). Governments and Big Tech assume that mobility data is essential to understanding proximity to infection during a pandemic. This section evaluates the feasibility of thoroughly addressing public health goals using individual location data—specifically call logs, device location tracking, and health data apps. We argue that these data sources collect rel-

---

[1]   Indeed, the industry has made a considerable impact on various areas of the private and public sectors particularly with AI technology (see, e.g., Engstrom et al., 2020, p. 6 [federal agencies]; American Academy of Family Physicians, n.d., [medicine]: Antonio, 2018 [sales and marketing]; Heilweil, 2019 [hiring and recruitment). However, these advancements have not come without presenting issues of their own (see Turner-Lee et al., 2019). Biases stretch across sectors, from law enforcement to healthcare, and directly harm vulnerable populations (e.g., AI Now Institute, 2018). Researchers underscore the need for oversight and urge the AI industry to implement internal auditing structures to improve transparency and accountability (Whittaker et al., 2018).

evant information but are not sophisticated enough to work without manual contact tracing and mass testing (see section I.D; see also O'Neill, 2020).

Call logs and phone records have been important data resources in previous public health emergencies. Mobile phone providers have shared logs with public health authorities to help track the spread of disease or adherence to public health guidelines (see Grantz et al., 2020, p. 2; see also Buckee et al., 2020, p. 145). Analyses of mobile phone data have helped identify the source of malaria outbreaks in Namibia (see Ruktanonchai et al., 2016), cholera outbreaks in Senegal (see Finger et al., 2016), and dengue outbreaks in Pakistan (Wesolowski et al., 2015). Public health authorities forged partnerships with mobile phone providers to access call log data (see section I.D; see also O'Neill, 2020). Mobile phone providers give researchers aggregate information to establish which users are in communication with other users (see Grantz et al., 2020, p. 2). However, without testing for the virus, communications between people do not alone provide useful public health information.

Device location data tracks where devices go and how they travel. Assuming the person who owns the device is moving with it, device data location indicates individual movement. Mobile phones use a combination of a global positioning system (GPS), Bluetooth, and Wi-Fi to determine the "approximate" geospatial location of the device (Apple, 2021a). A mobile device records its location each time it pings a nearby cell phone tower for service or Wi-Fi network (see Nield, 2018).[2] The location of the device is recorded into the phone's operating system (Apple, 2021b).[3] The operating system and third-party apps have access to the device's location data, which indicates where the device has been and the places the owner visited (see Boshell, 2019). Device location data can provide a log of individual activity, but testing for the virus is necessary to understand the implications of the device location data. Otherwise, general mobility data may only be valuable for understanding adherence to public health guidelines such as shelter-in-place orders.

Another source of pandemic-related mobility data is health-specific smart technologies. Health-related mobile phone apps monitor physical fitness by collecting vital signs such as heart rate, pulse, and oxygen saturation (see, e.g., Dolan, 2015; Luks & Swenson, 2020). Smart health devices often also have their own third-party phone apps that interact with existing mobile health data

---

[2]   Cell phone pings collect data sets that store the precise daily movements of millions of people (see Thompson & Warzel, 2019). While technically sanitized of identifying information, aggregate location pings reveal identities with little effort.

[3]   Often, a user's full access to a third-party application is predicated on the user enabling the application to access the user's location (Boshell, 2019). In turn, third parties make conclusions or predictions based on the users' location data, forming a profile for each user that can be sold to interested parties.

(see, e.g., Phaneuf, 2021). Apps associated with smart health devices aggregate and analyze trends as well as capture location information (see, e.g., University of Illinois at Chicago, 2020). Proponents argued that smart health devices could provide real-time surveillance of COVID-19 outbreaks (see Warzel, 2020). Smart thermometer apps claimed to identify unexpected patterns of fever (Bloudoff-Indelicato, 2020), although regulatory barriers prevented users from sharing real-time data with medical professionals (see Mathews & Evans, 2020). However, mobile health data sources are particularly susceptible to privacy vulnerabilities (see, e.g., Spinks, 2017).

Call logs, device location, and health apps enable the collection and possible aggregation of information (see Human Rights Watch, 2020). In order to identify which locations are important in the pandemic, the technology would need testing information, which could only be accomplished through mass testing. In the end, many of the digital innovations in health data tracking did not translate into actual treatment (see Neff, 2013).

C   Contact Tracing and Relational Mobility Data

Public health officials limit the spread of the virus by identifying who has been in contact with a positive test case and asking them to isolate (CDC, 2021). Contacting anyone who may have been exposed to the virus is the traditional method of containing an outbreak (see CDC, 2020c). Digital contact tracing attempts to emulate this manual contact tracing process through digital and automated means (Human Rights Watch, 2020; see also Greenberg, 2020). Relational mobility data can identify a small group of people who were in the same physical location, and it can indicate the breadth of pathogen spread between individuals (see Wesolowski et al., 2016). Public health organizations need relational mobility data of small groups in order to make decisions to protect the health of everyone in the area.

Digital contact tracing leverages mobile phone applications that share networked resources (see Greenberg, 2020). The contact tracing project released by two Big Tech companies, Google and Apple, used Bluetooth to identify all devices within the vicinity of each other (Barber, 2020; Greenberg, 2020; Romm et al., 2020). Despite their initial plans to only provide the technology framework, Google and Apple decided to build the entire application and permit states to use the technology (see Barber, 2020). A central server operated by the Association of Public Health Laboratories in addition to a single application infrastructure can track people across state lines.

Digital contact tracing apps deploy an "exposure notification" strategy (Spivak et al., 2020). Advocacy groups have collaborated with privacy and technology organizations to develop a set of principles to govern the collection and distribution of user information to alert the user to potential COVID-19 exposure (see Spivak et al., 2020). An exposure is determined by a combination of time and distance between individuals, but the exact cutoffs depend on the country and the app (see Leslie, 2020). For example, in Australia, the exposure threshold is 1.5 meters for 15 minutes whereas in Ireland the threshold is set at 2 meters for 15 minutes (Leslie, 2020). The use of Bluetooth to connect with all phones in a 1.5- or 2-meter radius assumes that Bluetooth is specific enough to properly trace exposure. Bluetooth relational mobility data intends to establish when people are breathing the same source of air, which is critical to understanding a respiratory virus.

Epidemiological models need proximity data to inform critical allocation decisions and medical responses. For instance, epidemiological models of COVID-19 determined where to concentrate resources for respirators (Oliver et al., 2020, p. 2). Predictive data technology for the pandemic has relied on four sources of data: call logs that assess population density, device location tracking from major mobile phone companies to understand population movement, third-party phone apps and health devices that share health and location data, and contact tracing data to estimate proximity to infection (see Washington & Rhue, 2021, footnotes 81–83; section I.C). Mobile location sources that track individual and group movements could provide actionable information for epidemiologists during a pandemic with the right assumptions.

D   Social and Technical Assumptions

Individual and relational mobility data expose several social and technical assumptions in addition to privacy concerns. Location data sources yield value insights, yet only for a limited population that own devices or show symptoms (see Pew Research Center, 2021).[4] Furthermore, assumptions that location data services have sufficient fidelity and accuracy for virus detection may not reflect reality. Together, these assumptions render some populations and behaviors invisible to public health authorities.

Public health interventions rely on the health of everyone in a community. However, current solutions that rely on data and technology may render some populations invisible and thus have limited application. Specifically, mobile phone adoption can vary greatly (see Deville et al., 2014). Several factors may correlate with less mobile device adoption, including economic, social, demographic, geographic, or cultural aspects of communities (see Pew Research

---

[4]   Even individuals who do own phones do not always have their phones with them while interacting with others. For example, students at school might be required to leave their phones in their lockers, and people entering a courthouse might need to leave their phones in their cars or elsewhere.

Center, 2021). Because of systematic social and geographic differences between users and non-users of mobile phones, mobile phone users reflect a non-representative sample of the population for public health observation (see, e.g., Blumenstock & Eagle, 2010; Wesolowski et al., 2012, pp. 1, 3). Reliance on expensive digital and internet-connected health devices suffers from the same challenges as reliance on mobile phones (see Liu et al., 2020, pp. 687, 689; McCullough, 2020). The adoption rates are less likely for people with less disposable income due to more limited knowledge of health systems and mobile applications and lack of trust in the healthcare system (Liu et al., 2020, p. 687). Solutions built on mobile devices will fail to account for areas with lower-income populations or less reliable mobile reception.

The presence of an outbreak in the population of mobile device owners may not be an appropriate proxy variable for a general outbreak. Conversely, an outbreak outside of this biased sample may be invisible within these data sources. A sampling bias means that the results of a study cannot be reliably applied to a general population because there may be something specific about that population that led to the results (Díaz-Pachón & Rao, 2021). Current mobile data solutions suffer from a sampling bias and would only be successful with widespread adoption.

Another reason these technologies have failed are assumptions about the spread of COVID-19. Originally, smart thermometers promised valuable information on the spread of the virus based on the presence of fever (Bloudoff-Indelicato, 2020; Warzel, 2020). However, a high body temperature, or fever, is not a primary indicator of the coronavirus infection, putting into question the value of aggregate temperature data (Reddy, 2020). As health officials expanded their understanding of COVID-19 (see Belluck, 2020), it became clear that some carriers could be asymptomatic (see Maragakis, 2021; Plater, 2020).[5]

Bluetooth contact tracing applications assume that all physical proximity is a meaningful approximation of air flow (see Anderson, 2020). However, location data that indicates the proximity of two devices cannot distinguish between two people in the same room or devices within the same distance on either side of a wall (Leith & Farrell, 2020). Relational location sources generated from Bluetooth could be potentially meaningless without adding information that makes a distinction between hazardous and non-hazardous interactions, and relational mobility data alone does not provide that information.

Digital contact tracing fails to reflect the realities of jobs that interact with the public. Some people can avoid contact with people outside their household,

---

[5]   Sources indicate that anywhere between 25 and 80 percent of individuals who contract COVID-19 are asymptomatic (Plater, 2020).

and other people cannot. Anyone whose work puts them into contact with hundreds of random people daily could easily be overwhelmed by notifications of possible exposure. Public employees and "essential workers," who may not have the economic choice to quarantine, face the extra burden of determining which notifications are viable threats.

Employees face an additional dilemma: health data collected by non-healthcare organizations do not qualify for HIPAA privacy protections (see Bari & O'Neill, 2019). Data collected through third-party apps can be aggregated and provided to employers in de-identified forms without violating HIPAA (Bari & O'Neill, 2019; see, e.g., Harwell, 2019; see generally 45 C.F.R. § 164.514 (2018). This leaves health-related pandemic data open for sharing among organizations that do not have a fiduciary responsibility to those employees.

Indeed, digital responses to the pandemic assume that people are willing to eschew their personal privacy in support of the public health effort. While Big Tech may enable data collection, governments may use those data sources in ways not anticipated by the public. For instance, the government in Singapore granted law enforcement access to contact tracing data to identify relationships between alleged criminals (Pierson, 2021). The reuse of data in both commercial and governmental contexts threatens the privacy of people who willingly volunteer their health data. The collection of data may persist after the emergency ends, further infringing on privacy rights (Oliver et al., 2020, p. 5).

The freedom of association, inscribed in the United Nations (1948) Declaration of Human Rights, means that there is no penalty for choosing to be with other people. Yet, during a pandemic, monitoring interpersonal associations is critical for public health. This tension between freedom and control underlies the many privacy concerns of deploying relational data solutions (Oliver et al., 2020, pp. 1, 4).

E   Summary

This extended analysis of call logs, device location tracking, health apps, and digital contact tracing demonstrates flawed social assumptions and technological limitations of these solutions for the pandemic. Although these technologies purport to provide solutions for public health, they generally only work within limited technical and social settings. This alone may be cause for concern, but the organizations representing this interest in pandemic data technology also have conflicts of interest.

II   CONFLICTS OF INTEREST

Proximity and health information is valuable outside of the pandemic context, making it vulnerable to misuse. Many organizations have financial interests that conflict with public health interests. It is plausible that private healthcare organizations and digital platforms would keep pandemic-related information to support their own predictive products. Any public health deployment of pandemic technology must recognize the reuse value of its data and the potential for exploitation.

A   Data Reuse

Data innovation interconnects new digital sources to derive predictive accuracy as a competitive advantage.[6] Drawing on the initial success of segmenting consumers geospatially by postal codes (see Byers, 2015, pp. 758–759; McGregor et al., 2013, pp. 1, 2), digital advertising inevitably will seek to use pandemic mobility data to improve marketing.

The reuse of data for a purpose outside of the original intention touches on many legal and ethical concerns, although it is a common practice. In one example, a DNA sample from a routine medical procedure connected the patient's relative to a crime scene (see Nakashima, 2008). The Chicago police maintains a database (Sweeney & Fry, 2018)[7] of *potential* gang members based on Facebook friends and photos of teenagers on the social networking site (Policing in Chicago Research Group, 2018).[8] Free mental health support in New York City funnels data into the algorithms that determine whether children will be removed from the home (Chapin Hall, 2019, p. 17).[9] Information

---

[6]   Data innovation uses traditional and non-traditional sources of data to obtain novel analyses on otherwise complex or impossible problems (United Nations Development Programme & UN Global Pulse, 2017). This process is commonly referred to as data analytics, which utilizes algorithms to derive conclusions from raw data (see, e.g., Petrozzino, 2020; Turner-Lee et al., 2019).

[7]   Juveniles who lose a relative or a friend to gun violence are put into the system as potential gang members even if they do not participate in any gangs (Sweeney & Fry, 2018). Similarly, individuals without criminal records may be identified in the database as gang members simply because of where they live (Dumke, 2018; Richardson et al., 2019).

[8]   The Office of the Inspector General for the City of Chicago (2019) found that Black, African American, and Latinx persons account for 95 percent of the 134,242 individuals designated as gang members (see also Complaint, *Chicagoans for an End*, 2019, pp. 2–3).

[9]   New York City's Administration for Children's Services (ACS) uses numerous public services to evaluate the competence of parents whose children will be put in

that was originally intended to support the needs of newly released prisoners instead calculates a risk assessment score that may curtail their future.[10] In these examples, the original purpose of the data collection was perverted to penalize instead of support. The data from the person seeking services, such as the teenager or the hospital patient, suddenly becomes the vehicle of a punitive system.

The crossover between public health and other uses is not theoretical. While many possible motivations for data reuse exist, it is inevitable that law enforcement, marketers, researchers, and the curious may want to know how people associate with each other. Reuse of pandemic data for financial profit is particularly concerning when it involves private healthcare organizations seeking to minimize costs or digital platforms seeking to improve digital advertising.

B   Profits and Patients

The U.S. healthcare system is built on a network of private healthcare organizations that bill for each unique health event (see generally Gross, 2019). This financial model is less than ideal when the volume of events is high with little monetary reward. A global pandemic exacerbates the challenges with the model further because everyone needs to be healthy for anyone to be healthy.

Private hospitals, healthcare maintenance organizations (HMOs), and individual physician practices are for-profit entities that are motivated to limit expenses and increase profits. Private businesses also select clients or market to certain groups over others. Private hospitals and healthcare organizations are motivated to limit access to care in order to manage budgets (see Gee, 2019).[11] Digital mobility data is invaluable for building actuarial models of

---

foster care (Chapin Hall, 2019, p. 17). Even parents who forgo public services to preserve their privacy run the risk of being turned over to ACS as neglectful or incompetent for not using the free city services (Glaberson, 2019, p. 350, footnote 233). Child protective agencies nationwide employ similar data analysis programs (Hurley, 2018).

[10]   The Correctional Offender Management Profiling for Alternative Sanctions (COMPAS) system was originally created within a university to help local communities (see Angwin et al., 2016). The software is used by courts as a risk assessment score to predict a defendant's likelihood to recidivate. The tool manipulates the offender's therapeutic *needs* as risks. For instance, if someone needs (or previously needed) addiction services, they are labeled as "at risk" (Northpointe, 2009; Northpointe, 2015.) Studies have found that the COMPAS tool suffers from analysis bias, scoring Black offenders higher on the risk assessment scale than white offenders with similar or worse backgrounds (Petrozzino, 2020, pp. 15–16).

[11]   For example, health insurers use "lifestyle data" from third-party sources to complement actuarial assessments, identify high-risk patients, and maximize profits (see Allen, 2018).

risk. While all healthcare organizations in the United States are subject to HIPAA laws that limit how they handle patient data (see HIPAA, 1996, § 221; Office for Civil Rights, 2015), they may use internal data to inform actuarial models (see 45 C.F.R. §§ 160.103, 164.501, 164.506, 2016; Office for Civil Rights, 2016). These organizations have a financial motivation, and possibly an obligation, to screen out or limit the number of sick people under their care (see footnote 11).

Particularly in the United States, patients with limited access to health insurance may be overrepresented in job categories that are considered essential during the pandemic: delivery services, transportation, education, or healthcare (Valentino-DeVries et al., 2020). People in these categories may be reasonably hesitant to share data with a healthcare system that might use a positive status to withhold, limit, or refuse healthcare (cf. Karampela et al., 2019). This means that the virus might continue in a vicious cycle if people who interact with a large number of other people do not have appropriate healthcare.

C   Advertising Models

All data sources are of interest to marketers and therefore to any large digital platform, including those of two popular mobile device manufacturers: Apple and Google. Digital businesses exploit new verified third-party data sources to improve advertisement delivery.

Advertising ecosystems leverage data to better target ads or find new clients, especially through existing clients. Friend of a Friend (FOAF) information is a mathematical and spatial representation of who is connected to whom (see Golbeck & Rothstein, 2008, pp. 1138–1139). FOAF reveals social connections and interpersonal associations usually based on voluntary data shared on a social networking site. Pandemic proximity sources that describe how people congregate provides valuable new information about interpersonal and FOAF relationships that may not be available elsewhere (see Gray, 2020).

Proximity data might not only be used for digital advertising. Insurance companies, credit reporting agencies, and other organizations that rely on risk calculations may be interested in evaluating who is in proximity to the virus. This might lead to an equivalent of health redlining that isolates neighborhoods deemed to be less profitable and more vulnerable to outbreaks (see generally Baradaran, 2017; Taylor, 2019). The reuse of pandemic proximity data as a punitive assessment would penalize people who live in densely populated locations or workplaces that interface with the public. Furthermore, this may limit the potential for tourism or locations that rely on positive promotion. For instance, New York City's Chinatown has suffered tremendous financial losses due to a false assumption that it has a risky proximity to the virus (see Bliss, 2020).

D   Summary

The financial conflicts of interest of large organizations that may offer pandemic data solutions cannot be ignored. Organizations with access to pandemic proximity information would improve their competitive edge over other businesses.[12] Organizations that share proximity data violate the trust of people whose movements are traced (see Washington & Rhue, 2021, footnote 124). The tension between valuable data assets and personal empowerment creates little incentive for individuals to share their information, assuming they have a choice.

The effectiveness of digital data is often limited by the effectiveness of public health interventions. Public health officials emphasize the importance of test-trace-treat as the three pillars of handling an infectious disease (e.g., Bicker, 2020); however, the data-driven pandemic technology only addresses the trace pillar. Information about positive tests is necessary in conjunction with location data to make digital contact tracing viable.

Even if all mobile device owners generated location data and chose to share their information, the limited and selective sample might still hamper the technology's full effectiveness. Effective public health monitoring requires acquisition of complete population information, which is the opposite of what occurs under the current system. To the extent that individual choice contributes to the lack of complete data, imposing a fiduciary responsibility upon those who possess proximity is a way to resolve the conflict-of-interest issue.

III   FIDUCIARY POLICY SOLUTIONS

A fiduciary has a legal responsibility to protect client confidentiality and interests. While fiduciaries have long standing in business and law, the concept of an information fiduciary is still hotly debated amongst legal scholars.[13] Pandemic data technology might be an opportunity to move information fiduciary theory into practice. We define trust within the context of pandemic data technology, and outline what issues an information fiduciary could solve.

---

[12]   This phenomenon is particularly concerning in the context of digital markets. Due to digital markets' complexity and reach, some view the technology industry as above supervision or "too big to audit" (Morar & Washington, 2020).

[13]   Compare Balkin, 2016, p. 1186, with Kahn & Pozen, 2019; and Haupt, 2020.

A   Trust

Without explicit guidelines or regulation, it would be very hard to investigate how data have travelled, to whom, or why. As well as regulators, journalists or interested citizens should be able to track the flow of public health information. The trust that exists between data aggregators and the public is essential to understanding why fiduciaries are necessary during a public health emergency.

Trust must exist throughout the data supply chain that moves data between organizations. Very often, companies do not share first-party data, but instead bundle interpretations of data, such as categories for targeted advertisements (Anderson & Jesdanun, 2018). As Mark Zuckerberg testified in response to congressional complaints about Facebook selling data, "Senator, we run ads" ("Facebook, social media privacy," 2018, p. 21). As long as data are exchanged within long chains of custody, a duty of care among all who may use the data is necessary to guarantee that trust. When data are held over long periods of time or held by different organizations, the potential for negative use later in the chain grows.

Trust must exist at the ends of the data supply chain as well. People depend on organizations to hold their public health-related data about them in trust. This is not about trust between one individual and one company, such as in a consumer–business relationship. Rather, people want to trust that organizations will not penalize them or negatively exploit their information (see, e.g., Colman et al., 2021; Emmer et al., 2020, pp. 23, 28; see generally Policing Project, 2020). Specifically, people need to be able to trust that organizations are not distracted by financial gain when creating public health solutions.

Trust in the government's ability to safeguard information or hire appropriate contractors is also at stake. Philly Fighting COVID switched from non-profit to commercial status after it obtained a contract with the City of Philadelphia (Scott, 2021). In its few short weeks as a vaccine distributor, Philly Fighting COVID gathered sensitive health data for thousands of local residents without delivering vaccines or appointments. Governments are trusting contractors to not exploit citizen information while delivering technology solutions (see Ferguson, 2021).

Data aggregation has been one means to protect consumers; however, public health officials need details, not aggregate data. A pandemic requires in-depth analysis to plan hospital allocation patterns, first responder staffing, or vaccine rollout schedules. The technology industry has no interest in sharing detailed information and would violate many laws and conventions if it did share it. Having this wealth of information only in the hands of a few commercial organizations reduces the ability of the data to make an impact on the public health crisis and potentially increases the incentive to profit off that data.

While the legal information fiduciary debate has focused on commercial businesses, the application in the public sector, and for public–private partnerships, has the most promise.

B   Information Fiduciaries

The legal scholar Jack Balkin introduced the concept of an information fiduciary in a 2016 law review article based on three laws of an algorithmic society (Balkin 2017; see generally Balkin, 2014). An information fiduciary, as Balkin (2017) suggests, would resolve potential abuses of power by anyone with the computational power to control large populations (pp. 1226–1227). Balkin (2017) emphasizes the asymmetries of information that make individuals vulnerable to and dependent on digital companies (pp. 1127–1129. In addition to Balkin's three laws, Frank Pasquale argued for a fourth law that grapples with issues of power based on the source, creator, or owner of the algorithm (see Pasquale, 2017, pp. 1253–1254; Pasquale, 2020, p. 11).

The legal debate on merits of an information fiduciary has considered the obligation of digital businesses, such as Google, Twitter, Amazon, and Facebook. David Pozen and Linda Khan are skeptical of information fiduciaries, emphasizing that their costs could easily lead to complacency (see Khan & Pozen, 2019, pp. 502, 537). They argue that information fiduciaries are largely immaterial because there is no way to test or confirm fiduciary responsibilities if a company exercises monopoly power within the industry (Khan & Pozen, 2019, pp. 537, 540). In a response to Pozen and Khan's skepticism of information fiduciaries in favor of antitrust actions, Balkin reiterated the importance of building trust between individuals and the institutions that use their data (see Balkin, 2020, pp. 11, 13, 22). Antitrust actions would not eliminate the desire of the resultant companies to earn a profit from their surveillance (Balkin, 2020, p. 22). We argue that if we cannot imagine information fiduciaries, we will not have successful antitrust. When AT&T split up, one "Ma Bell" dissolved into many "Baby Bells" that implemented similar business models and payment structures while competing for customers with innovations (Pagliery, 2014; see *United States v. AT&T*, 1982, pp. 200–201, 225). Trust could be further diminished if more companies repeat the same business models with few internal governance mechanisms and little regulatory oversight (see Morar & Washington, 2020; cf. Lande & Zerbe, 2020, pp. 564–566). Bringing the information fiduciary concept to the table in advance of antitrust enforcement action may support successful divisions of large companies.

In the case of healthcare, the premise of these arguments shifts. The information needs are by default wide-reaching and have to operate, not at the consumer level, but across the entire population. Information fiduciaries are essential to understanding the issues inherent in digital solutions to public health emergencies. Furthermore, implementing an information fiduciary for pandemic data serves to advance conversations about implementing this concept at a broader scale for social networking sites or other commercial services.

Health information, unlike other personally identifiable information (PII), consists of immutable characteristics that the patient has little control over changing, unlike details such as employment status. One person's health information might also impact the health status of the person's relatives, which escalates the stakes for sharing data. Anyone might naturally feel vulnerable sharing personal health details under these conditions. Vulnerabilities from sharing are exponential in a privatized healthcare system where every change in health status is a financial calculation (see section II.B). Patients who share personal health details are made vulnerable to a host of institutional data systems which have a clear financial conflict of interest (see section II.A).

Could an information fiduciary protect patients' interests during a pandemic?

C   Policy Solutions

We offer two tangible suggestions for implementing the information fiduciary concept in practice: conflict-of-interest notices and third-party stewards for pandemic-related health data.

1   Conflict-of-interest notices

Organizations that maintain access to any pandemic-related data must submit a digital public filing of conflict of interest. Journalists, litigators, or the public could use these filings for investigations like any other open data source. Organizations face a reputational cost when conflict-of-interest notices are released publicly (see, e.g., Willis, 2018; Ravitch, 2020; see also ProPublica, n.d.). This reduces the burden on the individual for misplaced trust (see Brennan-Marquez, 2015, pp. 637, 644, 646, 657, 659, & footnote 112), a known problem in consumer technology. The issue of misplaced trust in pandemic technology is similar to how the third-party doctrine placed the burden on consumers for trusting a deceitful actor with their data and communications.[14] In addition, to prevent the misuse towards surveillance by employers and government, public health officials may use these associations if—and

---

[14] Courts have long held that third-party reports to law enforcement do not violate Fourth Amendment protections of consumers who provide a third party with their data (see, e.g., *United States v. Jacobsen*, 1894, pp. 111, 125–26 [private freight carrier reports]; *Smith v. Maryland*, 1979, pp. 745–746 [telephone company reports]; *United States v. Miller*, 1976, p. 443 [bank reports]).

only if—the data does not penalize the subject of the data. Conflict-of-interest notices do not protect data but could be an essential mechanism to build trust.

2   Public health fiduciary

A public health fiduciary would have legal responsibility to protect data relevant to epidemiological outbreaks. It would protect patient interests and maintain confidentiality of location data related to the pandemic. A new public health entity would pledge a fiduciary responsibility to digital public health data and its distribution for only necessary medical reasons. A public health fiduciary would oversee who had access to the data in addition to tracking distribution and use. Active data distribution monitoring would allow for just-in-time access to data and discourage hoarding data for unknown future uses.

We recognize that it might be possible for an existing organization to commit to fiduciary responsibilities. However, large commercial organizations may struggle to establish that trust if they have marketing, risk management, or research teams that could benefit from access to the data. Government organizations may be distracted by politics and elections. Ideally a new public health entity would take on these responsibilities. Even a short-term pandemic-only organization would be useful to consider the impact of this data moving forward.

Regulatory enforcement or legal recourse could hold organizations to account for violating this trust. Additional policy instruments such as fines, organizational restrictions, antitrust, or other existing regulatory tools may enforce a duty of care.

CONCLUSION

Data-centric solutions may not limit the spread of the virus as intended if the technology relies on inaccurate assumptions and the organizations involved have financial interests that override other priorities. Any public health effort must have an ultimate goal of centering patient treatment and wellness.

It is imperative to develop mechanisms to protect the privacy of currently invisible populations, whether through increased political power, better privacy protections, or enhanced oversight. The act of sharing health data makes people vulnerable to institutions that may have interests in opposition to their own. Without the protection of all populations, public health goals using digital technology will fail. The visibility of all members of a community is essential to support public health efforts, but often that requires increasing surveillance with potentially negative consequences.

We believe that technology should be part of the public health solution; however, it should be led by a desire to meet the mission to serve all residents within a geographic area. A public health information fiduciary is the best solution to the conflicts of interest. Valuable proximity information could be used to fight the virus if it were not detrimental to the people whose locations are tracked.

NOTE

Originally published in a slightly different form as A. L. Washington & L. Rhue (2021). "Tracing the invisible: information fiduciaries and the pandemic." *American University Law Review*, 70(5), 1765–1797. Reprinted by permission of the publisher. This work draws on a presentation we made at the Future of Privacy Forum's International Tech & Data Conference in October 2020. We would like to thank Charles T. Stokes, 2019 graduate of Stevenson University in Baltimore, Maryland, for research assistance.

REFERENCES

45 C.F.R. § 160.103 (2016).
45 C.F.R. § 164.501 (2016).
45 C.F.R. § 164.506 (2016).
45 C.F.R. § 164.514 (2018).
AI Now Institute. (2018, October 16), AI Now 2018 Symposium. https://ainowinstitute.org/symposia/2018-symposium.html
Allen, M. (2018, July 17). "Health insurers are vacuuming up details about you—and it could raise your rates." ProPublica. www.propublica.org/article/health-insurers-are-vacuuming-up-details-about-you-and-it-could-raise-your-rates
Alter, C., & Villa, L. (2020, March 14). "'You must act now.' How states and cities have responded to the coronavirus pandemic." *Time.* https://time.com/5803334/coronavirus-pandemic-local-governments/
American Academy of Family Physicians. (n.d.). "AFP algorithms." www.aafp.org/afp/algorithms/viewAll.htm
Anderson, C. (2008, June 23). "The end of theory: The data deluge makes the scientific method obsolete." *Wired.* www.wired.com/2008/06/pb-theory/
Anderson, M., & Jesdanun, A. (2018, April 10). "AP fact check: Facebook doesn't sell data but profits off it." Associated Press. https://apnews.com/article/6f5156879a3a48218b509c97fcc28e39
Anderson, R. (2020, April 12). "Contact tracing in the real world." Light Blue Touchpaper. www.lightbluetouchpaper.org/2020/04/12/contact-tracing-in-the-real-world/
Angwin, J., Larson, J., Mattu, S., & Kirchner, L. (2016, May 23). "Machine bias." ProPublica. www.propublica.org/article/machine-bias-risk-assessments-in-criminal-sentencing
Antonio, V. (2018, July 30). "How AI is changing sales." *Harvard Business Review.* https://hbr.org/2018/07/how-ai-is-changing-sales
Apple. (2020, April 10). "Apple and Google partner on COVID-19 contact tracing technology." Apple Newsroom. www.apple.com/newsroom/2020/04/apple-and-google-partner-on-covid-19-contact-tracing-technology/

Apple. (2021a, February 2). "About privacy and Location Services in iOS and iPadOS." Apple Support. https://support.apple.com/en-us/HT203033

Apple. (2021b, April 26). "Location Services and privacy." Apple Support. https://support.apple.com/en-us/HT207056

Balkin, J. M. (2014, March 5). "Information fiduciaries in the digital age." Balkinization. https://balkin.blogspot.com/2014/03/information-fiduciaries-in-digital-age.html

Balkin, J. M. (2016). "Information fiduciaries and the First Amendment." *UC Davis Law Review*, 49, 1185–1232.

Balkin, J. M. (2017). "2016 Sidley Austin Distinguished Lecture on Big Data and Policy: The three laws of robotics in the age of big data" [Lecture]. *Ohio State Law Journal*, 78, 1217–1241.

Balkin, J. M. (2020). "The fiduciary model of privacy." *Harvard Law Review Forum*, 134, 11–33.

Baradaran, M. (2017). *The Color of Money: Black Banks and the Racial Wealth Gap*. Belknap Press.

Barber, G. (2020, September 1). "Google and Apple change tactics on contact tracing tech." *Wired*. www.wired.com/story/google-apple-change-tactics-contact-tracing-tech/

Bari, L., & O'Neill, D. P. (2019). "Rethinking patient data privacy in the era of digital health." Health Affairs Blog. https://doi.org/10.1377/hblog20191210.216658

Barua, A., & Levin, D. (2020, August 27). "What's weighing on consumer spending: Fear of COVID-19 and its economic impact." Deloitte Insights. www2.deloitte.com/us/en/insights/economy/spotlight/economics-insights-analysis-08-2020.html

Belluck, P. (2020, August 5). "CDC adds new symptoms to coronavirus list." *New York Times*. www.nytimes.com/2020/04/27/health/coronavirus-symptoms-cdc.html

Bicker, L. (2020, March 12). "Coronavirus in South Korea: How 'trace, test and treat' may be saving lives." BBC. www.bbc.com/news/world-asia-51836898

Bliss, L. (2020, December 7). "Chinatown businesses face a particularly brutal winter." Bloomberg. www.bloomberg.com/news/articles/2020-12-07/covid-19-has-been-a-disaster-for-u-s-chinatowns

Bloudoff-Indelicato, M. (2020, April 2). "This company claims its smart thermometer could help detect coronavirus hot spots faster than the CDC." CNBC. www.cnbc.com/2020/04/02/this-smart-thermometer-could-help-detect-covid-19-hot-spots.html

Blumenstock, J., & Eagle, N. (2010). "Mobile divides: Gender, socioeconomic status, and mobile phone use in Rwanda." In *ICTD '10: Proceedings of the 4th ACM/IEEE International Conference on Information and Communication Technologies and Development*, 1–10. https://doi.org/10.1145/2369220.2369225

Borchert, C. (2020, September 15). "Local robotics team makes, donates PPE for COVID-19 responders." *Center Times Plus*. www.utsouthwestern.edu/ctplus/stories/2020/technic-bots.html

Borgman, C. L. (2018). "Open data, grey data, and stewardship: Universities at the privacy frontier." *Berkeley Technology Law Journal*, 33, 365.

Boshell, P. M. (2019, March 25). "The power of place: Geolocation tracking and privacy." Business Law Today. https://businesslawtoday.org/2019/03/power-place-geolocation-tracking-privacy/

Brennan-Marquez, K. (2015). "Fourth Amendment fiduciaries." *Fordham Law Review*, 84, 611.

Buckee, C. O., Balsari, S., Chan, J., Crosas, M., Dominici, F., Gasser, U., Grad, Y. H., Grenfell, B., Halloran, M. E., Kraemer, M. U. G., Lipsitch, M., Metcalf, C.

J. E., Meyers, L. A., Perkins, T. A., Santillana, M., Scarpino, S. V., Viboud, C., Wesolowski, A., & Schroeder, A. (2020). "Aggregated mobility data could help fight COVID-19." *Science*, 368(6487), 145.2–146. https://doi.org/10.1126/science .abb8021

Bureau of the Census. (n.d.). "Population clock." U.S. Federal Statistical System. www .census.gov/popclock/

Byers, A. (2015). "Big data, big economic impact?" *A Journal of Law and Policy for the Information Society*, 10(3), 757–764.

Centers for Disease Control and Prevention. (2013, April 26). "CDC SARS response timeline." Department of Health and Human Services. www.cdc.gov/about/history/ sars/timeline.htm

Centers for Disease Control and Prevention. (2018, September 14). "Health Insurance Portability and Accountability Act of 1996 (HIPAA)." Department of Health and Human Services. www.cdc.gov/phlp/publications/topic/hipaa.html

Centers for Disease Control and Prevention. (2019, August 26). "Community NPIs: Flu prevention in community settings." Department of Health and Human Services. www.cdc.gov/nonpharmaceutical-interventions/community/index.html

Centers for Disease Control and Prevention. (2020a, September 1). "About COVID-19." Department of Health and Human Services. www.cdc.gov/coronavirus/2019-ncov/ cdcresponse/about-COVID-19.html

Centers for Disease Control and Prevention. (2020b, December 1). "What is Ebola virus disease?" Department of Health and Human Services. www.cdc.gov/vhf/ebola/ about.html

Centers for Disease Control and Prevention. (2020c, December 3). "Case investiga- tion and contact tracing: Part of a multipronged approach to fight the COVID-19 pandemic." Department of Health and Human Services. www.cdc.gov/coronavirus/ 2019-ncov/php/principles-contact-tracing.html

Centers for Disease Control and Prevention. (2020d, December 16). "Considerations for restaurant and bar operators." Department of Health and Human Services. www .cdc.gov/coronavirus/2019-ncov/community/organizations/business-employers/bars -restaurants.html

Centers for Disease Control and Prevention. (2021, March 12). "When you can be around others after you had or likely had COVID-19." Department of Health and Human Services. www.cdc.gov/coronavirus/2019-ncov/if-you-are-sick/end-home -isolation.html

Chapin Hall. (2019, June). "Strong Families New York City: Final evaluation report." University of Chicago. www1.nyc.gov/assets/acs/pdf/initiatives/2019/ CHFinalReport.pdf

Colman, T., Emmer, P., Ritchie, A., & Wang, T. (2021, January 6). "The data is in. People of color are punished more harshly for Covid violations in the US." *The Guardian*. www.theguardian.com/commentisfree/2021/jan/06/covid-violations -people-of-color-punished-more-harshly

Complaint, Chicagoans for an End to the Gang Database v. City of Chicago (N.D. Ill. 2018) No. 18-CV-4242.

Coveney, P. V., Dougherty, E. R., & Highfield, R. R. (2016). "Big data need big theory too." *Philosophical Transactions of the Royal Society A: Mathematical, Physical and Engineering Sciences*, 374(2080). https://doi.org/10.1098/rsta.2016.0153

"Design bias is harmful, and in some cases may be lethal." (2021, April 10). *The Economist*. www.economist.com/leaders/2021/04/10/design-bias-is-harmful-and-in -some-cases-may-be-lethal

Deville, P., Linard, C., Martin, S., Gilbert, M., Stevens, F. R., Gaughan, A. E., Blondel, V. D., & Tatem, A. J. (2014). "Dynamic population mapping using mobile phone data." *Proceedings of the National Academy of Sciences*, 111(45), 15888–15893. https://doi.org/10.1073/pnas.1408439111

Díaz-Pachón, D. A., & Rao, J. S. (2021). "A simple correction for COVID-19 sampling bias." *Journal of Theoretical Biology*, 512, 110556. https://doi.org/10.1016/j.jtbi.2020.110556

Dolan, B. (2015, September 10). "Apple shows off AirStrip's vital sign monitoring Apple Watch app." MobiHealthNews. www.mobihealthnews.com/46687/apple-shows-off-airstrips-vital-sign-monitoring-apple-watch-app

Dumke, M. (2018, April 19). "Chicago's gang database is full of errors—and records we have prove it." ProPublica. www.propublica.org/article/politic-il-insider-chicago-gang-database

Elflein, J. (2021, July 14). "COVID-19 cases and deaths among hardest hit countries worldwide as of July 14, 2021." Statista. www.statista.com/statistics/1105264/coronavirus-covid-19-cases-most-affected-countries-worldwide/

Emmer, P., Ervin, W., Purnell, D., Ritchie, A., & Wang, T. (2020). "Unmasked: Impacts of pandemic policing." Community Resource Hub. https://communityresourcehub.org/unmasked

Engstrom, D. F., Ho, D. E., Sharkley, C. M., & Cuéllar, M.-F. (2020, January). "Government by algorithm: Artificial intelligence in federal administrative agencies." Law and Policy Lab. www-cdn.law.stanford.edu/wp-content/uploads/2020/02/ACUS-AI-Report.pdf

"Facebook, social media privacy, and the use and abuse of data: Before the Senate Committee on Commerce, Science, and Transportation, and the Senate Committee on the Judiciary, 115th Cong." (2018). www.commerce.senate.gov/2018/4/facebook-social-media-privacy-and-the-use-and-abuse-of-data

Farzan, A. N., Noack, R., Taylor, A., Villegas, P., Bellware, K., Dupree, J., Shaban, H., Knowles, H., & Sands, D. (2020, October 24). "U.S. hits all-time high in new coronavirus cases, exceeding 80,000 in a day for the first time." *Washington Post*. www.washingtonpost.com/nation/2020/10/23/coronavirus-covid-live-updates-us/

Ferguson, C. (2021, January 30). "What went wrong with America's $44 million vaccine data system?" *MIT Technology Review*. www.technologyreview.com/2021/01/30/1017086/cdc-44-million-vaccine-data-vams-problems

Finger, F., Genolet, T., Mari, L., de Magny, G. C., Manga, N. M., Rinaldo, A., & Bertuzzo, E. (2016). "Mobile phone data highlights the role of mass gatherings in the spreading of cholera outbreaks." *Proceedings of the National Academy of Sciences*, 113(23), 6421–6426. https://doi.org/10.1073/pnas.1522305113

Gee, E. (2019, June 26). "The high price of hospital care." Center for American Progress. www.americanprogress.org/issues/healthcare/reports/2019/06/26/471464/high-price-hospital-care/

Glaberson, S. K. (2019). "Coding over the cracks: Predictive analytics and child protection." *Fordham Urban Law Journal*, 46, 307.

Golbeck, J., & Rothstein, M. (2008). "Linking social networks on the web with FOAF: A semantic web case study." Association for the Advancement of Artificial Intelligence, 1138–1143. www.aaai.org/Papers/AAAI/2008/AAAI08-180.pdf

Grantz, K. H., Meredith, H. R., Cummings, D. A. T., Metcalf, C. J. E., Grenfell, B. T., Giles, J. R., Mehta, S., Solomon, S., Labrique, A., Kishore, N., Buckee, C. O., & Wesolowski, A. (2020). "The use of mobile phone data to inform analysis of

COVID-19 pandemic epidemiology." *Nature Communications*, 11(1). https://doi
.org/10.1038/s41467-020-18190-5

Gray, S. (2020, December 17). "A closer look at location data: Privacy and pandemics."
Future Privacy Forum. https://fpf.org/blog/a-closer-look-at-location-data-privacy
-and-pandemics

Greenberg, A. (2020, April 10). "How Apple and Google are enabling COVID-19
Bluetooth contact-tracing." *Wired*. www.wired.com/story/apple-google-bluetooth
-contact-tracing-covid-19/

Gross, T. (2019, March 13). "Why an ER visit can cost so much—even for those
with health insurance." NPR. https://www.npr.org/2019/03/13/702975393/why-an
-er-visit-can-cost-so-much-even-for-those-with-health-insurance

Harpaz, J. (2020, May 22). "Apple iOS 13.5 is ready for COVID-19 contact tracing—
are you?" *Forbes*. www.forbes.com/sites/joeharpaz/2020/05/21/apple-ios-135-is
-ready-for-covid-19-contact-tracing

Harwell, D. (2019, April 10). "Is your pregnancy app sharing your intimate data with
your boss?" *Washington Post*. www.washingtonpost.com/technology/2019/04/10/
tracking-your-pregnancy-an-app-may-be-more-public-than-you-think/

Haupt, C. E. (2020). "Response, platforms as trustees: Information fiduciaries and the
value of analogy." *Harvard Law Review Forum*, 34, 36–37.

Health Insurance Portability and Accountability Act, Pub. L. No. 104-191, 110 Stat.
1936 (1996).

Heilweil, R. (2019, December 12). "Artificial intelligence will help determine if
you get your next job." Vox. www.vox.com/recode/2019/12/12/20993665/artificial
-intelligence-ai-job-screen

Hoban, V. (2020, July 30). "Science, uninterrupted: Will COVID-19 mark the end of
scientific publishing as we know it?" UC Berkeley Library News. https://news.lib
.berkeley.edu/covid-oa

Human Rights Watch. (2020, May 13). "Mobile location data and Covid-19: Q&A."
www.hrw.org/news/2020/05/13/mobile-location-data-and-covid-19-qa#

Hurley, D. (2018, January 2). "Can an algorithm tell when kids are in danger?" *New
York Times*. www.nytimes.com/2018/01/02/magazine/can-an-algorithm-tell-when
-kids-are-in-danger.html

Johns Hopkins Coronavirus Resource Center. (2021, July 21). "COVID-19 United
States cases by county." Johns Hopkins University & Medicine. https://coronavirus
.jhu.edu/us-map

Johnson, C. Y. (2020, November 17). "A vial, a vaccine and hopes for slowing
a pandemic—how a shot comes to be." *Washington Post*. www.washingtonpost
.com/health/2020/11/17/coronavirus-vaccine-manufacturing/

Karampela, M., Ouhbi, S., & Isomursu, M. (2019). "Connected health user willingness
to share personal health data: Questionnaire study." *Journal of Medical Internet
Research*, 21(11). doi:10.2196/14537

Karlamangla, S., Money, L., & Lin, R., II. (2020, December 24). "Coronavirus surge
slams L.A. hospitals, forcing ER rationing." *Los Angeles Times*. www.latimes.com/
california/story/2020-12-24/coronavirus-surge-hammering-los-angeles-hospitals

Khan, L. M., & Pozen, D. E. (2019). "A skeptical view of information fiduciaries."
Harvard Law Review, 133, 497–541.

Kornfield, M., & Jacobs, S. (2021, January 4). "As coronavirus death toll surpasses
350,000, Trump calls U.S. count 'far exaggerated.'" *Washington Post*. www
.washingtonpost.com/health/trump-calls-us-coronavirus-death-toll-fake-news-as

-count-surpasses-350000/2021/01/03/6bdc0b08-4e14-11eb-bda4-615aaefd0555
_story.html

Lande, R. H., & Zerbe, R. O. (2020). "The Sherman Act is a no-fault monopolization statute: A textualist demonstration." *American University Law Review*, 70, 497–588.

Leith, D. J., & Farrell, S. (2020). "Coronavirus contact tracing." *ACM SIGCOMM Computer Communication Review*, 50(4), 66–74. https://doi.org/10.1145/3431832.3431840

Leslie, M. (2020). "COVID-19 fight enlists digital technology: Contact tracing apps." *Engineering*, 6(10), 1064–1066. https://doi.org/10.1016/j.eng.2020.09.001

Lipton, E., Goodnough, A., Shear, M. D., Twohey, M., Mandavilli, A., Fink, S., & Walker, M. (2020, August 14). "The C.D.C. waited 'its entire existence for this moment.' What went wrong?" *New York Times*. www.nytimes.com/2020/06/03/us/cdc-coronavirus.html

Liu, P., Astudillo, K., Velez, D., Kelley, L., Cobbs-Lomax, D., & Spatz, E. S. (2020). "Use of mobile health applications in low-income populations." *Circulation: Cardiovascular Quality and Outcomes*, 13(9). https://doi.org/10.1161/circoutcomes.120.007031

Luks, A. M., & Swenson, E. R. (2020). "Pulse oximetry for monitoring patients with COVID-19 at home. Potential pitfalls and practical guidance." *Annals of the American Thoracic Society*, 17(9), 1040–1046. https://doi.org/10.1513/annalsats.202005-418fr

Maragakis, L. L. (2021, February 24). "Coronavirus symptoms: Frequently asked questions." Johns Hopkins Medicine. www.hopkinsmedicine.org/health/conditions-and-diseases/coronavirus/coronavirus-symptoms-frequently-asked-questions

Mathews, A. W., & Evans, M. (2020, March 9). "Sharing your digital health data: New rules ease access." *Wall Street Journal*. www.wsj.com/articles/sharingyourhealthdatanewdigitalrules-11583702453

Mazzocchi, F. (2015). "Could Big Data be the end of theory in science?" *EMBO Reports*, 16(10), 1250–1255. https://doi.org/10.15252/embr.201541001

McCullough, M. (2020, November 17). "Smart thermometers could help track COVID-19 surge in Philadelphia—if used in a smart way." *Philadelphia Inquirer*. www.inquirer.com/health/coronavirus/covid-19-outbreaks-kinsa-thermometers-track-fevers-early-warning-philadelphia-20201117.html

McGregor, V. K., Calderón, S. H., & Tonelli, R. D. (2013). "Big Data and consumer financial information." *Business Law Today*, 1–4. www.jstor.org/stable/businesslawtoday.2013.11.05

McNeil, D. G., Jr. (2020, March 18). "Can smart thermometers track the spread of the coronavirus?" *New York Times*. www.nytimes.com/2020/03/18/health/coronavirus-fever-thermometers.html

Morar, D., & Washington, A. (2020, September 3). "How a compliance mindset undermines antitrust reform proposals." Brookings Institute: Tech Stream. www.brookings.edu/techstream/how-a-compliance-mindset-undermines-antitrust-reform-proposals.

Nakashima, E. (2008, April 21). "From DNA of family, a tool to make arrests." *Washington Post*, A01.

Natanson, H., & Strauss, V. (2020, August 5). "America is about to start online learning, round 2. For millions of students, it won't be any better." *Washington Post*. www.washingtonpost.com/local/education/america-is-about-to-start-online-learning-round-2-for-millions-of-students-it-wont-be-any-better/2020/08/05/20aaabea-d1ae-11ea-8c55-61e7fa5e82ab_story.html

Neff, G. (2013). "Why Big Data won't cure us." *Big Data*, 1(3), 117–123. https://doi
.org/10.1089/big.2013.0029

New York Times. (n.d.). "Coronavirus in the U.S.: Latest map and case count." www
.nytimes.com/interactive/2021/us/covid-cases.html

Nield, D. (2018, September 3). "How location tracking actually works on your smartphone." Gizmodo. https://gizmodo.com/how-location-tracking-actually-works-on
-your-smartphone-1828356441

Northpointe Institute for Public Management, Inc. (2009, March). "Measurement and
treatment implications of COMPAS core scales." www.michigan.gov/documents/
corrections/Timothy_Brenne_Ph.D.__Meaning_and_Treatment_Implications_of
_COMPA_Core_Scales_297495_7.pdf

Northpointe Institute for Public Management, Inc. (2015, March). "Practitioner's guide
to COMPAS core." www.northpointeinc.com/downloads/compas/Practitioners
-Guide-COMPAS-Core-_031915.pdf

Office for Civil Rights. (2015, September 3). "Your health information privacy rights."
Department of Health and Human Services. www.hhs.gov/sites/default/files/ocr/
privacy/hipaa/understanding/consumers/consumer_rights.pdf

Office for Civil Rights. (2016, January). "Permitted uses and disclosures: Exchange for
health care operations." Department of Health and Human Services. www.hhs.gov/
sites/default/files/exchange_health_care_ops.pdf

Office of the Inspector General for the City of Chicago. (2019, April 11). "Review of
the Chicago Police Department's 'gang database.'" https://igchicago.org/2019/04/
11/review-of-the-chicago-police-departments-gang-database/

Oliver, N., Lepri, B., Sterly, H., Lambiotte, R., Deletaille, S., de Nadai, et al. (2020).
"Mobile phone data for informing public health actions across the COVID-19
pandemic life cycle." *Science Advances*, 6(23), 1–6. https://doi.org/10.1126/sciadv
.abc0764

O'Neill, P. H. (2020, August 19). "Contact tracing apps are only one part of the pandemic fight." *MIT Technology Review*. www.technologyreview.com/2020/08/19/
1007452/contact-tracing-apps-study

Pagliery, J. (2014, May 20). "How AT&T got busted up and pierced back together."
CNN. https://money.cnn.com/2014/05/20/technology/att-merger-history

Pasquale, F. (2017). "Response: Toward a fourth law of robotics: Preserving attribu-
tion, responsibility, and explainability in an algorithmic society" [Lecture]. *Ohio
State Law Journal*, 78, 1243–1255.

Pasquale, F. (2020). *New Laws of Robotics: Defending Human Expertise in the Age of
AI*. Belknap Press.

Perrigo, B. (2020, October 9). "U.S. states are rolling out COVID-19 contact tracing
apps. Months of evidence from Europe shows they're no silver bullet." *Time*. https://
time.com/5898559/covid-19-contact-tracing-apps-privacy/

Petrozzino, C. (2020). "Big Data analytics: Ethical considerations make a difference."
The SciTech Lawyer, 16(3).

Pew Research Center. (2021, April 7). "Mobile fact sheet." www.pewresearch.org/
internet/fact-sheet/mobile/

Phaneuf, A. (2021, January 11). "Latest trends in medical monitoring devices and
wearable health technology." Business Insider. www.businessinsider.com/wearable
-technology-healthcare-medical-devices?

Pierson, D. (2021, January 5). "Singapore says police can use COVID contact-tracing
data." *Los Angeles Times*. www.latimes.com/world-nation/story/2021-01-05/
singapore-coronavirus-contact-trace-data-criminal-investigations

Plater, R. (2020, May 28). "As many as 80 percent of people with COVID-19 aren't aware they have the virus." Healthline. www.healthline.com/health-news/50-percent -of-people-with-covid19-not-aware-have-virus

Policing in Chicago Research Group. (2018, February). "Tracked and targeted: Early findings on Chicago's gang database." http://erasethedatabase.com/wp-content/ uploads/2018/02/Tracked-Targeted-0217.pdf

Policing Project. (2020, May 20). "COVID-19: Stay-at-home and social distancing enforcement." NYU School of Law. www.policingproject.org/news-main/2020/5/ 20/covid-19-stay-at-home-and-social-distancing-enforcement

ProPublica. (n.d.). "A user's guide to democracy." ProPublica. www.propublica.org/ series/a-users-guide-to-democracy

Ravitch, D. (2020, January 17). "ProPublica exposes the big business of lobbying." Diane Ravitch's Blog. https://dianeravitch.net/2020/01/17/propublica-exposes-the -big-business-of-lobbying

Reddy, S. (2020, September 21). "Temperature isn't a good litmus test for coronavirus, doctors say." *Wall Street Journal*. www.wsj.com/articles/temperature-isnt-a-good -litmus-test-for-coronavirus-doctors-say-11600713159

Rhue, L., & Sundararajan, A. (2014). "Digital access, political networks and the dif-fusion of democracy." *Social Networks*, 36, 40–53. https://doi.org/10.1016/j.socnet .2012.06.007

Richardson, R., Schultz, J. M., & Crawford, K. (2019, December 17). "Dirty data, bad predictions: How civil rights violations impact police data, predictive policing systems, and justice." *NYU Law Review*. www.nyulawreview.org/online -features/dirty-data-bad-predictions-how-civil-rights-violations-impact-police-data -predictive-policing-systems-and-justice/

Romm, T., Dwoskin, E., & Timberg, C. (2020, March 17). "U.S. government, tech industry discussing ways to use smartphone location data to combat coronavirus." *Washington Post*. www.washingtonpost.com/technology/2020/03/17/white-house -location-data-coronavirus/

Rosenwald, M. S. (2021, February 22). "History's deadliest pandemics, from ancient Rome to modern America." *Washington Post*. www.washingtonpost.com/graphics/ 2020/local/retropolis/coronavirus-deadliest-pandemics/

Ruktanonchai, N. W., DeLeenheer, P., Tatem, A. J., Alegana, V. A., Caughlin, T. T., Zu Erbach-Schoenberg, E., Lourenço, C., Ruktanonchai, C. W., & Smith, D. L. (2016). "Identifying malaria transmission foci for elimination using human mobility data." *PLOS Computational Biology*, 12(4), e1004846. https://doi.org/10.1371/journal .pcbi.1004846

Sato, M. (2020, December 14). "Contact tracing apps now cover nearly half of America. It's not too late to use one." *MIT Technology Review*. www.technologyreview.com/ 2020/12/14/1014426/covid-california-contact-tracing-app-america-states/

Sauer, L. M. (2021, May 19). "What is coronavirus?" Johns Hopkins Medicine. www .hopkinsmedicine.org/health/conditions-and-diseases/coronavirus

Scholz, L. H. (2020). "Fiduciary boilerplate: Locating fiduciary relationships in infor-mation age consumer transactions." *Journal of Corporation Law*, 46, 143.

Scott, E. (2021, January 28). "What you need to know about the Philly Fighting COVID scandal." WHYY. https://whyy.org/articles/what-you-need-to-know-about -the-philly-fighting-covid-scandal

Smialek, J. (2020, June 18). "Major employers left out of government's coronavirus relief plan." *New York Times*. www.nytimes.com/2020/06/02/business/economy/ major-employers-coronavirus-relief.html

Smith v. Maryland, 442 U.S. 735 (1979).

Spinks, R. (2017, August 1). "Using a physical fitness app taught me the scary truth about why privacy settings are a feminist issue." Quartz. https://qz.com/1042852/using-a-fitness-app-taught-me-the-scary-truth-about-why-privacy-settings-are-a-feminist-issue/

Spivak, C., Trask, A., & Reed, H. (2020, May 20). "Data rights for exposure notification: Overview." Data Rights for Exposure Notification. http://exposurenotification.org

Sweeney, A., & Fry, P. (2018, August 9). "Nearly 33,000 juveniles arrested over last two decades labeled as gang members by Chicago police." *Chicago Tribune*. www.chicagotribune.com/news/breaking/ct-met-chicago-police-gang-database-juveniles-20180725-story.html

Taylor, K. (2019). *Race for Profit: How Banks and the Real Estate Industry Undermined Black Homeownership*. University of North Carolina Press.

Thompson, S. A., & Warzel, C. (2019, December 19). "Twelve million phones, one dataset, zero privacy." *New York Times*. www.nytimes.com/interactive/2019/12/19/opinion/location-tracking-cell-phone.html

Timberg, C., Harwell, D., & Safarpour, A. (2020, April 29). "Most Americans are not willing or able to use an app tracking coronavirus infections. That's a problem for Big Tech's plan to slow the pandemic." *Washington Post*. www.washingtonpost.com/technology/2020/04/29/most-americans-are-not-willing-or-able-use-an-app-tracking-coronavirus-infections-thats-problem-big-techs-plan-slow-pandemic/

Tovino, S. A. (2020). "Assumed compliance." *Alabama Law Review*, 72, 279.

Turner-Lee, N., Resnick, P., & Barton, G. (2019, May 22). "Algorithmic bias detection and mitigation: Best practices and policies to reduce consumer harms." Brookings. www.brookings.edu/research/algorithmic-bias-detection-and-mitigation-best-practices-and-policies-to-reduce-consumer-harms/

United Nations. (1948). Universal Declaration of Human Rights.

United Nations Development Programme & UN Global Pulse (2017, November 16). "A guide to data innovation for development: From idea to proof-of-concept." United Nations. www.undp.org/publications/guide-data-innovation-development-idea-proof-concept

United States v. AT&T, 552 F. Supp. 131 (D.D.C. 1982), *aff'd sub nom.* Maryland v. United States, 460 U.S. 1001 (1983).

United States v. Jacobsen, 466 U.S. 109 (1984).

United States v. Miller, 425 U.S. 435 (1976).

University of Illinois at Chicago. (2020, October 21). "Mobile health: Tools, benefits, and applications." UIC Online Health Informatics. https://healthinformatics.uic.edu/blog/mobile-health/

U.S. Food and Drug Administration. (2021, June 25). "Pfizer-BioNTech COVID-19 vaccine." Department of Health and Human Services. www.fda.gov/emergency-preparedness-and-response/coronavirus-disease-2019-covid-19/pfizer-biontech-covid-19-vaccine

Valentino-DeVries, J., Lu, D., & Dance, G. J. X. (2020, April 3). "Location data says it all: Staying at home during coronavirus is a luxury." *New York Times*. www.nytimes.com/interactive/2020/04/03/us/coronavirus-stay-home-rich-poor.html

Ventura, L. (2020, November 30). "World's largest companies 2020." *Global Finance Magazine*. www.gfmag.com/global-data/economic-data/largest-companies

Verily. (2021). "Baseline COVID-19 testing program." Project Baseline. www.projectbaseline.com/studies/covid-19/

Wakabayashi, D., & Singer, N. (2020, March 16). "Coronavirus testing website goes live and quickly hits capacity." *New York Times*. www.nytimes.com/2020/03/16/technology/coronavirus-testing-website-google.html

Warzel, C. (2020, June 29). "Can this thermometer help America reopen safely?" *New York Times*. www.nytimes.com/2020/06/29/opinion/coronavirus-kinsa-thermometer.html

Washington, A. L. (2019). "How to argue with an algorithm: Lessons from the COMPASS ProPublica Debate." *The Colorado Technology Law Journal*, 17, 131.

Washington, A. L., & Rhue, L. (2021). "Tracing the invisible: Information fiduciaries and the pandemic." *American University Law Review*, 70, 1765–1797.

Waters, M. (2019). "An examination of Facebook and its impact on the financial services and housing sectors: Hearing before the House Committee on Financial Services, 116th Cong." (statement of Rep. Maxine Waters, Chairwoman, House Committee on Financial Services).

Wesolowski, A., Eagle, N., Noor, A. M., Snow, R. W., & Buckee, C. O. (2012). "Heterogeneous mobile phone ownership and usage patterns in Kenya." *PLoS ONE*, 7(4), 1–6. https://doi.org/10.1371/journal.pone.0035319

Wesolowski, A., Qureshi, T., Boni, M. F., Sundsøy, P. R., Johansson, M. A., Rasheed, S. B., Engø-Monsen, K., & Buckee, C. O. (2015). "Impact of human mobility on the emergence of dengue epidemics in Pakistan." *Proceedings of the National Academy of Sciences*, 112(38), 11887–11892. https://doi.org/10.1073/pnas.1504964112

Wesolowski, A., Buckee, C. O., Engø-Monsen, K., & Metcalf, C. J. E. (2016). "Connecting mobility to infectious diseases: The promise and limits of mobile phone data." *Journal of Infectious Diseases*, 214(suppl 4), S414–S420. https://doi.org/10.1093/infdis/jiw273

Whittaker, M., Crawford, K., Dobbe, R., Fried, G., Kaziunas, E., Mathur, V., West, S. M., Richardson, R., Schulz, J., & Schwartz, O. (2018, December). "AI Now report 2018." AI Now. https://fd-binary-external-prod.imgix.net/zNYlk1ttnMpjXFuvyA6ifLlHov0.pdf?dl=AI_Now_2018_Report.pdf.pdf

Willis, D. (2018, June 6). "New in the Congress API: Lobbying registrations and more." ProPolitica. www.propublica.org/nerds/propublica-congress-api-lobbying-registrations-and-more

World Health Organization. (2020, July 9). "Transmission of SARS-CoV-2: Implications for infection prevention precautions." www.who.int/news-room/commentaries/detail/transmission-of-sars-cov-2-implications-for-infection-prevention-precautions

PART III

Legal and ethical considerations moving forward

11. Pandemic surveillance: ethics at the intersection of information, research, and health

Daniel Susser

This chapter provides a high-level overview of key ethical issues raised by the use of surveillance technologies, such as digital contact tracing, disease surveillance, and vaccine passports, to combat the COVID-19 pandemic. To some extent, these issues are entirely familiar. I argue that they raise old questions in new form and with new urgency, at the intersection of information ethics, research ethics, and public health. Whenever we deal with data-driven technologies, we have to ask how they fare in relation to important values like privacy, fairness, transparency, and accountability—values emphasized by information ethics scholars. Likewise, when such technologies put individuals at risk in order to drive scientific research and knowledge construction, we have to ask how they implicate values such as autonomy, beneficence and non-maleficence, and justice—values central to research ethics. And as researchers focusing on health information have long argued, when the data collected by these technologies pertain to individuals and public health, these ethical issues take on a special cast.

It is also true, however, that the pandemic has placed these questions in a new and revealing light. I highlight three insights from information ethics and research ethics that can help us navigate this difficult terrain. First, the value of privacy is instrumental, not absolute—there is nothing wrong with asking how to balance privacy against other important values. Second, privacy has both individual and social importance. Weighing privacy, on one hand, and public health, on the other, is not, therefore, a contest between individual and collective interests. Rather, it is an attempt to balance disparate public goods. Third, we ought to put these kinds of ethical decisions in the hands of third parties, rather than leaving them up to those who directly stand to benefit from them. In the case of pandemic surveillance technologies, this should mean more public, democratic oversight.

VALUES AT STAKE

Pandemic surveillance requires collecting, storing, analyzing, disseminating, and making decisions on the basis of huge amounts of information, raising critical questions that information and data ethicists have carefully studied. Several values tend to take center stage in these discussions: privacy, fairness, transparency, and accountability.

Questions about privacy ask how information about us flows. For example: Who collects information about us, by what means, and under which conditions? How to define privacy—and thus how to collect information in a manner that respects privacy—is the subject of significant controversy. Without trying to resolve these debates, here I draw attention to aspects of data collection that various approaches to privacy suggest are centrally important.

In US law and policy, information privacy is typically conceptualized as individual control over the flow of personal information (Westin, 2015). On this view, what matters most is that people are notified about data collection (digital or otherwise) and given the option to consent to or withhold consent from such collection at the initial point of capture (i.e., to "control" it) (Susser, 2019). The European Union's approach is more complicated. For present purposes, suffice it to say that it focuses on a more robust set of protections that aim not only to give individuals control over information about themselves (as the US approach does), but also to ensure that data collectors handle such information in ways that comport with European fundamental rights, and that third parties that buy and sell personal information are held to the same standards (Jones & Kaminski, 2021). A third approach to conceptualizing privacy is Helen Nissenbaum's theory of privacy as contextual integrity, which posits that norms governing how information ought to flow are intrinsically context-specific. On this view, the principal issue is whether data collectors gather and use information in ways that are contextually appropriate (Nissenbaum, 2010).

Thus, with respect to privacy, we might ask about pandemic surveillance technologies, such as contact tracing apps and vaccine passports, whether individuals are informed about the information that is being collected about them, about how it is used, and about the potential risks and benefits of its disclosure. Are they given the opportunity to choose whether to participate in these systems—to consent or withhold consent from data collection? Does data collection for the purposes of pandemic surveillance implicate European fundamental rights? Does data collection respect contextual norms, or is data collected in one context being put to use in others?[1]

In contrast with worries about privacy, worries about fairness generally focus less on information collection and more on its analysis and use as the basis for important decisions, especially when decision-making is automated.[2] Scholars have long argued that computational systems can perpetuate bias, whether by impacting people unfairly, encoding discriminatory attitudes of their designers, or reflecting unjust social conditions in which they are designed and deployed (Friedman & Nissenbaum, 1996). These concerns are especially salient in relation to machine learning and other artificial intelligence systems—technologies that work by inferring decision-making logics, statistically, from data about past decisions, rather than by following rules articulated explicitly in advance. Such systems have been shown to be particularly susceptible to bias, because the datasets they learn from mirror historical patterns of injustice pervasive in society.[3]

The COVID-19 pandemic has affected different communities in different ways, often reflecting and deepening preexisting disparities (Wood, 2020). Without care and attention to questions about fairness, the technologies introduced to end the pandemic could make these disparities worse. Organizations developing and deploying such technologies ought to ask questions like: How is the data driving our decision-making collected? Are datasets equally representative of different social groups? What kinds of biases might reasonably be expected in the data, and how can they be adjusted for? How are decision-making outcomes distributed across social groups? Is information about group status—especially membership in protected classes, such as those related to race, gender, religion, and so on—affecting the decisions that automated systems reach?

Lastly, abstract concerns about privacy and fairness are of little practical value if violations and inequities cannot be detected and redressed. The values of transparency and accountability emphasize the importance of structures and practices that enable individuals, organizations, and communities to ensure other values are upheld. Transparency, as we've seen, is core to how privacy is operationalized in US law and policy—to respect individual privacy is, on

---

[1]   For example, in Singapore, contact tracing data was appropriated by the police for law enforcement purposes (Illmer, 2021).

[2]   This is not to say the two values are entirely independent. Privacy protections are often unequally distributed—with marginalized groups subjected to more surveillance than privileged groups—raising fairness concerns about privacy (see, e.g., Bridges, 2020).

[3]   This issue has become the subject of a large and growing field of research (see, e.g., Mehrabi et al., 2021).

this approach, to make data collection and use transparent through privacy disclosures (i.e., "notice") and to seek individual consent in relation to it. But that is not the only relevant transparency requirement. Breach notification laws, for example, require data collectors to notify affected parties when information collected about them is exposed in a breach, and transparency requirements in the EU General Data Protection Regulation (GDPR) are designed to help people understand how automated decisions about them are reached (Bayamlıoğlu, 2018).

Worries about whether people subject to decision-making by automated systems can understand and contest decisions reached about them are becoming especially important as more decisions—both routine and significant—are delegated to computers. In the context of the COVID-19 pandemic, for example, we have seen some hospitals use automated decision-making systems to determine the order in which people were given access to vaccines (Harwell, 2020; Singer, 2021). To ensure that such systems and the organizations utilizing them are held to ethical standards, we should ask whether people know and understand that decisions about them are being made by automated systems, if the data and algorithms driving these systems are accessible to third-party auditors, and if their decision-making logics are explainable to the people they affect.

Pandemic surveillance implicates questions beyond those familiar to information ethics. Because one goal of pandemic surveillance is to advance scientific research on COVID-19, it also raises questions familiar to research ethics. These discussions generally focus on the values of autonomy, beneficence and non-maleficence, and justice.

Personal autonomy is the capacity for independent decision-making—the ability to choose for oneself, free from pressure, manipulation, or coercion (Roessler, 2021). It is a foundational value in liberal democratic societies, core to ideas of individual freedom and collective self-government. Research ethics, having developed partly in response to infamous cases of scientists experimenting on research subjects without their knowledge or against their will—such as Nazi medical experiments in World War II and the Tuskegee Syphilis Study, conducted for several decades in the middle of the 20th century—places significant emphasis on the right of individuals to choose freely, *autonomously*, to take part in scientific research. Usually, this right is operationalized through the mechanism of informed consent: before someone is implicated in scientific research, the person must be informed about it and given the opportunity to choose whether to participate (National Commission for the Protection of Human Subjects of Biomedical and Behavioral Research, 1979).

Where autonomy emphasizes free choice, the values of beneficence (i.e., "do good") and non-maleficence ("do no harm") point to the potential effects of scientific research or experimentation on people's welfare. Will taking part in a scientific study make someone better or worse off? What are the risks and benefits associated with participation, both to research subjects and society more broadly? Beyond respecting the autonomy of research subjects by creating conditions under which they can freely choose whether to take part in research, research ethics expects that participants in scientific research will not be subjected to disproportionate risks, relative to the potential individual and societal benefits of the study (National Commission for the Protection of Human Subjects of Biomedical and Behavioral Research, 1979).

And as with fairness in discussions about information ethics, the focus on justice in research ethics emphasizes the need to ensure that the risks and benefits of scientific research are evenly distributed across social groups. Historically, marginalized groups have often been the first to be burdened by scientific research and the last to benefit from it, subjected to disproportionate risk relative to other groups and deprived of access to new treatments, techniques, and other fruits of successful research and experimentation. For example, in the Tuskegee Syphilis Study, treatment for the disease was withheld from most of the research subjects harmed in the experiment, even after therapies were widely available (Corbie-Smith, 1999). In designing research programs, it is therefore crucial to consider not only the rights and welfare of individual research subjects, but also the distribution of costs and benefits across society.

Developing pandemic surveillance technologies that advance scientific understanding of COVID-19 and help test treatments and strategies for combating it while respecting the core values of research ethics—autonomy, beneficence and non-maleficence, and justice—requires asking difficult questions and being prepared to make complex trade-offs. Will individuals subjected to these technologies be clearly informed about their implication in research, and will they be given the opportunity to make autonomous decisions about whether to participate? What are the specific costs and benefits of research, both to individuals and society? Do the benefits of particular research efforts outweigh potential harms? How are risks and benefits distributed across social groups? Are some groups exposed to disproportionate risk and others given access to disproportionate benefit? These are difficult questions, which cannot be resolved in the abstract; they must be raised in relation to each particular research effort and answered by considering its concrete design, manner of deployment, and expected impacts. As I discuss briefly in the next section, weighing such trade-offs is especially difficult in the context of a public health emergency like the COVID-19 pandemic. But we have no choice but to weigh them.

Finally, as if these ethical questions were not difficult enough, they are complicated further by the fact that they involve health information.

Obviously, health information can be highly sensitive, and the harms people suffer from its misuse are severe. Disclosing someone's health status can provoke powerful social stigma. Consider, for example, the stigma historically suffered by people who are HIV positive—especially gay men. Moreover, such disclosures can serve as the basis for harmful forms of discrimination in the provision of important goods, such as housing and employment. It is not difficult to imagine the kinds of stigma and discrimination that might result from careless stewardship of COVID-related health information, such as test results, vaccination status, or contact tracing data. Although other kinds of personal information, such as location information or internet browsing histories, can be very revealing and deserve significant protection, disclosure of health information threatens particularly acute harms.

In addition to being highly sensitive, health information raises complex ethics and policy challenges because its disclosure exposes not only the individuals it was collected from but also potentially their family members and other close associates. Genetic information provides the classic illustration of this problem: Given that our family members share a great deal in common with us genetically, revealing information about one person's genetic profile can be equally revealing of the person's parents, siblings, and children. Information about COVID diagnoses, vaccination status, and contact tracing creates similar dynamics: for example, knowledge that someone is COVID positive plausibly implicates people the person lives and works with. The nature of health information complicates the preceding discussion because, as we've seen, information ethics and research ethics often focus on empowering individuals. Yet it isn't clear that individuals should be empowered to decide whether to disclose information that might implicate their roommates or close kin.

LESSONS FOR AND FROM COVID-19

The ethical issues described in the previous section are complex and demanding. I want to highlight three insights from information ethics and research ethics that can help guide discussions about how to meet these challenges.

First, although privacy is often discussed in a way that suggests its value is absolute—that is, that it should never be traded off against other goods—most privacy scholars and advocates argue otherwise (see, e.g., Moore & Katell, 2016). Privacy is deeply important, for both individual and collective flourishing, but it is not good *in itself*. Rather, privacy is an instrumental value, something we pursue for what it affords us—the space for free thought and expression, reprieve from the judgmental gaze of others, the conditions for intimacy, and other essential goods (Warren & Brandeis, 1890; Fried, 1968, pp. 478–480). When privacy and other values conflict, trade-offs have to be weighed.

COVID-19 furnishes a compelling case in point: many have argued that to bring the pandemic under control, we ought to give up privacy in the name of more accurate, granular contact tracing and disease surveillance. In other words, some argue that privacy is in tension with another centrally important (perhaps more important) value: public health. Others disagree. Privacy and public health are mutually compatible, they argue, because researchers have developed strategies for conducting contact tracing in a manner that is simultaneously accurate and privacy preserving (Apple & Google, 2021; Wacksman, 2021). Who has it right remains a subject of much debate. But if there really is a tension between privacy and public health, we need not commit to any particular resolution in advance. Even the most committed privacy proponents would likely concede that compelling people to disclose information about themselves—sacrificing some privacy—could be worth it for the sake of bringing the pandemic to an end, especially in conjunction with safeguards that ensure the information isn't used for other purposes.[4]

Second, there is a temptation to frame the ethical trade-offs described above as a conflict between an individual right (privacy) and a collective one (public health). Given the way that privacy is often theorized—especially in US law and policy—it is easy to understand why. However, this framing makes it very difficult, in practice, to resolve questions about how to balance these different kinds of goods. In pluralistic, liberal democratic societies there are deep disagreements about whether individual or collective interests ought to be given pride of place. Those on the libertarian side of the political spectrum argue that individual rights trump collective ones, while those on the social-democratic side argue the reverse. Thus, when framed as a contest between individual and collective pursuits, deciding whether to prioritize individual privacy or public health requires first resolving these more fundamental—perhaps intractable—tensions.

Yet privacy scholars have long argued that privacy is not *merely* good for individuals; it is also a social good (see, e.g., Cohen, 2012; Regan, 2000, pp. 212–217; Reidenberg, 1992; Nissenbaum, 2010). Which is to say, not

---

[4]   Of course, privacy advocates can offer many other reasons against adopting invasive forms of surveillance and tracking, even under emergency conditions and in the name of public health. For example, technology studies scholars have long pointed out that surveillance infrastructures built for one purpose tend to be put to other uses—so-called "surveillance creep" (Marx, 1988). Indeed, we have already seen this in the context of pandemic technologies, in the Singapore case mentioned above. The point here is that privacy is something that *can* be balanced against other important values. Whether it ought to be has to be determined case by case.

only are we individually worse off without privacy, but society as a whole is worse off without it. Absent privacy, societies are more conformist and less open. They do not benefit from the new, challenging ideas people are able to advance when they have the privacy to entertain and develop them. And such societies can easily give way to authoritarian forms of power, if individuals are not allowed to live significant parts of their lives free from unwanted surveillance. Framing the problem this way helps us see that we are not dealing with a problem of reconciling two different kinds of interests—individual privacy versus public health. Rather, it's a question of balancing two public goods: How should we trade off the social benefits of privacy against the social benefits of public health? In this way, emphasizing the social value of privacy can help us avoid unproductive debates about the relative importance of individual and collective goods.

Third and finally, research ethics reminds us that when arbitrating between competing values, it is often important to solicit the perspective of a neutral third party, a person or an institution that does not stand to benefit directly from the decision. In research ethics, that third party is usually an institutional review board, or IRB. We do not ask the scientists proposing sensitive research to determine for themselves whether its potential benefits outweigh potential costs—to experimental subjects or society at large. We task a panel of peer scientists, ethicists, and members of the public to independently make that determination.

In the case of pandemic surveillance technologies, we may want to create similar decision-making structures. Rather than expecting individual companies, health departments, and other institutions to make these ethical decisions on their own, we should place them in the hands of third parties—for example, independent ethics boards or regulatory agencies. Better yet, we should demand democratic oversight. This could take many different forms: opportunities for public comment and debate, citizen juries or so-called "minipublics," or formal votes in local or national legislatures (Greitens, 2020, pp. 182–185; Fung, 2007). Whatever the mechanism, we could decide collectively how to navigate the difficult ethical challenges raised by these difficult circumstances.

REFERENCES

Apple & Google. (2021, April). "Exposure Notification Privacy-preserving Analytics (ENPA)" [White Paper]. https://covid19-static.cdn-apple.com/applications/covid19/current/static/contact-tracing/pdf/ENPA_White_Paper.pdf

Bayamlıoğlu, E. (2018). "Transparency of automated decisions in the GDPR: An attempt for systemisation." http://dx.doi.org/10.2139/ssrn.3097653

Bridges, K. M. (2020). *The Poverty of Privacy Rights*. Stanford University Press.

Cohen, J. E. (2012). "What privacy is for." *Harvard Law Review*, 126, 1904–1933.

Corbie-Smith, G. (1999). "The continuing legacy of the Tuskegee Syphilis Study: Considerations for clinical investigations." *American Journal of the Medical Sciences*, 317(1), 5–8. https://doi.org/10.1016/S0002-9629(15)40464-1

Fried, C. (1968). "Privacy." *Yale Law Review*, 77(3), 475–493. https://doi.org/10.2307/794941

Friedman, B., & Nissenbaum, H. (1996). "Bias in computer systems." *ACM Transactions on Information Systems*, 14(3), 330–347.

Fung, A. (2007). "Minipublics: Deliberative designs and their consequences." In S. Rosenberg (ed.), *Deliberation, Participation and Democracy: Can the People Govern?* (pp. 159–183). Palgrave Macmillan. https://link.springer.com/chapter/10.1057/9780230591080_8

Greitens, S. C. (2020). "Surveillance, security, and liberal democracy in the post-COVID world." *International Organization*, 74(S1), E169–E190.

Harwell, D. (2020, December 23). "Algorithms are deciding who gets the first vaccines. Should we trust them?" *Washington Post*. www.washingtonpost.com/technology/2020/12/23/covid-vaccine-algorithm-failure/

Illmer, A. (2021, July 5). "Singapore reveals Covid privacy data available to police." BBC. www.bbc.com/news/world-asia-55541001

Jones, M. L., & Kaminski, M. E. (2021). "An American's guide to the GDPR." *Denver Law Review*, 98, 93–128.

Marx, G. (1988). *Undercover: Police Surveillance in America*. University of California Press.

Mehrabi, N., Morstatter, F., Saxena, N., Lerman, K., & Galstyan, A. (2021). "A survey on bias and fairness in machine learning." *ACM Computing Surveys*, 54(6), 1–35. https://doi.org/10.1145/3457607

Moore, A., & Katell, M. (2016). "Introduction." In A. Moore (ed.), *Privacy, Security, and Accountability: Ethics, Law, and Policy*. Rowman and Littlefield.

National Commission for the Protection of Human Subjects of Biomedical and Behavioral Research. (1979). "The Belmont Report: Ethical Principles and Guidelines for the Protection of Human Subjects of Research." US Department of Health and Human Services.

Nissenbaum, H. F. (2010). *Privacy in Context: Technology, Policy, and the Integrity of Social Life*. Stanford University Press.

Regan, P. M. (2000). *Legislating Privacy: Technology, Social Values, and Public Policy*. University of North Carolina Press. www.jstor.org/stable/10.5149/9780807864050_regan

Reidenberg, J. R. (1992). "Privacy in the information economy: Fortress or frontier for individual rights." *Federal Communications Law Journal*, 44(2), 195–244.

Roessler, B. (2021). *Autonomy: An Essay on the Life Well Lived*. Polity Press.

Singer, N. (2021, February 7). "Where do vaccine doses go, and who gets them? The algorithms decide." *New York Times*. www.nytimes.com/2021/02/07/technology/vaccine-algorithms.html

Susser, D. (2019). "Notice after notice-and-consent: Why privacy disclosures are valuable even if consent frameworks aren't." *Journal of Information Policy*, 9, 148–173. https://doi.org/10.5325/jinfopoli.9.2019.0148

Wacksman, J. (2021). "Digitalization of contact tracing: Balancing data privacy with public health benefit." *Ethics and Information Technology*, 1–7.

Warren, S., & Brandeis, L. (1890). "The right to privacy." *Harvard Law Review*, 4(5), 193–220. https://doi.org/10.2307/1321160

Westin, A. (2015). *Privacy and Freedom*. IG Publishing.

Wood, D. (2020, September 23). "As pandemic deaths add up, racial disparities persist—and in some cases worsen." NPR. www.npr.org/sections/health-shots/ 2020/09/23/914427907/as-pandemic-deaths-add-up-racial-disparities-persist-and-in -some-cases-worsen

12. Using personal data and data-driven technologies for research and public health in the context of the COVID-19 pandemic

Bethânia de Araújo Almeida

Scientific research involving humans requires ethical approval from a review board and the permission of study participants, who are informed of the potential risks and benefits of their participation and reserve the right to withdraw consent at any time. Research conducted in the field of health to address scientific issues has traditionally employed data containing personal information, for example, populational characteristics and laboratory and hospital data, among others, in accordance with ethical and legal guidelines. The ethical evaluation of research is based on a set of fundamentals, including the social relevance of the research in question and a commitment to providing maximum benefits while minimizing possible damage and risks.

In scientific research, data are treated, visualized, and interpreted using models and theories specific to disciplines and areas of knowledge in order to serve as confirmation or empirical refutation of a study's hypothesis. The coherence and validation of observations and experiments are demonstrated by data that corroborate findings, which are then evaluated by peers. The growing production and use of data in an increasingly digitized world has prompted the emergence of new forms of knowledge production that use information not originally collected for research purposes, but which can be prepared and integrated to respond to scientific questions (Barreto et al., 2019, p. 181).

Because of the impossibility of obtaining informed consent in these cases, waivers may be requested if justified. The request for a waiver of consent must be based on and evaluated with regard to the responsibilities assumed by researchers to mitigate risks and ensure the rights of study participants, including the implementation of procedures aimed at preserving the confidentiality and privacy of data subjects, as well as at preventing the stigmatization of individuals or groups.

Aspects related to privacy, information security, and the use of data containing personal information for scientific and public health research purposes are considered by some general data protection laws, such as those in Brazil and Europe (Lei Geral de Proteção de Dados Pessoais [LGPD], 2018; Regulation (EU) 2016/679 [GDPR], 2016). Data protection laws are designed to protect the fundamental rights of freedom and privacy, and aim to establish guiding principles and concepts to preserve the balance between effectively protecting the rights of data subjects while still allowing for the processing of personal and sensitive data for certain purposes under specified conditions. The struggle between preserving rights and exploiting valuable data also represents an opportunity to stimulate the debate surrounding the consequences of the use of data-driven technologies and increasingly sophisticated surveillance techniques by public and private entities.

Large-scale data analytics has gained increasing relevance for scientists and health authorities, mainly for data related to behaviors and health conditions in the face of the COVID-19 pandemic. The collection and processing of data via applications and digital devices (mobile technologies) has been highlighted as a means of monitoring quarantine compliance, conducting probabilistic contagion assessments, and managing permissions to go out in public, in addition to other aspects of individual and collective life. Partnerships between governments and technology companies aimed at developing applications that permit the collection of personal data, such as location, contact, and health information, have become more frequent in efforts to contain the COVID-19 pandemic (Almeida et al., 2020, pp. 2488–2489; Editorial, *Nature*, 2020; *Economist*, 2020).

From this perspective, political, regulatory, and societal aspects related to privacy, information security, and basic human rights must be considered. Policies should be aligned and implemented with regard to the development and use of data-driven technologies, especially in the context of the COVID-19 pandemic (Ada Lovelace Institute, 2020). The collection and processing of data has taken place—supposedly in the name of public health and public interest—while circumventing proper scrutiny during the rushed process of adopting technological solutions to social and public health problems (Almeida et al., 2020, pp. 2490–2491).

Ethical, legal, and social questions about the use of data-driven technologies have been raised more frequently during the pandemic because of threats to privacy and other aspects, including the potential for consequences, intentional or not, on civil and political rights in light of risks for abuse. It is important to note the lack of transparency and accountability regarding the types of data collected, as well as an absence of efforts to minimize data collection and processing, such as restricting these activities to exclusively achieve stated purposes. Moreover, data subjects are often unaware with whom their information has been shared, whether the data collected will continue to be stored after the health crisis, and under what conditions (Almeida et al., 2020, p. 2490).

DATA-GUIDED TECHNOLOGIES AND THE COVID-19 PANDEMIC

Increased data collection and use of data have generated new methods of producing knowledge that utilize algorithms and sophisticated computational models to generate and extract information from large volumes of data from a single source or linked from multiple sources. Thus, it becomes necessary to reflect on the potential advantages of using different data sources as well as associated impacts and challenges.

Technology companies, such as Google and Facebook, possess a considerable amount of all personal data generated worldwide, as well as the means to extract the maximum value from this data. Their power has become even greater because of the volume of data generated by the migration of users from personal computers to cell phones, whose applications often continually collect data about users' locations and behaviors. The ability to monitor and infer information about users, or to dispense specific information that may influence or manipulate behaviors, is an unsettling predicament that can imply negative consequences for both individuals and society as a whole (Zuboff, 2019, pp. 8–12; Naughton, 2019). In the context of the COVID-19 pandemic, these companies have become even more powerful thanks to exponential increases in online activity and consequent increases in the generation and collection of citizens' digital data worldwide (Kind, 2020).

Additionally, considering the growing use of both Big Data analytics and artificial intelligence (AI), there are new risks for data subjects' rights related to inferential analysis used to support important decisions. As the EU data protection law provides an inadequate legal basis to assess decision-making processes based on these technologies, some authors argue that a new right to reasonable inferences must be considered to provide accountability on high-risk inferences that cause harm or have low verifiability. Among the recommendations for EU policy are a focus on how data is evaluated; not just focusing on identifiable data, which is fluid and can change over time because of technological progress; the justification of data sources and intended inferences before the deployment of inferential analytics at scale; and the granting of data subject rights to challenge unreasonable inferences (Wachter & Mittelstadt, 2019).

The potential usefulness of inferences generated by Big Data and AI should be subject to scrutiny and adhere to responsible, regulated ethical and moral standards. Digital trends and transformations have become accelerated during the COVID-19 pandemic, including our relationship with digital technologies, through the need to follow protocols and adopt new behaviors to avoid infection, illness, and death. In this newly reconfigured society, algorithms now play a central role as a result of increased use of platforms and new applications.

To prevent abuse or unintended negative consequences because of COVID-19-related data collection and use in the name of public health, some authors argue that sharing accumulated experiences on data protection in the context of humanitarian crises may prove valuable. For example, the Red Cross International Committee produced a data protection manual for use in humanitarian actions, which applies to applications that track user location, collect biometric information, and monitor the use of cloud-based services (Kuner & Marelli, 2020). These authors note that location data can be very useful in epidemiological analysis; yet in the context of political crises, this can also be used to target individuals and groups, placing democratic ideals and human rights at risk (Zwitter & Gstrein, 2020, pp. 1, 3).

Other initiatives have upheld the central role of the use of data and accumulated experiences to achieve humanitarian objectives while protecting personal data. For example, the resolution adopted by the Global Privacy Assembly (2020) brings together the authorities charged with data protection of practically every nation, and the regimented documentation specified in the UN Global Pulse (2020) project also respects individual privacy while permitting data collection and processing.

It is important to note that historically, data access and data-sharing principles in the context of international health emergency responses have been delineated by research funders and multilateral agencies, mainly with respect to scientific data (see, e.g., Wellcome, 2016; Littler et al., 2017, p. 243; GloPID-R, 2018, pp. 4–6). However, the COVID-19 pandemic has intensified this discussion and expanded its scope to include other sources of data. A recent statement on governance, operations, and skills was published by the science academies of the Group of Seven (G7) nations, the world's seven biggest economies. It states, among other points, that national rules and regulations on data governance regimes will be required to ensure a global legal interoperability among countries (Royal Society, 2021).

Regulations represent the only mechanism capable of controlling data access in emergency situations while establishing permissions and limits on the processing of personal data (Almeida et al., 2020, p. 2490). This will shape roles, rules, and protocols among researchers, corporations, regulators, and policymakers in an attempt to avoid negative impacts resulting from temporary abeyance.

Data has always been an important asset in the production of knowledge and evidence. For this reason, it is important to call attention to the great potential of the growing production and use of data, supported by ever-more-powerful and specialized digital technologies. Thus, it becomes necessary to reflect on

the potential of using different data sources for public health research purposes, as well as to address associated societal impacts and challenges.

In this sense, the establishment of novel legal concepts regarding personal
data processing is part of this regulatory process, as it is important to denom-
inate this phenomenon in order to understand it, as well as to guide the social
and economic logic that defines how we use these technologies (Naughton,
2019). Narratives, discourses, and concepts about data shape the way we
think about it (Patel, 2020), whether as a raw material (i.e., commodities),
as a private product, or as a public good. The establishment of updated legal
concepts related to data-driven technologies will help us understand and deal
with the complex dynamics of social phenomena as they arise or become
established.

FINAL CONSIDERATIONS

The collection, processing, and analysis of data, including personal data,
are central and universal to public health actions and to the actions being
implemented to control the current devastating pandemic. However, the establishment of a data governance system, in an ethical, transparent, responsible,
and equitable manner, is also a global demand that cannot be undertaken by
a single country or jurisdiction. The use of digital technologies to respond
to the challenges posed by the COVID-19 pandemic may not just represent
a means of containing the health crisis, but could also represent an opportunity. It may be possible to overcome the current ethical and social dilemmas
faced by an increasingly data-driven world, characterized by immense asymmetries of power and knowledge that favor the large companies that dominate
data-driven technology sectors.

Technologies that utilize personal data in the context of monitoring the pandemic provide evidence of dilemmas, which are not restricted to health crises,
but have become more evident as a result. These dilemmas require collective
action and multidisciplinary approaches.

The definition of guiding concepts and values is central to the establishment of universal policies, regulations, and practical recommendations in
the defense of individual privacy, collective autonomy, and the rights and
obligations of those who develop, utilize, and are affected by these types of
technologies. Appropriate governmental structures that transparently articulate
information regarding decision-making aimed at coordinating and balancing
distinct, and sometimes conflicting, interests are essential to implement protective mechanisms against abuse and uphold accountability.

Technologies are tools, and their uses, applications, and effects assume
distinct forms depending on the social, political, and economic realities and
values that shape them. There is a need to create frameworks capable of ena-

bling reflection on and governance of the emerging technologies that employ personal data in an ever more digitally oriented world. These technologies could constitute powerful resources in the search for answers to the current humanitarian and health crisis provoked by COVID-19, and could serve to address other current or future health, societal, and environmental challenges.

REFERENCES

Ada Lovelace Institute. (2020, May 4). "Provisos for a contact tracing app: The route to trustworthy digital contact tracing." www.adalovelaceinstitute.org/evidence-review/provisos-covid-19-contact-tracing-app/

Almeida, B. A., Doneda, D., Ichihara, M. Y., Barral-Netto, M., Matta, G. C., Rabello, E. T., Gouveia, F. C., & Barreto, M. (2020). "Personal data usage and privacy considerations in the COVID-19 global pandemic." *Ciência & Saúde Coletiva*, 25(S1), 2487–2492. https://doi.org/10.1590/1413-81232020256.1.11792020

Barreto, M. L, Almeida, B. A., Doneda, D. (2019). "Uso e proteção de dados pessoais na pesquisa científica" [Use and protection of personal data in scientific research]. *Public Law Magazine*, 16(90), 179–194.

Economist (2020, April 18). "App-based contact tracing may help countries get out of lockdown. But only as part of a bigger system." *The Economist*. www.economist.com/science-and-technology/2020/04/16/app-based-contact-tracing-may-help-countries-get-out-of-lockdown

Editorial, *Nature* (2020, April 29). "Show evidence that apps for COVID-19 contact-tracing are secure and effective." *Nature*. www.nature.com/articles/d41586-020-01264-1

Global Privacy Assembly. (2020, October). "Adopted resolution on the role of personal data protection in international development aid, international humanitarian aid and crisis management." https://globalprivacyassembly.org/wp-content/uploads/2020/10/FINAL-GPA-Resolution-International-Aid-EN.pdf

GloPID-R. (2018, June). "Principles of data sharing in public health emergencies." www.glopid-r.org/wp-content/uploads/2018/06/glopid-r-principles-of-data-sharing-in-public-health-emergencies.pdf

Kind, C. (2020, April 2). "What will the first pandemic of the algorithmic age mean for data governance?" Ada Lovelace Institute. www.adalovelaceinstitute.org/what-will-the-first-pandemic-of-the-algorithmic-age-mean-for-data-governance/

Kuner, C., & Marelli, M. (eds.) (2020). *Handbook on Data Protection in Humanitarian Action* (2nd edn). International Committee of the Red Cross. www.icrc.org/en/data-protection-humanitarian-action-handbook

Lei Geral de Proteção de Dados Pessoais [General Personal Data Protection Law] (LGPD). Law No. 13.079 (2018, August 14). www.planalto.gov.br/ccivil_03/_ato2015-2018/2018/lei/L13709.htm

Littler, K., Boon, W., Carson, G., Depoortere, E., Mathewson, S., Mietchen, D., Moorthy, V. S., O'Connor, D., Roth, C., & Segovia, C. (2017). "Progress in promoting data sharing in public health emergencies." *Bulletin World Health Organization*, 95, 243. http://dx.doi.org/10.2471/BLT.17.192096

Naughton, J. (2019, January 20). "'The goal is to automate us': Welcome to the age of surveillance capitalism." *The Guardian*. www.theguardian.com/technology/2019/jan/20/shoshana-zuboff-age-of-surveillance-capitalism-google-facebook

Patel, R. (2020, January 23). "Changing the data governance ecosystem—through nar-ratives, practices and regulations." Ada Lovelace Institute. www.adalovelaceinstitute .org/changing-the-data-governance-ecosystem-through-narratives-practices-and -regulations/

Regulation (EU) 2016/679 of the European Parliament and of the Council of 27 April 2016 on the protection of natural persons with regard to the processing of personal data and on the free movement of such data and repealing Directive 95/36/EC (General Data Protection Regulation). 2016 O.J. (L 119). https://gdpr-info.eu/

Royal Society. (2021, March 31). "Data for international health emergencies: Governance, operations and skills." https://royalsociety.org/-/media/about-us/ international/g-science-statements/G7-data-for-international-health-emergencies-31 -03-2021.pdf

UN Global Pulse. "UN Global Pulse principles on data protection and privacy." (2020, February 5). UN Executive Office of the Secretary-General. www.unglobalpulse .org/policy/ungp-principles-on-data-privacy-and-protection/

Wachter, S. & Mittelstadt, B. (2019). "A right to reasonable inferences: Re-thinking data protection law in the age of Big Data and AI." *Columbia Business Law Review*, 2019(2).

Wellcome. (2016). "Statement on data sharing in public health emergencies." https:// wellcome.org/press-release/statement-data-sharing-public-health-emergencies

Zuboff, S. (2019). *The Age of Surveillance Capitalism: The Fight for a Human Future at the New Frontier of Power*. Public Affairs.

Zwitter, A., & Gstrein, O. J. (2020). "Big data, privacy and COVID-19—learning from humanitarian expertise in data protection." *Journal of International Humanitarian Action*, 5(1), 1–7. https://doi.org/10.1186/s41018-020-00072-6

13. Pandemic ethics: the intersection of technology, trust, and privacy, and implications for marginalized communities

Jolynn Dellinger

Since the beginning of 2020, the world as we know it has undergone tumultuous change. While privacy, security, and data ethics have been growing areas for decades, the COVID-19 pandemic brought heightened attention and new dimensions to these fields. Our daily lives and work have become even more digitally mediated than usual, and we have increasingly relied on a number of emerging technologies to respond to this international crisis.

Throughout 2020, as we set about dealing with COVID-19 as a global community, countries implemented different approaches designed to assess, monitor, trace, and constrain the virus. Many of those approaches were limited, to some degree, by local laws and regulations. But to a substantial extent, no existing laws applied or, where laws did exist, the manner in which they applied to COVID-19 responsive technologies was unclear. In the absence of external constraints like laws and regulations, and in our effort to interpret applicable laws, ethical considerations must guide our multifaceted response to the pandemic. The questions we must answer implicate both privacy and trust and entail significant implications for marginalized communities and vulnerable populations. This chapter reviews the pre-pandemic trust environment; trust and privacy issues that have been raised by various manual and technological responses to the pandemic, and the implications of these responses for marginalized groups; best data practices and ethical obligations; and policy recommendations pertaining to the rebuilding of trust and the protection of data that could ultimately promote participation in public health initiatives. Trust and privacy matter. Our societal trust deficit and our failure to protect privacy have impaired our ability to respond as effectively as possible to a global pandemic.

ETHICAL OBLIGATIONS

Thinking broadly about pandemic ethics, an argument can be made that each individual has an ethical obligation to participate in measures that contain the spread of the virus. Such measures could include wearing a mask, social distancing, testing, providing personal information to contact tracers or using digital contact tracing applications, quarantining in some circumstances—forgoing both work and social interaction—and getting a vaccine when vaccines are available. Some measures may involve the sharing and disclosure of sensitive, personal information about our health, our interactions with other people, our social networks, our whereabouts, and our daily activities. Surveillance technologies may include digital contact tracing applications and the use of cell phone location information, social media monitoring, wearable devices that collect and communicate health and location data, internet search monitoring and analysis, symptom monitoring, and immunity or vaccine passports. Using these technologies, government entities may be able to collect and use COVID-related data to inform public health responses. In the context of a global pandemic, some degree of surveillance may be necessary to protect public health. Some may argue that we each have an obligation to use any and all technology at our disposal to help stop the spread of the virus.

Sometimes, however, our ability to take recommended actions or use specific technology is limited by our circumstances, age, degree of economic security, or access to technology. And sometimes, taking action designed to protect public health can compromise or threaten privacy and civil liberties. I use the term "privacy" here to mean the following: the right to be let alone, the ability to make autonomous decisions, freedom from unnecessary surveillance, and the right to control access to, and use of, personal information. Protecting privacy, like protecting public health, is a public good. As we continue to determine the best, most effective ways to respond to COVID-19, and as we encourage individuals to cooperate in public health measures, we have a countervailing ethical obligation to collect and use the data that we need to protect public health in a manner that does not cause harm to individuals or subject them to unnecessary risks. From an ethical perspective, we want to avoid causing harm: we also want affirmatively to do good; to respect autonomy; and to enable trust and promote justice. In a public health response primarily reliant on voluntary participation, which is the situation in the United States, trust is crucial. The more that people trust the system and the decision-makers, the more likely it is that they will choose to participate, and we affirmatively want people to participate in responses, technological and otherwise, that we believe will contain the virus—for individuals' own health and for the public good. To a degree, we cannot effectively help people if they do not have that trust. Various COVID-19 responses have raised concerns about the secondary use of collected location and health data, law enforcement access, hacking and security, and the normalization and continuation of both the collection and use of data and of tracking technologies adopted for purposes of the pandemic.

In 2020, as we struggled to find ways to stop the spread of COVID-19, trust in public institutions and private corporations was remarkably low in the United States (Rainie & Perrin, 2019; Brooks, 2020). While a thorough discussion of the trust deficit and its numerous causes is beyond the scope of this chapter, four specific factors illustrate the larger point and highlight the aspects of the problem particularly relevant to COVID-19 responsive measures: (a) the historical misuse and abuse of data by governments, corporations, and public–private partnerships in an environment lacking data protection regulations; (b) the discriminatory treatment of marginalized groups; (c) the misuse and abuse of data pertaining specifically to marginalized groups; and (d) the historically justified fear of mission creep and the normalization of surveillance.

THE PRE-PANDEMIC TRUST LANDSCAPE

First, historical events provide reasons for the erosion of trust in public institutions in the context of data use and surveillance. The use, misuse, and abuse of personal information by the government have contributed to general distrust and suspicion (see, e.g., Madden & Rainie, 2015).[1] Think back to the findings of the Church Committee in the 1970s and the FBI's now well-documented surveillance of Martin Luther King Jr. and other individuals involved in the civil rights movement, and consider the more recent, expansive post-9/11 surveillance, the Snowden disclosures, and the spotlight on pervasive surveillance of citizens that ensued.

Likewise, corporate conduct with respect to personal data has contributed to increasing popular concern about privacy and distrust of commercial actors (Auxier et al., 2019).[2] We are living in a data economy populated by platforms,

---

[1]   As Madden & Rainie (2015) write,
    when asked to think about the data the government collects as part of anti-terrorism efforts, 65% of Americans say there are not adequate limits on "what telephone and internet data the government can collect." ... Those who are more aware of the government surveillance efforts are considerably more likely to believe there are not adequate safeguards in place; 74% of those who have heard "a lot" about the programs say that there are not adequate limits.

[2]   Some 81% of the public say that the potential risks they face because of data collection by companies outweigh the benefits, and 66% say the same about government data collection. At the same time, a majority of Americans report being concerned about the way their data is being used by companies (79%) or

service providers, and data brokers that are lightly regulated or wholly unregulated when it comes to privacy. These companies tend to push the envelope in favor of innovation and growth and fail to reliably take responsibility for data protection or the ways their technologies are being used. This self-regulatory approach in the United States has enabled a commercial landscape dominated by Big Tech and powered by behavioral advertising business models featuring an unrestrained appetite for data. Incidents like the Equifax breach, Facebook's repeated privacy violations (Federal Trade Commission, 2019), and the Cambridge Analytica scandal are on people's minds, and documentaries like *The Social Dilemma* generate popular discussion and concern. Corporate commitment to growth at all costs and disregard for the privacy of individuals do not inspire trust. Add to these factors the growing number of public–private partnerships—relationships between law enforcement or national security entities like the Department of Homeland Security and corporations like Amazon (Ring Doorbells and the Neighbors app), Clearview AI (facial recognition technology), and data brokers—as well as reports of government entities purchasing data from private companies (Clark, 2021; Edelman, 2020; Morrison, 2020). Americans who read the news are understandably concerned.

Here in the United States, we are navigating this risk-riddled landscape in the absence of comprehensive data protection laws. Notably, even if we did have comprehensive laws protecting data, such laws would likely have exceptions for public health emergencies like the COVID-19 pandemic. Indeed, because of the pandemic and the needs created by this global emergency, we have seen the relaxation of some privacy protections and of the enforcement of some aspects of the Privacy Rule of the Health Insurance Portability and Accountability Act (HIPAA; Office for Civil Rights, n.d.). While such accommodations are positive from an efficiency perspective, they too can exacerbate trust issues. A stopgap protective measure would have been COVID-specific data protection legislation like the Public Health Emergency Privacy Act proposed by Representatives Eshoo, Schakowsky, and DelBene and Senators Blumenthal and Warner (Offices of Reps. Eshoo et al., 2020), but Congress has, to date, failed to act on any such proposals.

Another major contributing factor to the trust deficit in the United States is the historical and current treatment of marginalized, oppressed, and vulnerable populations. Discriminatory and unequal treatment in the context of the criminal justice system and healthcare are particularly relevant in the COVID context. And a third factor arises from a combination of the first two issues—the use, misuse, and abuse of data, specifically with respect to margin-

---

the government (64%). Most also feel they have little or no control over how these entities use their personal information. (Auxier et al., 2019) alized, oppressed, and vulnerable populations. A few recent examples include Immigration and Customs Enforcement (ICE) obtaining access to Motel 6 registration information about undocumented individuals (Paris, 2019), ICE's purchase of utility customers' service and use data from a private commercial database (Harwell, 2021), a variety of predictive policing techniques (Heaven, 2020), the use of biased facial recognition technologies (Najibi, 2020), automated risk assessments in criminal justice and healthcare contexts (Angwin et al., 2016; Edes & Bowman, 2018), the FBI's surveillance of Black Lives Matter (Joseph & Hussain, 2018), and the surveillance of protests and protesters after the murder of George Floyd (Ng, 2020; Powers, 2020[3]), to name only a few.

Finally, many people fear that new forms of surveillance, enabled and carried out for ostensibly emergency purposes, will be repurposed and normalized, compounding civil liberties and privacy incursions in an already overly surveilled society. Historical precedent supports such concerns about both normalization (Vladeck, 2021) and mission creep, and both of these phenomena compromise trust.

In sum, the 2020 landscape in the United States featured low trust, low data protection, high perceived risk, and high need for data. Crafting an effective, equitable, privacy-protective public health response posed a substantial challenge and required us to consider, among other things, how to rebuild trust.

REBUILDING TRUST IN THE CONTEXT OF COVID-19

The enactment and reliable enforcement of robust data protection legislation would unquestionably help rebuild trust in the United States. However, our obligation to act ethically and carefully in our attempt to promote public health exists independently of such laws.[4] The fact that something is legal does not make it ethical. Specifically, where our public health strategy involves surveillance, such as manual or digital contact tracing, we must consider what acting carefully and ethically means in practice and in context. In a world where

---

[3]   In an interesting entanglement between civil rights concerns and COVID-related technologies, law enforcement officials in Minnesota claimed to be using "contact tracing" to track protesters after the murder of George Floyd. The claim was later retracted but nevertheless contributed to general confusion about contact tracing and an increasing level of distrust. Powers (2020) quotes health security professor Caitlin Rivers, who replied to an NBC video of Minnesota law enforcement with a tweet: "This is not contact tracing! What is described in the video is police work. To see the two linked jeopardizes the credibility of public health, which needs community trust to work effectively" (Rivers, 2020).

[4]   Data ethics and research ethics frameworks, several of which have been outlined by the World Health Organization (2020), may provide some guidance (pp. 1–2).

surveillance technologies have had a demonstrably more severe impact on marginalized communities, we need to evaluate explicitly the interests of and risks for these groups of people.

Ideally, we want COVID-19 responsive measures to be effective, protective, equally available to all people, and not unnecessarily invasive of privacy. The best scenario for public health would be one in which our responsive technology, testing, tracing, isolation opportunities and requirements, and ultimately vaccines are equally available to and used by all people. Whether responsive measures are perceived as privacy protective or privacy invasive will likely affect different communities' willingness to adopt those measures, and to the extent that the efficacy of a measure is reliant on pervasive use, privacy implications can affect efficacy as well.

Digital contact tracing (DCT) is one example of a technology that numerous countries adopted to help contain the spread of the virus. DCT applications allow individuals to learn whether they have been exposed to the virus based on their proximity to infected individuals, to report positive COVID tests, and to permit notification of individuals with whom they have come into contact if they have tested positive for COVID (Zittrain et al., 2020).[5] Some digital contact tracing apps use GPS technology and collect both health and location information in a centralized manner. In spring 2020, Apple and Google worked together to engineer and provide an exposure notification system (ENS), essentially a decentralized alternative to digital contact tracing that facilitates exposure notification in a relatively privacy-protective manner. The ENS option arguably provides less helpful information to public health officials because the system was designed to work without collecting location and health data. Even as these technologies were being developed and implemented, debates were taking place about the efficacy of contact tracing applications and ENS and the extent to which they created or mitigated privacy risks (Bambauer & Ray, 2020; Soltani et al., 2020).

For the best public health outcome, every individual's participation in COVID responses clearly matters, but we must also recognize that the use of location and health data creates more privacy risks and has potentially more severe consequences for members of marginalized communities and vulnerable populations. As a society, we have ethical responsibilities to all people. An assessment of the disparate risks and potential exposure of individuals in marginalized communities is necessary for a holistic evaluation of DCT technology.

---

[5]   For more information about digital contact tracing, see "Digital contact tracing: A primer," by Zittrain et al. (2020). The resources include an informative nine-minute video.

In the United States, marginalized groups and historically disenfranchised groups are at greater risk of contracting COVID-19, of hospitalization, and of death because of the illness (Centers for Disease Control and Prevention, n.d.; Zamarripa & Roque, 2021). The numbers in the United States generally show that Latinx individuals and Black Americans have greater chances of exposure, higher infection rates, and higher rates of death from COVID (Ford et al., 2020). In North Carolina, for example, Black Americans—only 22% of the state's population—comprised 30% of the cases and 34% of the deaths from COVID at one point in the summer of 2020 (NC Governor Roy Cooper's Office, 2020). The Latinx community makes up less than 10% of the population here in North Carolina; yet this group comprised, at one point in the summer of 2020, 39% of the COVID cases (NC Governor Roy Cooper's Office, 2020).[6] North Carolina undertook targeted measures to address the situation (Kissick, 2020; NC Governor Roy Cooper's Office, 2020), and this disparity has since improved, but the inequities remain of concern (Green & Kummerer, 2021; Off & Sánchez-Guerra, 2021). Data analyzed more recently indicates inequity in vaccination rates and fewer individuals receiving available vaccinations in these same communities (Smoot & Bell, 2021).

Reports have indicated that people in marginalized groups are at a higher risk for exposure, infection, and death because of factors pertaining to work, living conditions, and access to healthcare (Off & Sánchez-Guerra, 2021). Individuals in these groups may do work that cannot be done from home or remotely. They are more likely to hold jobs classified as "essential" work and may need to continue to work to maintain employment and income (Off & Sánchez-Guerra, 2021). Less spacious living conditions may provide less privacy, less individual space, and accordingly, reduced ability to quarantine within the home. Urban living environments and neighborhoods are more populous and make social distancing more challenging. Among other contributing factors, less reliable access to healthcare; limited insurance coverage; more limited access to testing for a variety of reasons, including cost and time off work, as well as requirements to provide personal information to get tests and, later, vaccines all contribute to disproportionate effects of COVID (Centers for Disease Control and Prevention, 2021). Lack of cultural competence and language proficiency within the ranks of manual contact tracers may have also played a role in discouraging personal interactions designed to limit the spread of the illness.

---

[6]   Similar disparities can be observed in other states as based on current (June 2021) numbers provided by public health departments in California, Oregon, Utah, and Washington (California Department of Public Health, n.d.; Oregon Health Authority, n.d.; Utah Department of Health, n.d.; Washington State Department of Health, n.d.).

Of course, it is because of data and data analytics that we know all of this information. So data use is an incredibly important response to COVID; data helps us understand how to inform public policy, direct resources, and allocate testing efforts. While data use is crucial, it is important to collect and use data carefully and intentionally. We don't want participation in a public health response and the use of personal health and location data to create yet another arena of harm for groups of people already at higher risk.[7]

Data can be used in harmful ways, and enforcement of laws can be carried out in discriminatory ways. Potential deportation, discretionary enforcement of immigration laws, discriminatory over-policing for social distancing violations, and exploitation of COVID technologies for other types of tracking, implicating severe consequences for already overpoliced, over-surveilled communities, are just some examples of such problems.

We have to consider how we might work to build trust in these circumstances and create an environment in which all people will participate in our public health response. As an initial matter, we need to convey a clear and accurate understanding of the health benefits that can be gained from various responses. Educational campaigns around digital technologies like DCT applications and ENS could be helpful as well. Early on in the development of DCT technologies, at least one publication suggested that 60% of people would need to adopt and use contact tracing technology for it to have any beneficial effect on stopping the spread of COVID. Subsequently, a group from MIT corrected that statement, noting that we could benefit from a far lower adoption rate, but that the more people who use it, the better (O'Neill, 2020). These numbers are important because individuals who assess associated risks and recommend these technologies look to this kind of data to evaluate efficacy. Also, if data could be collected and used responsibly in a manner that protects privacy, DCT technologies could have the capacity to provide a higher degree of perceived privacy than manual contact tracing efforts. Some individuals may be more comfortable using an app to monitor exposure than they are speaking one-on-one with a contact tracer.

Working with leaders and representatives of specific communities to make our responses more meaningful within those communities can also increase participation. Engaging culturally competent manual contact tracing services, surmounting language barriers, and working carefully with leaders who are trusted within communities to share important health messages all contribute to effective communication.

---

[7]   Arguably, our ethical obligations are intensified by the fact that oppression, discrimination, and social injustice have created this marginalization.

Avoiding and actively working to combat the politicization of COVID-19 responses like mask wearing that are fundamental, low-tech, effective actions is also imperative. Wearing a mask should not be a political statement; it's simply health-protective conduct when most of the population has not been vaccinated. While vaccinations present a more complicated issue and a higher degree of risk than mask wearing, it is still important that the response not be politicized.

Reliably engaging in preadoption ethical review of surveillance and other COVID-19 responsive technologies for consent and voluntariness, for privacy concerns, and specifically, for risks to vulnerable and marginalized populations is a crucial step in this global effort (Ranisch et al. 2020). As I have written previously,

> Whenever we consider using emerging tech that involves surveillance ... we should recognize the implications for privacy and civil liberties and engage in a deliberate ... five-step analysis as follows: 1) What is the problem we are trying to solve? 2) What is the proposed solution? 3) Will the proposed solution be effective? 4) If so, will it intrude on our privacy/civil liberties? And 5) If so, what controls could be put in place to sufficiently minimize those risks for all people? (Dellinger, 2020)

We should focus on promoting and actuating fair information practices like transparency, accountability, purpose specification, and use limitation. We should also insist on COVID data-specific legal protections, explicitly barring non-COVID uses of health and location data collected for COVID purposes. We should mandate confidentiality and, where possible, anonymity. With respect to efficacy, if something is unlikely to work or to be of minimal help, let us not ask people to sacrifice privacy or civil liberties for it. Our balancing of efficacy and privacy must be informed by an understanding of the different risks various technologies pose for different groups within the country, the Latinx community and Black Americans in particular.

The most important of these data management suggestions is the absolute, unconditional prohibition of the use of data collected for purposes of COVID for any other purpose, especially law enforcement. Law enforcement officials and federal agents, including ICE, should not have access to any data collected for COVID purposes. Full stop. No exceptions. Strict explicit prohibitions should also prevent all commercial and health entities from repurposing COVID-19 related data for sale.

Whatever we ultimately decide in the United States about our willingness to enact a comprehensive federal data protection scheme, ethical practices and regulations to protect data shared or used for pandemic response purposes should be non-negotiable. Creating such protections on the basis of an evaluation of the impact of COVID-19 responsive measures on all segments of society would ultimately allow a more effective balancing of our ethical obligation to share data to promote public health with our ethical obligation not to do harm. It is unlikely that we have seen our last pandemic. Getting to work on these proposals now, and importantly, on the larger effort in the United States to rebuild trust and protect privacy generally, will put us in a better position to respond effectively and ethically the next time we find ourselves in this situation.

REFERENCES

Angwin, J., Larson, J., Mattu, S., & Kirchner, L. (2016, May 23). "Machine bias." ProPublica. www.propublica.org/article/machine-bias-risk-assessments-in-criminal-sentencing

Auxier, B., Rainie, L., Anderson, M., Perrin, A., Kumar, M., & Turner, E. (2019, November 15). "Americans and privacy: Concerned, confused and feeling lack of control over their personal information." Pew Research Center: Internet, Science & Tech. www.pewresearch.org/internet/2019/11/15/americans-and-privacy-concerned-confused-and-feeling-lack-of-control-over-their-personal-information/

Bambauer, J., & Ray, B. (2020, November). "COVID-19 apps are terrible—they didn't have to be." The Digital Social Contract: A Lawfare Paper Series. https://s3.documentcloud.org/documents/20424830/bambauer-and-ray-final-2.pdf

Brooks, D. (2020, October 5). "America is having a moral convulsion." *The Atlantic*. www.theatlantic.com/ideas/archive/2020/10/collapsing-levels-trust-are-devastating-america/616581/

California Department of Public Health. (n.d.). "COVID-19 Race and Ethnicity Data." California Health and Human Services Agency. Retrieved June 13, 2021, www.cdph.ca.gov/Programs/CID/DCDC/Pages/COVID-19/Race-Ethnicity.aspx

Centers for Disease Control and Prevention. (n.d.). "Risk for COVID-19 infection, hospitalization, and death by race/ethnicity." Department of Health and Human Services. Retrieved June 17, 2021, from www.cdc.gov/coronavirus/2019-ncov/covid-data/investigations-discovery/hospitalization-death-by-race-ethnicity.html

Centers for Disease Control and Prevention. (2021, April 19). "Health equity considerations and racial and ethnic minority groups." Department of Health and Human Services. www.cdc.gov/coronavirus/2019-ncov/community/health-equity/race-ethnicity.html

Clark, M. (2021, January 22). "US Defense Intelligence Agency admits to buying citizens' location data." The Verge. www.theverge.com/2021/1/22/22244848/us-intelligence-memo-admits-buying-smartphone-location-data

Dellinger, J. (2020, July 14). "Digital contact tracing tools." Triangle Privacy Research Hub. www.triangleprivacyhub.org/digital-contact-tracing-responses-to-covid-19/

Edelman, G. (2020, February 11). "Can the government buy its way around the Fourth Amendment?" *Wired.* www.wired.com/story/can-government-buy-way-around-fourth-amendment/

Edes, A., & Bowman, E. (2018, February 19). "'Automating inequality': Algorithms in public services often fail the most vulnerable." NPR. www.npr.org/sections/alltechconsidered/2018/02/19/586387119/automating-inequality-algorithms-in-public-services-often-fail-the-most-vulnerab

Federal Trade Commission. (2019, July 24). "FTC imposes $5 billion penalty and sweeping new privacy restrictions on Facebook." www.ftc.gov/news-events/press -releases/2019/07/ftc-imposes-5-billion-penalty-sweeping-new-privacy-restrictions

Ford, T. N., Reber, S., & Reeves, R. V. (2020, June 16). "Race gaps in COVID-19 deaths are even bigger than they appear." Brookings. www.brookings.edu/blog/up -front/2020/06/16/race-gaps-in-covid-19-deaths-are-even-bigger-than-they-appear/

Green, M., & Kummerer, S. (2021, January 15). "As COVID-19 surges, disproportion-alities in infections shrink." ABC11 Raleigh-Durham. https://abc11.com/covid-19 -latino-medical-racism-resources/9691481/

Harwell, D. (2021, March 1). "ICE investigators used a private utility database covering millions to pursue immigration violations." *Washington Post*. www.washingtonpost .com/technology/2021/02/26/ice-private-utility-data/

Heaven, W. D. (2020, July 17). "Predictive policing algorithms are racist. They need to be dismantled." *MIT Technology Review*. www.technologyreview.com/2020/ 07/17/1005396/predictive-policing-algorithms-racist-dismantled-machine-learning -bias-criminal-justice/

Joseph, G., & Hussain, M. (2018, March 19). "FBI tracked an activist involved with Black Lives Matter as they traveled across the U.S., documents show." The Intercept. https://theintercept.com/2018/03/19/black-lives-matter-fbi-surveillance/

Kissick, C. (2020, October 15). "Privacy issues at the heart of North Carolina's coronavirus response." Lawfare. www.lawfareblog.com/privacy-issues-heart-north -carolinas-coronavirus-response

Madden, M., & Rainie, L. (2015, May 20). "Americans' attitudes about privacy, security and surveillance." Pew Research Center: Internet, Science & Tech. www .pewresearch.org/internet/2015/05/20/americans-attitudes-about-privacy-security -and-surveillance/

Morrison, S. (2020, December 2). "A surprising number of government agencies buy cellphone location data. Lawmakers want to know why." Vox. www.vox.com/ recode/22038383/dhs-cbp-investigation-cellphone-data-brokers-venntel

Najibi, A. (2020, October 24). "Racial discrimination in face recognition technology." Science in the News. https://sitn.hms.harvard.edu/flash/2020/racial-discrimination -in-face-recognition-technology/

NC Governor Roy Cooper's Office. (2020, June 4). "Governor Cooper signs executive order to address disproportionate impact of COVID-19 on communities of color." [Press release]. https://governor.nc.gov/news/governor-cooper-signs-executive -order-address-disproportionate-impact-%EF%BB%BF-covid-19-communities

Ng, A. (2020, June 1). "Contact tracers concerned police tracking protesters will hurt COVID-19 aid." CNET. www.cnet.com/news/contact-tracers-concerned-police -tracking-protesters-will-hurt-covid-19-aid/

Off, G., Alexander, A., & Sánchez-Guerra, A. (2021, June 9). "Black, Latino NC workers had to play 'Russian roulette' during COVID. The toll was steep." *Charlotte Observer*. www.charlotteobserver.com/news/state/north-carolina/article251871898 .html

Office for Civil Rights. (n.d.). "HIPAA and COVID-19." Department of Health and Human Services. Retrieved April 2, 2021, from www.hhs.gov/hipaa/for -professionals/special-topics/hipaa-covid19/index.html

Offices of Reps. Eshoo, Schakowsky, DelBen, Sens. Blumenthal. & Warner (2020, May 14). "Protecting civil liberties during COVID-19: Reps. Eshoo, Schakowsky, DelBene, and Sens. Blumenthal, and Warner introduce Public Health Emergency

Privacy Act" [Press release]. https://eshoo.house.gov/media/press-releases/protecting-civil-liberties-during-covid-19-reps-eshoo-schakowsky-delbene-and

O'Neill, P. H. (2020, June 5). "No, coronavirus apps don't need 60% adoption to be effective." *MIT Technology Review.* www.technologyreview.com/2020/06/05/1002775/covid-apps-effective-at-less-than-60-percent-download/

Oregon Health Authority. (n.d.). "COVID-19 updates: Oregon Health Authority. NIC GovStatus—Emergency Response Solution." Retrieved June 22, 2021, from https://govstatus.egov.com/OR-OHA-COVID-19

Paris, F. (2019, April 5). "Motel 6 to pay $12 million after improperly giving guest lists to ICE." NPR. www.npr.org/2019/04/05/710137783/motel-6-to-pay-12-million-after-improperly-giving-guest-lists-to-ice

Powers, B. (2020, June 15). "Minnesota official alarms privacy advocates with contact tracing comments." CoinDesk. www.coindesk.com/minnesota-official-alarms-privacy-advocates-with-contact-tracing-comments

Rainie, L., & Perrin, A. (2019, July 22). "Key findings about Americans' declining trust in government and each other." Pew Research Center. www.pewresearch.org/fact-tank/2019/07/22/key-findings-about-americans-declining-trust-in-government-and-each-other/

Ranisch, R., Nijsingh, N., Ballantyne, A., van Bergen, A., Buyx, A., Friedrich, O., Hendl, T., Marckmann, G., Munthe, C., & Wild, V. (2020, October 21). "Digital contact tracing and exposure notification: Ethical guidance for trustworthy pandemic management." *Ethics and Information Technology*, 23, 285–294. https://dx.doi.org/10.1007%2Fs10676-020-09566-8

Rivers, C. [@cmyeaton]. (2020, May 30). "This is not contact tracing! What is described in the video is police work. To see the two linked jeopardizes" [Video attached] [Tweet]. Twitter. https://twitter.com/cmyeaton/status/1266877404544450561

Smoot, H., & Bell, A. (2021, February 11). "Pervasive vaccine inequity for minorities persists all over NC, new records show." *Charlotte Observer.* www.charlotteobserver.com/news/coronavirus/article249093495.html

Soltani, A., Calo, R., & Bergstrom, C. (2020, April 27). "Contact-tracing apps are not a solution to the COVID-19 crisis." Brookings. www.brookings.edu/techstream/inaccurate-and-insecure-why-contact-tracing-apps-could-be-a-disaster/

Utah Department of Health. (n.d.). "Case counts: Coronavirus." Retrieved June 22, 2021, from https://coronavirus.utah.gov/case-counts/

Vladeck, S. I. (2021, January 11). "The normalization of the post-Sept. 11 regime." *Tablet.* www.tabletmag.com/sections/news/articles/patriot-act-2001-homeland-security-20-years

Washington State Department of Health. (n.d.). "COVID-19." Retrieved June 22, 2021, from www.doh.wa.gov/Emergencies/COVID19

World Health Organization. (2020, June 26). "Ethical considerations to guide the use of digital proximity tracking technologies for COVID-19 contact tracing." United Nations. www.who.int/publications/i/item/WHO-2019-nCoV-Ethics_Contact_tracing_apps-2020.1

Zamarripa, R., & Roque, L. (2021, March 5). "Latinos face disproportionate health and economic impacts from COVID-19." Center for American Progress. www.americanprogress.org/issues/economy/reports/2021/03/05/496733/latinos-face-disproportionate-health-economic-impacts-covid-19/

Zittrain, J., Nagy, A., Rosenberg, L., & Ross, H. (2020, July 8). "Digital contact tracing: A primer." Berkman Klein Center. https://cyber.harvard.edu/story/2020-07/digital-contact-tracing-primer

14. Of pandemics and progress

Andrea M. Matwyshyn

The COVID-19 pandemic is neither our first nor our last major international health event. In reviewing the impact of past pandemics on societies and economies, a contradiction of sorts becomes apparent: while past pandemics have brought unexpected aggregate and individual harms, they have also spurred scientific advancement at an accelerated pace. In particular, these catastrophic health events have catalyzed novel reuses of health information to bolster public health and epidemiology.

In what may be two of the earliest cases of "big data" health analytics, Florence Nightingale and Dr. John Snow traced patterns of illness and death, harnessing the information to develop successful public health interventions. In 1854, Florence Nightingale documented and analyzed infection and death data in the hospital she managed in Turkey during the Crimean War (Science Museum, 2018). Her novel health data statistical visualizations led her to create a set of new treatment practices (Kopf, 1978; McDonald, 1998). Meanwhile, in London, her contemporary, Dr. John Snow, demonstrated that a cholera outbreak in Soho, which killed over 600 people, was caused by water supplies contaminated by raw sewage (Centers for Disease Control and Prevention [CDC], 2017; Tuthill, 2003).[1] Later, building on these prior pioneering public health insights, the tracking practices developed during the outbreak of typhoid between 1900 and 1907 in the United States drove the evolution of modern

---

[1]   As I have written previously (Matwyshyn & Pell, 2019, pp. 508–509), Snow constructed a map to plot deaths from the outbreak and examined possible contamination sources for each case. Five hundred cases in ten days were concentrated around the same Soho intersection, leading Snow to conclude that the outbreak source was a specific water pump.

Snow's peers discounted his theory, believing that breathing vapors or a "miasma in the atmosphere" was the cause of the outbreak (this reflected the conventional medical wisdom of the time). Five years earlier, Snow authored a controversial article about his water contamination theory. He noted that untreated sewage and animal waste from homes and businesses were dumped in the River Thames, and that water companies bottled and sold that same river water. Ultimately, contamination of the Soho pump allegedly occurred because a baby's diaper had been washed in a town well (CDC, 2017; Tuthill, 2003).

hygiene practices and epidemiology as a discipline (CDC, 2012; *Encyclopedia Britannica*, 2021).[2]

Today, we live in a time when new technologies offer the potential to advance public health and epidemiology once again. Yet computing has both enhanced treatment options and simultaneously introduced new categories of threats to human health (see, e.g., Leveson & Turner, 1993). We are now struggling not only with traditional health epidemics but also with novel digital "infodemics" that exacerbate them.[3] Indeed, rampant health disinformation spread through social media has necessitated the World Health Organization's (2020) formalization of the field of "infodemiology." Meanwhile, ransomware and malware plague hospital systems and the companies developing pharmaceutical and device interventions (Newman, 2020; Terry, 2020). Thus, today's technology enables us to develop vaccines and other interventions with unprecedented speed, and it simultaneously threatens to undermine that development. In other words, the questions of traditional threats to health now merge with a new generation of infectious threats introduced by computing (Perlroth, 2020).

I have previously argued (see Matwyshyn, 2019) that modern technologies are a double-edged sword for new health interventions: they offer both tremendous potential and significant risks, especially as we enter an era where human bodies are functionally becoming some of the "things" reliant on the internet—an Internet of Bodies. In other words, the Internet of Things involves not merely recreational gadgets but also devices and processes that have a direct impact on humans' physical safety and health. As a consequence, these concerns push us to evaluate various health tech intervention proposals with a keener eye on privacy and security. They also push us to examine at

---

[2]   Infamously, a cook named Mary Mallon, better known as "Typhoid Mary," accidentally transmitted typhoid fever to people who ate her meals. Before she was found to have been the source of the outbreak in New York City, Mallon allegedly infected approximately a dozen people with typhoid (CDC, 2013; *Encyclopedia Britannica*, 2021). Snow's work demonstrated the importance of simultaneously tracking infection in real time and adopting mitigation strategies that operate both on an individual level and in the aggregate, targeting groups and societies.

[3]   For example, as I have described previously (Matwyshyn & Pell, 2019, p. 483), in 1988, a graduate student at MIT lost control of a worm he had created as a proof of concept. While he had intended the worm to self-replicate across systems by exploiting a security vulnerability, he made a mathematical error that resulted in a bug: the worm self-replicated at a disastrously fast rate. Much like Typhoid Mary's contaminated food, the student's worm caused unintended harm. It substantially slowed down approximately 10 percent of the (admittedly few) machines on the internet at the time because the worm usurped their computing power. This was the first known self-replicating malware and the first Computer Fraud and Abuse Act prosecution—thanks to an infection and a bug.

least five types of inquiries: (a) our understandings of (various definitions of) progress; (b) the implications of new technologies on fundamental human dignity concerns; (c) the ethics of certain revenue models; (d) the technological and social sustainability of particular health technologies; and (e) the specific threat models of technology-reliant implementations.

A   DEFINING PROGRESS

As I will explain elsewhere (Matwyshyn, 2022a), the word "progress" and its lesser cousin "innovation" often dominate policy discussions about technology, but rarely are they defined.[4] This deficit matters: meaningful variation exists across individual definitions of progress, and the variation has ripple effects in our analysis of desirable policy outcomes. Turning briefly to the philosophy literature, we discover that theories of progress diverge along three axes or types of claims implicit in every definition: normative claims, social science claims, and methodological or epistemological claims. Thus, an articulation of the specifics of each of these three types of claims should be at the forefront in our discussions of new health technologies.

On the point of normative claims, as I have discussed in earlier scholarship, there are multiple possible end points in the relationship between technology and the human body (see Matwyshyn, 2019). On the one side of the sliding scale sits a corporeal supremacy model that views the body as its core and technology as merely a convenient enhancement. On the other side of the scale sits a corporeal inferiority model of humanity, where the human body is merely an inferior carbon-based operating system ripe for upgrade. Absent from our conversations are robust discussions of which point on the sliding scale underpins various technologies. Exactly what normative, social science, and methodological/epistemological claims drive this research? The same normative baseline and end point of development may not be shared by technology builders and policymakers. Yet in the absence of a clear, shared normative baseline, the two subsequent elements of "progress"—social science claims (what gaps exist in our knowledge that can be rigorously investigated?) and methodological/epistemological claims (did the implementation of the inquiry yield trustworthy results?)—will inevitably become muddled. Different visions of the future of the human body and "progress" will lead us to different policy responses in our present moment.

For example, how invasive should we permit health data collection to become? An always-on health surveillance system hardwired into human

---

[4]   For a discussion of the definitions of progress in the Founding Era, see, e.g., Matwyshyn (2022c).

bodies, for example, would in theory provide the highest quality information. But in practice, it would come with high risk of potential repurposing or abuse to the detriment of the surveilled human and potential over-trust of some-times faulty sensors (DoItYourself, 2021). Some entrepreneurs advocate for a model of humanity that involves optional, recreational self-augmentation with real-time information from the cloud and, ostensibly, live third-party monitoring of those feeds (Lewis, 2020). A public health emergency might provide an excuse to fast-track such (potentially undesirable) technologies. But it is noteworthy that such companies often view the human body on the far side of the normative sliding scale—as functionally a last-generation, carbon-based operating system and simply another "platform" upon which to build, commodify, and upgrade. Imagine a world where chips or sensors are embedded in (some) bodies, performing instantaneous data collection (that may or may not be accurate) (Yuste et al., 2017). Is that a desirable health data enhancement or a limit on autonomy? Both? What constitutes meaningful consent in such a context, where pushed upgrades can influence the extent of real-time surveillance? Conflicting models of next-generation humanity con-tinue to cause debate in both medical and non-medical contexts (Matwyshyn, 2022a), and the absence of shared normative baselines presents an increasing challenge. Importantly, they hold varying consequences for the future of delib-erative democracy and potential for authoritarian abuses. These questions also guide us to broader concerns about human dignity.

B   DEFENDING DIGNITY

As I explain elsewhere, co-creation of the relationship between new tech-nologies and human body quantification for health reasons is not new (see discussion in Matwyshyn, 2022a). Indeed, a review of history reveals that new modes of technology (and the subsequent quantifications) tend to present a double-edged sword, and the experimentation they facilitate has sometimes led us into ethically problematic territory (see, e.g., Boissoneault, 2017). Consider the "better babies" contests of the eugenics movement in the early 1930s, whose winners met particular quantified metrics for allegedly "supe-rior" bodies (Ferrari, 2018). On the one hand, more rigorous tracking with the help of new technologies can lead to better outcomes for the target population (Palmer, 2018). But on the other hand, greater quantification sometimes results in our deciding that some bodies are "better" than others, and we have some-times used metrics of "correctness" that do not stand up to rigorous scientific scrutiny in historical retrospect (Palmer, 2018).

New body-tracking technologies and metrics have always been bound up with sensitive questions of social hierarchy, invidious discrimination, and risks to human dignity (see, e.g., Sutherland, 2020). Technology-assisted hyper quantification has sometimes created "winners" and "losers" in ways that we, in retrospect, deem deeply problematic (Ferrari, 2018). As human bodies become tracked by always-on technologies, the potential for dignitary harm escalates. Thus, as in the past, risks to principles of equality or due process could arise from new tracking technologies; the specifics of design and deployment and how derivative information is used and reused will prove dispositive. Consider, for example, the infamous eugenics exhibit at the 1933 World's Fair (Laughlin, 1935). These issues around information repurposing, in particular, direct us to examine revenue models that support various technologies.

C   DISSECTING REVENUE

If the past is the prologue, the uses of aggregated data will continue to evolve and expand alongside technological capability. As I discuss elsewhere, cautionary tales of (in)famously well-funded Silicon Valley product failures such as the Juicero highlight the repeating disconnect between the revenue models that fuel venture capital investment and the revenue models that advance value in the eyes of consumers (Matwyshyn, 2022b).[5] These streams of sensitive health data will likely be viewed, first and foremost, as presenting a potentially viable secondary revenue stream for short-run return on investment for health tech companies. Negative consequences and risks that arise for the bodies generating the data may be viewed as merely a secondary, less pressing concern as compared to profit. Indeed, the truth of a health technology enterprise's ethics lies in a careful examination of its revenue model. To wit, the data reuse patterns of first-generation internet business models point to the risks of this maximum data exploitation by health-related technologies: health data reuse and repurposing presents a lucrative secondary revenue stream. This information could be merged into various forms of social credit databases and used for "matching audiences," privileging some users' bodies and downgrading others (see, e.g., Sutherland, 2020; Facebook, 2015). In particular, as databases are repurposed for future uses that were undisclosed with particularity to consumers at the time of information collection (Zuboff, 2019), data collected for ostensibly limited health-ish purposes is unlikely to remain limited to health

---

[5]   As Thompson (2017) reports, the Juicero was an internet-enabled juicer. From the standpoint of the investors, the machine offered many fruitful paths for user data collection and identification of future marketing opportunities. For a portion of users, the utility of the juicing device was not significantly greater than simply squeezing the packets of pulped fruits and vegetables themselves. Thus, Juicero became a quasi-infamous example in tech circles of a product that was designed with the investors in mind rather than the users and perhaps without a thorough analysis of the return on buyers' investment in purchasing and using this particular technology.

usage. Legal constraints are few, as the scope of the last generation of privacy law, such as the Health Insurance Portability and Accountability Act (1996), is limited.

D   DETERMINING SUSTAINABILITY

A related fourth set of inquiries involves technology sustainability, design suitability, and technical substantiation. These three standards connect with the two secondary questions in defining "progress" that were introduced above—the social science and methodological/epistemological claims that support the chosen normative point on the sliding scale of techno-humanity. These are questions that the law can engage relatively readily in terms of connecting prior lines of technology regulation, fair market practices, and assessing the veracity of medical claims (Federal Trade Commission, n.d.). The criterion of sustainability pushes us to ask whether the technologies we build and use today can be reframed in ways that reduce social and environmental impact tomorrow.

As a concrete example, in furtherance of COVID-19 monitoring, some researchers have turned to monitoring wastewater in sewer systems to try to identify hot spots of COVID outbreak (Michael-Kordatou et al., 2020). Using sewer water creates a layer of anonymization and a degree of privacy enhancement that provides real-time snapshots. Perhaps surprisingly, these snapshots are potentially more accurate on the aggregate level in terms of identifying at-risk populations, yet they require less work on the part of the affected population. Additionally, the unit of analysis—the neighborhood or block—is more in the spirit of historical public health models of intervention. Thus, such a research model is arguably a win–win without the same degree of technical and privacy issues presented by individual user-focused models, the models that have often dominated the technology conversation. It also negates various implementation issues. For example, users might not launch an app properly, a phone might not successfully interoperate with the code base that a particular COVID app uses, unintended interactions or security compromise might occur because of the other apps on the phone, or the user may be subject to unexpected resale and repurposing of the information. Many of the technology problems that have been at the forefront of the conversations around COVID-19 apps disappear when we collect data at an aggregated level—a level that is potentially more sustainable.

E   DELIBERATING IMPLEMENTATION

Finally, the specifics of implementation matter. Consider the acclaimed science fiction series *Battlestar Galactica*, in which an intergalactic war takes place in the distant future. A single battleship, *Galactica*, is still functional specifically because it was intentionally "air gapped" (see, e.g., Unknown Lamer, 2014). Despite relying on computing in some aspects of its operation, the *Galactica* was kept off the grid by its captain, Commander Adama, as an information security measure (Moore et al., 2003, 8:25, 29:40).[6] This science fiction series reminds us that because of information risk, the newest technologies are not always the best fit for specific environments (see, e.g., Matwyshyn, 2017). Indeed, this "Adama principle," as I have elsewhere dubbed it, helps underscore that each point of interconnection can simultaneously be a point of exploitation and catastrophic compromise (Matwyshyn, 2019; for a different but related version of this idea, see Panjwani, 2018). The accuracy of threat modeling and the specifics of implementation sit at the heart of whether a technology becomes a productive tool or a threat to human well-being.

In prior work, I have explained the unique technology and legal challenges of the Internet of Bodies, or IoB (Matwyshyn, 2019). For example, consider the choice of then Vice President Dick Cheney to have his physician disable the wireless function of his pacemaker (Fredericks, 2013). Cheney was allegedly concerned that his implanted defibrillator—a lifesaving technology—could be compromised by attackers and used to assassinate him (Fredericks, 2013). Most consumers do not possess Cheney's sophistication in threat modeling; they also live within a different threat landscape. But informed health choices always become more complex with each additional layer of technology (Horrigan, 2019)

In place of the Adama principle, we are at risk of embracing an inferior model—what I have called the problem of "mandatory soup" (Matwyshyn, 2019, pp. 125–129). At a banquet with a preset menu, despite the appearance of many choices, everyone receives the same soup—sometimes even when the soup is not wanted. By analogy, consider the IoT marketplace: even as robust competition appears to superficially exist in the market, if all implementations result in the most connected variant, in reality, competition becomes impoverished. In other words, all implementations end up with the same threat model and the same categories of exploitable problems. Competition on degree of interconnectivity is an axis that is currently neglected in traditional competition policy discussion. Yet it will play an increasingly important role as a differentiating implementation choice as products continue to default to the maximum degrees of connectedness (Matwyshyn, 2019, pp. 125–129).

---

[6]   Commander Adama knew that the enemy Cylons were masters at disabling battlestars by compromising their wireless networks and then attacking the whole ship. Consequently, he ordered that his ship never be networked (Moore et al., 2003, 29:40).

Less-connected technologies present not only lowered risk of compromise, but also lower risks of detrimental information repurposing.

As new technologies are proposed to track, diagnose, and mitigate public health emergencies, they warrant robust scrutiny. While builders and policy-makers may enjoy the efficiency of allegedly one-size-fits-all/"silver bullet" technology strategies, successful technology implementation varies across implementation environments and users. In other words, not all contexts will present a uniform threat model and set of social challenges. The reality of social problems such as public health emergencies is rarely uniform. The most promising technologies will recognize the variation in risk across social contexts, the likelihood of technology failures, and the need for flexibility in implementation.

REFERENCES

Boissoneault, L. (2017, March 8). "A spoonful of sugar helps the radioactive oatmeal go down." *Smithsonian Magazine*. www.smithsonianmag.com/history/spoonful-sugar-helps-radioactive-oatmeal-go-down-180962424/

Centers for Disease Control and Prevention. (2012). *Principles of Epidemiology in Public Health Practice* (3rd edn). Department of Health and Human Services. www.cdc.gov/csels/dsepd/ss1978/index.html

Centers for Disease Control and Prevention. (2017, March 14). "John Snow: A legacy of disease detectives." Department of Health and Human Services. https://blogs.cdc.gov/publichealthmatters/2017/03/a-legacy-of-disease-detectives/

DoItYourself. (2021, March 13). "5 common oxygen sensor problems." www.doityourself.com/stry/5-common-oxygen-sensor-problems

Encyclopedia Britannica. (2021, June 6). "Typhoid Mary." In *Britannica.com*. www.britannica.com/biography/Typhoid-Mary

Facebook. (2015, November 30). "More matching capabilities with Custom Audiences." www.facebook.com/business/marketing-partners/partner-news/more-matching-capabilities-with-custom-audiences/

Federal Trade Commission. (n.d.). "Health claims." Retrieved August 6, 2021, from www.ftc.gov/tips-advice/business-center/advertising-and-marketing/health-claims

Ferrari, M. (Director). (2018). *The Eugenics Crusade: What's Wrong with Perfect?* [Film]. American Experience.

Fredericks, B. (2013, October 19). "Cheney feared terrorists would 'hack' pacemaker." *New York Post*. https://nypost.com/2013/10/19/cheney-feared-heart-gizmo-hack-attack/

Health Insurance Portability and Accountability Act, Pub. L. No. 104-191, 110 Stat. 1936 (1996).

Horrigan, D. (2019, January 7). "The Internet of Bodies: A convenient—and, yes, creepy—new platform for data discovery." Yahoo Finance. https://finance.yahoo.com/news/internet-bodies-convenient-yes-creepy-113031037.html

Kopf, E. W. (1978). "Florence Nightingale as statistician." *Research in Nursing & Health*, 1(3), 93–102. https://doi.org/10.1002/nur.4770010302

Laughlin, H. H. (1935). "The eugenics exhibit at Chicago: A description of the wall-panel survey of eugenics exhibited in the Hall of Science, Century of Progress

Exposition, Chicago, 1933–34." *Journal of Heredity*, 26(4), 155–162. https://doi
.org/10.1093/oxfordjournals.jhered.a104061

Leveson, N., & Turner, C. (1993). "An investigation of the Therac-25 accidents."
Computer, 26(7), 18–41. https://doi.org/10.1109/mc.1993.274940

Lewis, T. (2020, September 2). "Elon Musk's pig-brain implant is still a long way from
'solving paralysis.'" *Scientific American*. www.scientificamerican.com/article/elon
-musks-pig-brain-implant-is-still-a-long-way-from-solving-paralysis/

Matwyshyn, A. M. (2017, March 13). "The big security mistakes companies make
when buying tech." *Wall Street Journal*. www.wsj.com/articles/the-big-security
-mistakes-companies-make-when-buying-tech-1489372011

Matwyshyn, A. M. (2019). "The Internet of Bodies." *William & Mary Law Review*,
61(1). https://scholarship.law.wm.edu/wmlr/vol61/iss1/3/

Matwyshyn, A. M. (2022a). "Internet of Latour's things" [unpublished manuscript].
Penn State Law.

Matwyshyn, A. M. (2022b). "iTrust Antitrust" [unpublished manuscript]. Penn State
Law.

Matwyshyn, A. M. (2022c). "Our founding hackers" [unpublished manuscript]. Penn
State Law.

Matwyshyn, A. M., & Pell, S. K. (2019). "Broken." *Harvard Journal of Law &
Technology*, 32(2), 481–574. https://jolt.law.harvard.edu/assets/articlePDFs/v32/
32HarvJLTech479.pdf

McDonald, L. (1998). "Florence Nightingale." *Journal of Holistic Nursing*, 16(2),
267–277. https://doi.org/10.1177/089801019801600215

Michael-Kordatou, I., Karaolia, P., & Fatta-Kassinos, D. (2020). "Sewage analysis
as a tool for the COVID-19 pandemic response and management: The urgent need
for optimised protocols for SARS-CoV-2 detection and quantification." *Journal of
Environmental Chemical Engineering*, 8(5), 104306. https://doi.org/10.1016/j.jece
.2020.104306

Moore, R. D. (Writer), James, C. E. (Writer), & Rymer, M. (Director). (2003,
December 8). "Part 1" [TV miniseries episode]. In R. D. Moore & D. Eick
(Executive Producers), *Battlestar Galactica*. David Eick Productions; R&D TV
Enterprises; Studios USA.

Newman, L. H. (2020, September 28). "A ransomware attack has struck a major US hospital chain." *Wired*. www.wired.com/story/universal-health-services-ransomware
-attack/

Palmer, J. (2018, November 1). "The strange case of Dr. Couney." *Jewish Standard*.
https://jewishstandard.timesofisrael.com/the-strange-case-of-dr-couney/

Panjwani, R. [@occamsraza]. (2018, June 27). "The Adama Doctrine of Security—the
only safe device is an unnetworked device. Cc @amatwyshyn" [Tweet reply].
Twitter. https://twitter.com/occamsraza/status/1011982726113759232?s=20

Perlroth, N. (2020, October 28). "Officials warn of cyberattacks on hospitals as
virus cases spike." *New York Times*. www.nytimes.com/2020/10/28/us/hospitals
-cyberattacks-coronavirus.html

Science Museum. (2018, December 10). "Florence Nightingale: The pioneer statistician." www.sciencemuseum.org.uk/objects-and-stories/florence-nightingale
-pioneer-statistician

Sutherland, M. (2020, January). "China's Corporate Social Credit System."
Congressional Research Service. https://crsreports.congress.gov/product/pdf/IF/
IF11342

Terry, M. (2020, October 5). "Clinical trial software company hit by massive ransomware attack." BioSpace. www.biospace.com/article/clinical-trial-software-company-eresearchtechnology-hit-by-ransomware-attack/

Thompson, D. (2017, April 21). "The very serious lessons of Juicero." *The Atlantic.* www.theatlantic.com/business/archive/2017/04/juicero-lessons/523896/

Tuthill, K. (2003, November). "John Snow and the Broad Street pump: On the trail of an epidemic." *Cricket*, 31(3). www.ph.ucla.edu/epi/snow/snowcricketarticle.html

Unknown Lamer. (2014, March 18). "Is analog the fix for cyber terrorism?" [online forum post]. Slashdot. https://it.slashdot.org/story/14/03/18/021239/is-analog-the-fix-for-cyber-terrorism

World Health Organization. (2020, June 30). 1st WHO Infodemiology Conference. United Nations. www.who.int/news-room/events/detail/2020/06/30/default-calendar/1st-who-infodemiology-conference

Yuste, R., Goering, S., y Arcas, B. A., Bi, G., Carmena, J. M., Carter, A., et al. (2017). "Four ethical priorities for neurotechnologies and AI." *Nature*, 551(7679), 159–163. https://doi.org/10.1038/551159a

Zuboff, S. (2019). *The Age of Surveillance Capitalism: The Fight for a Human Future at the New Frontier of Power*. Public Affairs.

Index

9/11 terrorist attacks 95

abusive surveillance 95
actor-network theory 89
Adama principle 222
advertising ecosystems leverage data 170
algorithm-driven suspicionless mass
        surveillance 98
Al Sur 141
Amazon 31
American Convention on Human Rights
        (ACHR) 137
Android operating system 33, 67, 91, 140
Android smartphone 66, 75
antitrust actions 173
Apple 31, 36–8, 54, 65–8, 74, 97,
        114–16, 124, 140
    engineering practices 30
    smartphones 67, 115
Apple-Google API platform 29, 30, 67
Apple/Google-based app 35, 75, 116,
        117, 121, 123
application program interface (API) 65,
        68
    battery sipping 30
    smartphones indefinitely 68
arbitrary power 13
Argentine apps 139, 141
artificial intelligence (AI) 189, 199
AT&T, data aggregation 10
authoritarian proof 86
auto-test systems 138

Baby Bells 173
Backer, Larry 70–71
bank fraud 56
Battlestar Galactica 221
behavioral modifiers 64
Biden administration's legislative agenda
        152
big data 27, 31, 37–8, 69, 71

Big Data analytics 199, 216
Big Tech companies 32–4, 33, 36, 37,
        38, 72, 161, 162
    coronavirus mobile app models 38
    COVID-19 models 34
    surveillance systems 72
    technological innovation 105
Big Tech tools 28
Birchfield v. North Dakota 20
Black Americans 210, 212
Black and Minority Ethnic (BAME) 124
Black, Indigenous, and people of color
        (BIPOC) 95
Black Lives Matter, FBI's surveillance
        208
Bluetooth 74, 124
    contact tracing 140
    contact tracing applications 166
    data 19
    digital contact tracing 67
    digital tracing, COVID-19 65–8
    handshake technology 66, 75
    low-energy 66
    proximity data 159
    proximity tracing 66
    signals 115, 143
    tracing 30
    tracking 18, 76
body-tracking technologies 219
Bolsonaro, Jair 143
Boyd v. United States 13
Brazil
    app 54
    authorities 42
    Bar Association 58
    bureaucracy 52
    health system 53
    independence, declaration of 43
    nationality 51
    oil company 105
    19th century society 45
    population of 55, 56

Buenos Aires 144
Bush, George W. 106
business obligations 154

California Bankers Association v. Shultz
   13
California Consumer Privacy Act
   (2018/2020) 153
California Privacy Rights Act 152, 153
California v. Greenwood 13
call logs 163, 164
Camargo, A. P. R. 48, 50
carbon-based operating system 218–19
Carpenter v. United States 6, 11, 13, 18,
   20
Carvalho reports 43
cellphone 6, 7
   alerts 6
   search data 12
   service 12
cellphone location data 9
   contact tracing purposes 7, 8
   for public health surveillance 6, 7
   use of 7
cell site location 11, 13, 76
cell tower location data 18
Centers for Disease Control (CDC) 12
   prevention 22, 158, 210, 216
centralization, standards-based
   technology 30
Centre for Data Ethics and Innovation
   120
Centro de Estudos e Pesquisas de Direito
   Sanitário (CEPEDISA) 42
Chalhoub, S. 52
Chandler v. Miller 14
Chilean CoronApp 139
China
   contact tracing apps 70
   governance models 78
   pandemic surveillance systems 65,
      70, 79
   smartphone app 6
   surveillance of COVID-19 pandemic
      64, 68–71, 76
China Social Credit System 64, 65,
   69–70, 72, 73, 76, 77, 79, 80, 93
   pandemic surveillance 68–71
Chinese Communist Party (CCP) 71
Chinese Exclusion Act (1882) 34

cholera 32
civil registration 44, 46, 49
civil right, to privacy 137
civil society 119
conflict-of-interest notices 174
conflicts of interest
   advertising models 170
   data reuse 168–9
   profits/patients 169–70
Congress (US) 21, 106, 152, 153, 207
   public health data surveillance
      and analytics infrastructure
      modernization 7
   USA Freedom Act (2015) 20
constant threats to freedom 46
consumer rights 154
contact tracing 7, 16, 18, 22, 136
   apps 38, 42, 54, 150
      China's implementation of 70
   cellphone location data 7, 8
   data aggregation 10
   programs 20
   traditional human-based 65
   traditional methods 8
   UK see United Kingdom, contact
      tracing apps
Conviva 148
Coronavirus Aid, Relief, and Economic
   Security (CARES) Act (2020) 7
Coronavírus SUS app 42, 54, 55, 143
Court of Justice of the European Union
   (CJEU) 107, 108
COVID-19 apps 35, 37, 66, 73–5, 78, 90,
   137, 144
   tracing apps 30, 87, 88, 90
      data capacities 74
      timeline 118
COVID-19 Community Mobility Reports
   7
COVID-19 pandemic 1, 8, 15, 27, 28, 33,
   42, 43, 53, 60, 67, 88, 105, 120,
   128, 159, 187, 189, 199, 216
   5G networks 96
   automated decision-making systems
      190
   Bluetooth-based digital tracing 65–8
   in Brazil 42
   brought dramatic changes 148
   China's surveillance 68–71
   contact tracing 136

containment measures 42
crisis of 27, 33
data collection 34
data-driven technologies 198–201
data protection legislation 207
Delta variant 128
digital apps see COVID-19 apps
digital technologies, use of 201
digital tracing tools 66
digital trends and transformations
        199
ethical approval 197
exposure notifications 129
global coronavirus 136
Group of Seven (G7) nations 200
health information 192
humanitarian and health crisis 202
infection 17
information apps 56
Latin America 138
mass surveillance 6–22
monitoring 221
non-COVID uses, of health/location
        data 212
outbreaks 164, 221
politicization of 212
privacy and public health 125, 193
public health emergencies 207
public health outcome 209
risk parameters 129
surveillance technologies 28, 89
        techno-social loops of 90
survey, online public services 56
testing 16, 115
tracing applications 86
        data 95
        as techno-social installations
                90–91
tracking technologies 105, 149
transparency, lack of 54
travel restrictions 69
US law and policy 188
vaccination 88
virus 20
credit-card history 6
creditworthiness 71
Crimean War 216
cultural resources 88
cybersecurity 1

data aggregation 10, 16, 22, 172
data collection 1–2, 20, 28, 32–4, 38–9,
        43, 48–52, 49, 56, 59–61, 70, 80
data consent controls 31
data dump/flip-switch 31
data privacy, questions 1
Data Protection Act (2018), UK 121
*Data Protection Commissioner v.
        Facebook Ireland, Ltd. and
        Maximilian Schrems* 108
Data Protection Impact Assessment
        (DPIA) 126
data sharing 2–3, 58, 76, 111, 120
data surveillance 3, 7, 15, 72, 80
data technology 3, 158–62, 165, 167, 171
decentralized data model 29
deliberating implementation 221–3
demographer-sanitarians 48–50
demographic-sanitary statistics 50
Demographic Statistics Service 48
Department of Health and Social Care
        (UK) 114, 122, 123
Department of Homeland Security (US)
        21, 207
Department of Justice (US) 21, 110
Diaz v. Google 74
digital authoritarianism 76, 80
digital bodies 28, 31, 38
digital businesses 170, 173
digital companies 154
digital contact tracing (DCT) 8, 16–19,
        66, 164, 166, 209
        technology 28
        tools 65, 66
digital innovation 4
digital mobility data 169
digital privacy policy
        pandemic experience 148–9
        pandemic surveillance perspectives
                149–50
        post-pandemic 154
                digital nation 150–52
                government initiatives 152–4
digital public health surveillance
        program 16
digital rights organizations 140
digital surveillance 137
        apparatuses 144
digital technologies 136, 138, 141, 143,
        149, 199, 201, 211

digital tracing methods 18
digital tracking methods 65
digital transformation 114
digital transparency 150
dignity, defending 219–20
dot-com crash in 2000 and 2001 29
Duncan, Thomas Eric 17

Ebola crisis
    in Liberia 125
    in United States 17
    West African outbreak 17
e-commerce 69
Economic Commission for Latin
    America and the Caribbean
    (ECLAC) 138
economic shift, mortgage crisis of 2008
    29
educational campaigns 211
Emergency Aid 42
epidemiological surveillance programs 9,
    11–14, 19
ethical pandemic surveillance see
    pandemic surveillance systems
Ethics Advisory Board 120, 126
    members 120
    principles 121
European Commission (EU) 108–10
European Union
    digital contact tracing 20
    EU–US Privacy Shield Framework
    108
    General Data Protection Regulation
    (GDPR) 119
Exposure Notification Application
    Programming Interface 66
"Exposure Notification: Frequently
    Asked Questions" 124
exposure notification system (ENS) 65,
    124, 164, 209

Facebook 31, 98, 168, 172, 199, 207
Falun Gong-owned media 93
federal public health policies, fragility
    of 55
Federal Trade Commission 97
Ferguson v. City of Charleston 14
fever epidemic see yellow fever epidemic
fiduciary policy solutions 171–5

conflict-of-interest notices 174–5
    information fiduciaries 173–4
    policy solutions 174
    public health fiduciary 175
    trust 172–3
Fischhof, Adolf 32
FluPhone screenshots, for influenza
    symptom reporting 127
foreign intelligence 2, 105–10
Foreign Intelligence Surveillance Act
    (FISA) 106
    Amendments Act of 2008 106
    Section 702 program 88
Foreign Intelligence Surveillance Court
    106, 107
foreign surveillance power, lack of time
    106
Fourth Amendment thresholds 9, 10
frictionless pandemic surveillance
    comparative perspective 72–7
    social credit systems 64–80

GAEN system 69, 74
    decentralization 68
    framework 91
    logs, Google's implementation 75
Gallup survey 151
General Census of Empire 46
General Data Protection Regulation
    (GDPR) 74, 108, 119, 190
General Personal Data Protection Law
    (Lei Geral de Proteção de Dados
    [LGPD]) 43, 57, 58, 59, 60, 198
geolocational tracking 105
Germany, digital contact tracing 20
global pandemic 4, 27, 38, 158
    emergency 65
global positioning system (GPS) 6, 18,
    163
    data 18, 19
    technology 209
    tracking 11
Global Privacy Assembly 200
Global Wireless Solutions 148
Google 31, 35–8, 54, 65, 66–68, 74, 97,
    114, 115, 124, 140, 170, 199
    app 78
    data aggregation 10
    Google-Apple API 29, 30, 67
    location data 7

motto 34
system 115
government affairs 69
government-based problem-solving 93
Government Communications
    Headquarters (GCHQ) 105
government-funded academic research
    126
government-managed algorithms process
    73
government servers, user data 68

hard surveillance systems 71
Hasbajrami case 107
healthcare maintenance organizations
    (HMOs) 169
Health Insurance Portability and
    Accountability Act of 1996
    (HIPAA) 159, 167, 221
health-related mobile phone apps 163
health surveillance system 218
healthy tension 77
Helen Nissenbaum's theory of privacy
    188
HIV positive 192
House of Commons Public Accounts
    Committee 123
House of Representatives (US) 152
HTTPS/TCP/IP/TLS 36
Human Rights Watch 164
humans' physical safety 217

Immigration and Customs Enforcement
    (ICE) 208
infectious disease mitigation 17
infodemiology 217
informational alienation 58, 59
Information Commissioner's Office 119
information fiduciaries 160
    conflicts of interest
        advertising models 170
        data reuse 168–9
        profits/patients 169–70
    COVID-19 pandemic 159
    data technology 160
    fiduciary policy solutions 171–5
        conflict-of-interest notices
            174–5
        information fiduciaries 173–4

policy solutions 174
public health fiduciary 175
trust 172–3
global pandemic 158
interpreting data 158
pandemic data technology 160
    contact tracing/relational
        mobility data 164–5
    individual mobility data 162–4
    public health crisis 161–2
    social/technical assumptions
        165–7
privacy-related challenge facing 160
technology industry 159
information security 197–8, 222
instant digital contact tracing 8, 16–17
Institute for Computational and Data
    Sciences (ICDS) 1
Instituto Brasileiro de Geografia e
    Estatística (IBGE) 57
intelligence and security agencies 122
intelligence apparatus 92
Inter-American Commission on Human
    Rights (IACHR) 138
International Association of Privacy
    Professionals (IAPP) 138
International Health Regulations (IHR)
    58
international human rights 137
international marketing intelligence
    service 148
Internet of Bodies (IoB) 222
iOS devices 67
iOS operating systems 33, 66–67, 91,
    140
iPhones 115
Isle of Wight trial 116, 126

Johns Hopkins Center for Health
    Security 8
Johns Hopkins Coronavirus Resource
    Center 158
Johnson, Boris 114

Kennedy, Robert 106
Khan, Linda 173
KMPG survey 149
Kuhn, Thomas 96

large-scale data analytics 198
Latin American
    civil society organizations 141
    COVID-19 apps 142
Latinx community 210
Law of Captivity 46
legislating digital contact tracing
    data access/analysis/use 21
    data gathering/aggregation 19–20
    data storage 20
    Fourth Amendment 15–22
    pre-deployment review 16–19
    program designed 21–2
    recursive review 22
linguistic communities 93, 96–7, 99
location data 56
    smartphones 6
    tracking data 150
Loveman, M. 46, 47

"mandatory soup" 222
mask wearing 128
mass surveillance, in COVID-19
    pandemic 6–22
    cellphone location data 7
    COVID-19 Community Mobility
        Reports 7
    Fourth Amendment
        frameworks 9–15
        legislating digital contact
            tracing 15–22
    public health benefits 8
    United States 6
McDonald, Sean 123
McKinsey Global Institute 151
Meaker, M. 71
medical-sanitary network 50
Mexican COVID-19MX 139
Microsoft 31, 151
minipublics 194
mobile device applications 159
mobile phones 162, 163
    analyses of 163
    applications 164
    geospatial location 163
    location 165
    users and non-users of 166
mobility data 141, 163–5, 168–9
modernization projects 46

multiple pandemic surveillance
    technologies 75

National Commission for the Protection
    of Human Subjects of Biomedical
    and Behavioral Research 191
National Data Protection Agency
    (ANPD) 57
National Data Protection Authority 43
National Health Service (NHS) 119
National Health Service Volunteer
    Responders (NHSV) 115
nationalization, difficulties of 50
National Security Agency (NSA) 21, 105
    spying on Petrobras 105
    telephony metadata program 20
    USA Freedom Act (2015) 20
National Technology Adviser 126
Nazi medical experiments 190
negotiation, social movement of 47
Neoabsolutist government 32
New Zealand app 90
next-generation humanity, conflicting
    models of 219
NHS app 119
    Test and Trace 123
    tracing app, much-larger-scale study
        of 123
NHSX app 115, 126
    centralization 68, 115
    digital transformation 114
    Ethics Advisory Board 120
    version of 117
non-pharmaceutical interventions (NPIs)
    161
No Such Agency/Never Say Anything
    107

Office for National Statistics 124
Oliver v. United States 13
Ordem dos Advogados do Brasil (OAB)
    58
Organization of American States (OAS)
    137
Oswaldo Cruz Institute 49

Painel TIC COVID-19 43, 56
pandemic data technology 160

contact tracing/relational mobility
data 164–5
individual mobility data 162–4
public health crisis 161–2
social/technical assumptions 165–7
pandemic ethics
COVID-19 responsive technologies
204
ethical obligations 205–6
pre-pandemic trust landscape 206–8
rebuilding trust, of COVID-19
208–13
technology/trust/privacy 204
pandemics, and progress
COVID-19 pandemic 216
defending dignity 219–20
defining progress 218–19
deliberating implementation 221–3
determining sustainability 221
dissecting revenue 220–21
pandemic surveillance, developing
narratives of
contingency/incommensurability
contingency 93–5
incommensurability 96–7
COVID tracing applications, as
techno-social installations
90–91
global event 99
language of trust, reestablishing of
97–9
technology 86–7
techno-social loop 87–90
trust, as technological affordance
92–3
pandemic surveillance systems 27, 64,
73, 76, 77, 93–5, 97, 190
acceleration of 77
apps, privacy in Latin America
see privacy/pandemic
surveillance apps, in Latin
America
in China 70
ethics 187–94
lessons for/from, COVID-19 192–4
technologies 28, 86, 94, 194
US see United States, foreign
surveillance
values, at stake 188–92

Pan-European Privacy-Preserving
Proximity Tracing (PEPP-PT) 68
Paraguayan War 46
Parliament's Joint Committee on Human
Rights 119, 121
Pasquale, Frank 173
Patriot Act 97
personal autonomy 190
personal data/data-driven technologies
data governance system 201–2
data-guided technologies,
COVID-19 pandemic
199–201
research/public health 197–202
personally identifiable information (PII)
174
PILOT Lab 4
pilot users 116
policymakers 9, 19, 78
post-pandemic government digital
privacy policy initiatives 152–4
Pozen, David 173
privacy-intrusive system 64
privacy laws 66, 108, 150, 152–3, 221
privacy/pandemic surveillance apps, in
Latin America 136
app characteristics 138–40
concerns, about surveillance 140–41
contact tracing 136
COVID-19 apps
global coronavirus pandemic
136
impact of 141–2
limited use, reasons 142–4
theoretical/methodological approach
137–8
privacy preservation
balanced approach, to forward
progress 33–6
centralized platforms 29–31
history vs. technology 38–9
knowledge, pursuit of 27
lessons from past 31–3
privacy vs. public health 27–9
solutions framework 37–8
privacy-related challenges 160
Privacy Rule of the Health Insurance
Portability and Accountability
Act 207
private surveillance technologies 96

progress, defining 218–19
proximity data 170
proximity tracing, Bluetooth-driven 66
public health
    benefits 8
    challenges 14
    crises 111, 159, 160
    data surveillance
        analytics infrastructure
            modernization 7, 51
        cellphone location 6, 7
        traditional methods 7, 16, 18
    emergency demands 65, 75, 76, 160
    fiduciary 175
    interventions 165
    needs 27
    officials limit 164
    recommendations 150
    risk 6
    solutions 51, 160
    trade-off privacy 27–28, 159, 191,
        193, 205
Public Health Emergency Privacy Act
    (US) 207
public–private partnerships 10, 55, 173,
    206–7

QR codes 90
Quarantine Act 54

Rapporteurs for Freedom of Expression
    of the UN 140
rebuild immunity 98
Red Cross International Committee 200
Republic of Ireland 116
research ethics 190–2, 194, 208
ResetWork 151
revenue, dissecting 220–21
Revolt of the Vaccine (1904) 52
Rorty, Richard 96

sanitary-informational apparatus 52
São Paulo Intelligent Monitoring
    Information System (SIMI-SP) 55
Schneier, Bruce 77
"secret law" system 72
self-isolation 17–18, 22, 116, 122, 123,
    128, 129
Semmelweis, Ignaz 32, 37

separation of powers 2, 79, 128
service delivery models 56
Sesame Credit scores 69
silent data governance revolution 78–80
Sistema Único de Saúde (SUS) 53
skilled workers 8, 16
smart medical devices, for monitoring
    symptoms 159
smartphones
    app 6, 86, 105, 114, 148
    location data 6, 89, 105
    software 66, 67–68, 74, 75
    users 66, 87, 91, 128, 148
Snow, John, Dr. 32, 216
social challenges 223
social contacts 12
social control, tools of 8
social credit systems 70, 71, 73, 76, 79,
    93
    databases 220
    ratings systems 69
Social Dilemma, The 207
social distancing 17
    contact between infected and
        non-infected people 161
    controlling 43
    instant digital contact tracing 16
social isolation index 56
social media 69, 78, 89, 150, 205, 217
social media privacy 172
social regulatory systems 70
social science claims 218
societal trust deficit 204, 206, 207
soft social credit systems 65, 72–3,
    79–80
South Korea, cellphone alerts 6
Spanish government's tracing app 123
standard contractual clauses (SCCs) 109
    data protection 111
    data transfer, against government
        surveillance 109
Stored Communications Act (US) 76
surveillance abuses, US officials 111
surveillance/pandemic, in Brazil 42–59
    contact tracing apps 42
    containment measures 42–3
    COVID-19 pandemic 53–9
        cases 42
        data protection 57–9
        Federal Constitution 53

health emergency 53
    technologies to fight 54–7
data processing 43–7
racism/population management
    43–7
yellow fever see yellow fever
    epidemic
surveillance powers, emergency 8
surveillance technologies 1, 71
sustainability, determining 221
Swisher, Kara 150

TCP/IP 36
technology theatre 123
techno-social Möbius strip 94
telephonic metadata 20, 21
Terrorist Surveillance Program 97, 106
thermal imaging 66, 68
tools of legibility 47
Total Information Awareness 97
tracing app 29, 66, 116, 117, 121, 122,
    123, 129
Track and Trace program 126
transparency 16, 31, 39, 47, 54, 58, 70,
    107, 119–20, 139, 142, 149–50,
    154, 189–90, 201
travel restrictions, COVID-19 pandemic
    69
trust
    government's ability 172
    pre-pandemic trust environment 204
trustworthiness 39, 71
Tuskegee Syphilis Study 190–91
Twitter 31, 173

ubiquitous surveillance technologies,
    terrorist attacks of 78
United Kingdom (UK)
    contact tracing apps
        Apple/Google system 114, 117
        broader questions raised 123–8
        controversy, over organizations
            122–3
        COVID-related DPIAs 126
        COVID tracing app timeline
            118
        ethics advisory board principles
            121

FluPhone screenshots, for
    influenza symptom 127
institutional mechanisms, for
    oversight/regulation
    119–21
Isle of Wight trial 116
NHSX app 68, 115, 117
    pilot users 116, 117
COVID-19 cases 114
Department of Health and Social
    Care 123
England and Wales tracing app 126
Government Communications
    Headquarters (GCHQ) 122
internet use among residents 125
United Nations (UN) 137
Declaration of Human Rights 167
freedom of association 167
Global Pulse 200
Organization of American States
    137
Universal Declaration of Human
    Rights 138
United States (US) 66
after 9/11 106
corporate surveillance infrastructure
    72
COVID-19 pandemic 6
democratic traditions 88
epidemiological surveillance
    programs 8
foreign surveillance 3
    after 9/11 106
    Big Tech innovation 105
    CJEU's expectations, of
        privacy 111
    cumbersome process 109
    essential equivalence 109
    Foreign Intelligence
        Surveillance Act (FISA)
        106
    national security surveillance
        110
    national security threat 105
    Privacy Shield 111
    standard contractual clauses
        (SCCs) 109
    US federal law 105
healthcare organizations 170
intelligence community 107

legal language of 97
New Zealand fail 88
pandemic surveillance policy 64, 65
phone tracking 76
self-regulatory approach 207
social credit systems 65, 73, 76
soft surveillance system 79
surveillance capitalism 79
United States v. AT&T 173
United States v. Hasbajrami, 2019 107
United States v. Miller 13
USA Freedom Act (2015) 20

venture capitalists 29
video monitoring 64
Virginia Department of Health 90, 91
Virginia smartphone users 91
virus transmission 7, 65, 114, 136

W3C Solid 31
web-based shopping companies 29

Weber, Rosa 58
Western credit systems 69
Wi-Fi 6, 163
wiretapping 64
Work Trend Index 151
World Health Organization (WHO) 7,
    217

yellow fever epidemic 47–52
    data collection/processing 50
    nationalization 50
    Oswaldo Cruz Institute 49
    political authority, centralization of
        50–51
    sanitary-informational apparatus 52
    statistical reasoning/data collection
        47–52
    transitions 48

ZIP codes 67
Zuboff, Shoshana 78, 96